DREAMS
COMING TRUE...

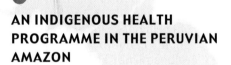

**AN INDIGENOUS HEALTH
PROGRAMME IN THE PERUVIAN
AMAZON**

Compiled and edited by Søren Hvalkof

© 2004 Karen Elise Jensen Foundation and NORDECO.

Dreams Coming True...

An Indigenous Health Programme in the Peruvian Amazon

Compilation and editing: Søren Hvalkof

Interviews: Søren Hvalkof

Cover, typesetting and lay-out: Rikke Aamann-Christensen

Maps: Jorge Monrás and CPTI, Peru.

Vignettes: Noé Silva Morales (Shenkare)

English translation: Elaine Bolton

English copyediting and proofreading: Birgit Stephenson, Christina Gadiel and Søren Hvalkof

Logistic coordination: Mirtha Castillo Andrade

Typing of transcripts: Daisy Zapata

Prepress and print: Eks-Skolens Trykkeri, Ltd., Copenhagen, Denmark.

Library publication data:
Dreams Coming True...
An Indigenous Health Programme in the Peruvian Amazon/edited by Søren Hvalkof
1. Health - rural health - international health - alternative medicine - tropical medicine
2. Latin America - Peru - Amazonia - Ucayali - Amazonas - Madre de Dios
3. Indigenous peoples - Amazon - Ashéninka - Asháninka - Yine - Conibo - Shipibo
4. Amazon region - Ucayali River - Urubamba River - Gran Pajonal
5. Development research - participatory approaches - community development
6. Anthropology - ethnography - medical anthropology - shamanism - healing
7. Social movements - indigenous organisations

I. Hvalkof, Søren, 1951-

ISBN 87-986168-7-0

EAN   9788798616870

NORDECO

Skindergade 23³ - DK-1159 Copenhagen K - Denmark

Ph.: (+45) 33 91 90 30 - Fax: (+45) 33 91 90 32

E-mail: sh@nordeco.dk - nordeco@nordeco.dk

Contents

Maps

Asháninka design

Preface

By Søren Hvalkof, compiler and editor

Introduction

This is a book about an exceptional indigenous health project in the Peruvian Amazon. The project was invented, designed and implemented by the indigenous organisations themselves, with funding and support from a private Danish foundation. The book gives a kaleidoscopic insight into the multi-faceted universe of indigenous/non-indigenous relations, and into an attempt to merge the best health practices of both worlds with multiple actors and ethnic identities. It is neither an attempt to present an academic analysis of the medical and anthropological dimensions of this process, nor to offer an intellectual statement for post-modern contemplation. Rather it aims to present an optimistic testimony to the practical possibilities of developing an indigenous health system within the modern state in a globalised setting, hopefully inspiring and motivating other indigenous peoples and organisations, NGOs, government institutions and international organisations to engage and cooperate on similar endeavours.

The Project

The project was born in the wake of a very successful land titling process following years of indigenous peoples' struggle for their rights. The success of the indigenous communities in obtaining legal collective titles to their territories aroused an awareness on the part of the native Amazonians to the fact that indigenous rights existed within the Peruvian State, that it was possible to change the *status quo* and that international support was available. Excited by this new scenario after centuries of oppression and abuse by successive colonists and patrons, the indigenous people finally demanded what was rightfully theirs: their own education, their own health system, their own government, their own religion and a new sustainable economy. They wanted to become an active part of modern Peruvian society and of the world.

Armed with new optimism, in 1992 the indigenous umbrella organisation of the Peruvian Amazon, AIDESEP[1], approached a small Danish consultancy company, NORDECO[2], enquiring about support and funding for the development of an indigenous health programme that was of the highest priority for the indigenous organisations. Serving as a mediator, NORDECO made contact with a larger Danish medical foundation, the Karen Elise Jensen Foundation, which normally funds high-tech medical research and, after a period of project formulation, a proposal was submitted. The Karen Elise Jensen Foundation approved the project and donated the funds necessary to launch a pilot project. AIDESEP and its regional member organisations were to implement it on a daily basis and NORDECO was given responsibility for technical supervision and financial control. An unusual condition of this support was, however, that board members of the Karen Elise Jensen Foundation would participate in the monitoring visits, and report their findings and observations on the project's development back to the Foundation. This turned out to be a decisive factor in the success of the project.

The project was named The Indigenous Health Programme - "Programa de Salud Indígena" in Spanish - with the acronym PSI-AIDESEP. It began operating as a pilot phase in 1993, initially with three different projects in three different regions, one in northern Peru in the area of San Lorenzo on the Lower Marañon River, one in the Upper Ucayali around the provincial capital of Atalaya in the Central Amazon, and one around Puerto Maldonado on the Madre de Dios river system in the southernmost part of Peru. All three regions represented different ethnic, social and geographical characteristics, as the Programme wanted to gain comparative experiences that could be used to improve the health programme's development and methodology. After an initial three years of health work in the three areas, a second phase was approved by the Karen Elise Jensen Foundation. Based on the experience of the first phase, it was decided to concentrate the work in the Atalaya province and discontinue the work in the other two regions. After completion of the second phase, a third phase was approved, aimed at consolidating the Programme, extending its coverage and promoting its continuation through the public health system in Peru. The Indigenous Health Programme was eventually phased out during the year 2000, having succeeded in involving, training and establishing a health service system in 119 indigenous communities. A proposal for an institutionalised indigenous health technician training system was subsequently developed by the PSI and is presently being considered for funding by the public Peruvian health system and a multilateral development agency. The Karen Elise Jensen Foundation has agreed to support this new project in its initial activities until international funding is secured and transfer of experience is completed.

The book

This book reflects the reality in which the health programme has developed. A reality that articulates a number of different and often contradictory positions, cultural backgrounds, political views and cosmologies, creating a new indigenous authenticity out of this conglomerate of meanings. Outside spectators may comment on the impossibility of managing a project involving so many different actors and power relations: a number of different indigenous groups all with their own particular and frequently unrelated languages, different cosmologies and belief systems, all with their particular understanding of sickness and cure and of cause and effect, indigenous groups ranging from small nomadic units with only very sporadic and recent contact with Peruvian national society, speaking no Spanish at all, to large and well-organized groups with centuries of experience of contact with the ever expanding and aggressive national and non-indigenous society. A team of nurses and physicians, professionally trained in the conventional western biomedical system, who have to communicate, mediate and work together with shamans and other specialists in indigenous medicine and accept medical practices and rituals completely alien to western tradition and logic. Another group of indigenous leaders and politicians with yet other agendas, but simultaneously supposed to coordinate, organize and take responsibility for the implementation and administration of funds. On top of this there are a number of other interests and power brokers, such as the colonist *mestizo* population, which has traditionally distanced itself from any attempts to develop indigenous capacity but which, on the other hand, is equally interested in health issues and a better life, and also represents the public health sphere in Peru, including the staff and management of hospitals and health posts. And, finally, we have the funding and support institutions, based at the extreme opposite side of the globe and with a completely different background within an old and well-functioning European democracy but, nonetheless, insisting on taking personal part in the development of the Programme despite the logistical complications and conceptual contradictions.

This book aims to represent this multiplicity of positions and views by giving representatives from many of the different groups of actors an opportunity to voice their views, either in the form of written contributions or via interviews. The various articles and chapters are thus very diverse and uneven in their approach, language and style, reflecting the empirical reality of the project.

The contributions

The book contains articles by AIDESEP's Programme Director and its indigenous leadership documenting the political and organisational background and motivation for developing an integrated health approach and decentralised implementation strategy. The same indigenous leadership also contributes with interpretations of indigenous health practices and shamanism and of the philosophy behind the restitution and integration of such practices and, finally, with their vision for a future continuation of the PSI in the form of an official Peruvian indigenous health technician training system.

The technical staff of the Programme present a number of contributions. The physician and medical coordinator in the field has written a lengthy article on the medical perspectives of the Programme, taking a more conventional western approach to the topic. He presents statistical information as well as reflections on the effects of the projects. The nurses are represented by a number of interviews. As these key staff spent 11 months in the field each year, it would have been an overwhelming challenge to make each of them write a piece for this volume. The interview form was chosen to ensure that their points of view and their experiences were heard. As it turned out, these interviews are probably the most vivid part of the book.

Other sets of interviews represent the positions and opinions of the indigenous specialists, such as the shamans, vapour and herbal healers, midwives and others. Also, patients and community members, as well as indigenous leaders, health promoters and project coordinators, have all contributed with their views and voices. All the interviews were tape recorded in the field between July and August 2000 by the editor, and subsequently transcribed and edited. Some of the names mentioned have been substituted with pseudonyms, but only in cases where it was crucial to protect the privacy of the persons concerned.

Representatives of the Karen Elise Jensen Foundation and the NORDECO staff involved in the Programme have all contributed with articles covering different aspects of the ethnographic and historical background, the project's history and structural development, personal experiences of their encounter with an unfamiliar world, and reflections on the attempts to integrate indigenous health practices and western medicine.

Finally the book contains a number of photos, drawings, designs and other illustrations all originating from people involved in the Programme.

Acknowledgements

It would be an impossible task to mention all the people who, in one way or another, have supported the compilation and production of this book. However, special thanks must go to the following: Mrs. Mirtha Castillo, Andrade Programme Administrator, based in the AIDESEP office in Pucallpa, who willingly undertook innumerable and often impossible tasks and put enormous efforts into coordinating and ensuring often complicated logistics and who helped the editor out with typing assistance etc. We are also grateful to Mrs. Daisy Zapata, OIRA's secretary in Atalaya, who took on the arduous task of typing out interviews from the original tapes, working with an old tape deck and a manual typewriter with a worn-down ribbon. The boat pilots who transported the editor safely around, day and night, in all kinds of weather on the fast and tricky Ucayali and Urubamba rivers and tributaries during the collection of material for the book, also deserve applause for their efforts. Of these we would particularly like to mention Mr. Luis Cushmariano, who put extraordinary efforts into helping to coordinate our activities. The Asháninka artist, Noé Silva Morales, from Atalaya drew all the indigenous designs shown in the vignettes and also supported the publication by sending us two excellent paintings of shamanic experiences during Ayahuasca sessions, which greatly improve the quality of the book.

Thanks also go to the regional indigenous organisations, OAGP, OIRA and ORDECONADIT, their leaders and staff, who were always helpful, supporting us in any way we needed, and were indispensable to the success of this project; as well as to the many communities visited, which always received us with warm hospitality

We owe a particular debt of gratitude to the graphic designer, Mrs. Rikke Aaman Christensen, from Denmark, who volunteered to undertake the enormous work involved in designing the cover and helping with the layout of the book. Thanks also to Alejandro Parellada, of IWGIA, for helping with the editing of the many Spanish language interviews, and Jorge Monrás, also of IWGIA, for his support with the drawing of maps. During the entire period of implementation, we received excellent cooperation from IWGIA (International Work Group for Indigenous Affairs), and this has been greatly appreciated. Nor should we forget the translators, Elaine Bolton in England and Mario di Lucci in Uruguay, who have put much dedication and enthusiasm into this project.

Andrew Gray on the Ucayali River.   Photo: *Dorte M. Jensen*

Both the health project and this book are in certain ways spin-offs from anthropological research carried out by the editor in the regions of Gran Pajonal and Ucayali in the 1980s and 90s. Hence it seems appropriate to thank the Danish Council for Development Research (RUF-Danida) and the Danish Social Science Research Council (SSF) for funding that research in various periods. The editor also appreciates the support from the Danish Institute for International Studies in Copenhagen for having offered office space and facilities in the last editorial stage of the book's elaboration.

Finally, we would like to dedicate this book to our friend and colleague, Andrew Gray, who lost his life after the plane he was travelling on crashed in the Pacific around Vanuatu one stormy night in May 1999, during a networking trip to indigenous organisations on the Pacific islands.

Andrew dedicated his whole life to the indigenous cause, and was particularly supportive of AIDESEP's Indigenous Health Programme. He helped to supervise the initial project component in Madre de Dios, and accompanied the team on one of its visits to Peru. Andrew's departure is more than an irreparable loss to the indigenous world; we all miss him and his high spirits, which turned many exhausting and stressful trips and events into positive experiences. These will always be remembered with pleasure.

Notes

1. The Asociación Interétnica del Desarrollo de la Selva Peruana (AIDESEP) - the Interethnic Association for the Development of the Peruvian Amazon - was established around 1980 with three different indigenous organisations as members. Today (2003) it covers more than 40 indigenous federations and regional organisations from all over the Peruvian Amazon, and is the largest indigenous organisation in the country, playing a very active role in national and international politics with regard to indigenous rights.
2. The Nordic Agency for Development and Ecology (NORDECO) is a small consultancy company based in Copenhagen, Denmark. It specialises in integrated conservation and community development in Third World countries and Eastern Europe, and has for many years been working with indigenous organisations and peoples in Latin America, Asia and Africa. It is registered as a non-profit making foundation that supports initiatives in developing countries within the areas of the environment, sustainability, biodiversity, participatory monitoring and community support. (cf. www.nordeco.dk)

Shipibo-Conibo design

1. Introduction

AIDESEP and the Indigenous Perspective

*By Gil Inoach Shawit, Ex-president of AIDESEP
and Juan Reátegui Silva, Director of PSI-AIDESEP*

The indigenous reality

The history of the indigenous peoples of the Peruvian Amazon during colonial times is already common knowledge. The continuity of colonial policy throughout a large part of the Republic is also well-known, and it was during this time that the dark history of the rubber boom of the early 1900s unfolded. What remains to be written, however, is the history of the Amazonian peoples and the "developmentalist policies" of the Peruvian state, from 1960 to the rise in drug trafficking and terrorism of the last two decades of the 20th century.

Prior to AIDESEP's creation, the indigenous peoples of the Amazon had their own tradition of organising, according to their objective development conditions and the tasks to be done. The centralisation of these forms of organisation began with the support and guidance of religious groups (Catholic orders and evangelical churches) but generally disappeared when the organising group left. The first real attempts at independent organisation began as a defence against the penetration of settlers and companies exploiting raw materials. These organisations were, initially, local, communal and then, later, regional or basin-level. The Asháninka, Amuesha of the Selva Central and Aguaruna of the Alto Marañón were the ones who initiated the federative movement among the communities in the late 1960s/early 1970s.

The socio-political context of the early 1970s was highly favourable to the development of indigenous peoples' organisation. On the one hand, social upheaval was occurring within broader society and, in Peru, a populist military experiment was underway. This led to the enactment of the Law of Native Communities in 1974 and began the process of titling community lands. As part of this process, indigenous organisational development progressed, the Coordinating Body of Native Communities of the Peruvian Rainforest (COCONASEP) being formed in 1979, changing its name a year later (1980) to the Inter-Ethnic Association for Development of the Peruvian Rainforest (AIDESEP).

AIDESEP

The Association for the Inter-Ethnic Development of the Peruvian Rainforest is a national-level organisation of Amazonian indigenous peoples whose aim is to fight to defend the territory, natural resources, culture, language and other human and political rights of indigenous peoples. It also challenges actions being carried out, by the state itself or by individuals, that violate other rights accorded them in terms of legal order, bilingual intercultural education, respect for their customs, world view, history, identity, language and affirmation of their free self-determination, given that the Constitution acknowledges that Peru is a multicultural country.

Reasons for establishing AIDESEP

It was the requirements of the Law of Native Communities (1974) that was behind the indigenous peoples' search for more complex organisational forms. The answer, in 1980, was AIDESEP, the result of ten years of grass-roots experience. Whilst it is clear that the peoples themselves are the main protagonists in their history, it is also clear that, at each historic moment, the peoples are reflected in their leaders. This first generation of AIDESEP's leaders is engraved in the memory of all those who know and love the history of the Amazonian peoples.

AIDESEP's path

Since its early days, AIDESEP has directed its efforts towards formulating a basic platform that guarantees respect for the fundamental rights of Amazonian indigenous peoples. AIDESEP has done so based on an awareness of the need to unite the communities around common objectives in the face of adverse circumstances, demanding their recognition, legalisation of their lands and territories, and implementing actions that boost indigenous presence in the country's political, social and economic activities, for the first time raising the banner of indigenous demands, under the leadership of their own organisations.

AIDESEP also promotes the coordination of intercultural and interethnic spaces aimed at recovering their rights as peoples, developing mechanisms for formulating proposals and negotiating the implementation of indigenous cultural and economic activities, interacting with civil society, public organisations and national and international bodies involved in indigenous daily life.

AIDESEP has promoted the formation of other indigenous federal organisations and, in 1982, was the driving force behind the creation of the Coordinating Body of Indigenous Organisations of the Amazonian Basin (COICA), which now acts as umbrella organisation to associations in nine countries of the Basin, namely: Venezuela, Surinam, Colombia, Ecuador, Bolivia, Peru, Brazil, French Guyana and British Guyana.

AIDESEP's efforts to improve the living conditions of indigenous men and women have been considerable and are praiseworthy given the current context of such issues within the country. Administrative and legislative acts are issued with no consideration for the provisions of ILO Convention 169 regarding consultation and participation, and the attitude of the judiciary and the Attorney-General's office when administering justice fails to respect customary law, which is constitutionally recognised. Nonetheless, AIDESEP continues to work tenaciously to achieve its objectives.

AIDESEP's organisational strength has enabled it to become a main player, with a key role in representing indigenous peoples before the various state sectors responsible for designing action policies. It proposes initiatives and legislative reforms, such as the proposed Indigenous Law, Regulations Governing Hydrocarbon Activities on Indigenous Territories, and Tax Regulations governing indigenous peoples. Furthermore, AIDESEP has made significant contributions to the Proposed System for Protecting Indigenous Peoples' Collective Knowledge of Biodiversity and Access to Genetic Resources.

It has contributed to strengthening harmonious relations between indigenous peoples on both sides of the border with neighbouring Ecuador and Colombia, proposing state action to support exchanges between the indigenous Huitoto, Bora, Achuar, Shuar, Aguaruna and Huambisa peoples.

It has participated actively within the country, in the Selva Central region, contributing to the defence of the Asháninka people in the face of subversive action. In addition, the organisation has been involved in international peace initiatives, organising two binational meetings between the indigenous peoples from Peru and Ecuador who were involuntarily involved in the border conflict between the two countries.

AIDESEP's aims

Based on experience gained during the struggle for their own autonomous organisation, AIDESEP's federations and grassroots organisations have set themselves the following overall objectives:

1. To represent the immediate and historic interests of all indigenous peoples of the Amazon.
3. To guarantee the preservation and development of the cultural identity, territory and values of each of the indigenous peoples of the Amazon.
4. To make the exercise of indigenous self-determination viable, within the context of national Peruvian law and international law.
5. To promote the human and sustainable development of the indigenous peoples.

AIDESEP's legal status in Peru

The Inter-Ethnic Association for Development of the Peruvian Rainforest (AIDESEP) is a non-profit making organisation with legal status under national private law, recorded in the Public Registry of the Book of Associations of Lima on sheet no. 6835, entry A-1, dated 27th May 1985.

AIDESEP's grassroots

AIDESEP can be found the length and breadth of the Peruvian Amazon, in six decentralised bodies located in the north, centre and south. At a secondary level, there are 53 federations and territorial organisations representing 1,340 indigenous communities throughout the federations' territory. These federations group together communities belonging to 64 Amazonian indigenous peoples, including: the Maijuna, Secoya, Bora, Huitoto, Yagua, Jebero, Achuar, Kichwaruna, Wangurina, Shipibo, Cacataibo, Ashaninka, Cashinahua, Sharanahua, Culina, Amahuaca, Amarakaeri, Kechuas, Aguaruna, Chayahuita, Cocama, Cocamilla, Huambisa, Shapra, Candoshi, Yíne, Yami, Matsiguenga, Yanesha, Arasaire, Toyoeri, Harakmbut, Ashéninka, Nomatsiguenga, Ese-eja, Huachipaeri, Ocaina, Ticuna, Urarina, Yaminahua, Yora, Nahua and Muratu.

AIDESEP's institutional development

AIDESEP is working to find a solution to improve the quality of life of indigenous peoples through the following actions:

Territory and natural resources

In this area of work, AIDESEP endeavours to put an end to encroachment onto its territories through education, organisational strengthening, self-demarcation, legal defence, titling, and through agreements with the Ministry of Agriculture and Regional Agrarian Departments. It puts effort into raising awareness among the authorities, and national society as a whole, of the basis of the indigenous relationship with their territories, territories that cannot be exchanged for other land and which are the basis of their ethnic, material and spiritual reproduction, guaranteeing their survival as peoples.

Another important activity in this area of work is that of training promoters on legal issues in order to manage and defend the territory and promote a good use of the Amazonian forest's natural resources.

In the last few years, this type of work has achieved the demarcation of a high percentage of the communities and the titling of 40% of the indigenous territories of the Peruvian Amazon.

In terms of technical support for this territorial work, AIDESEP liaises with an organisation known as the Centre for Territorial Information and Planning (CIPTA), which enables adequate information to be obtained on natural resources, their location and correct management, such as:

- Defence of the ethnic territory, natural resources and the environment.

AIDESEP's organisational structure

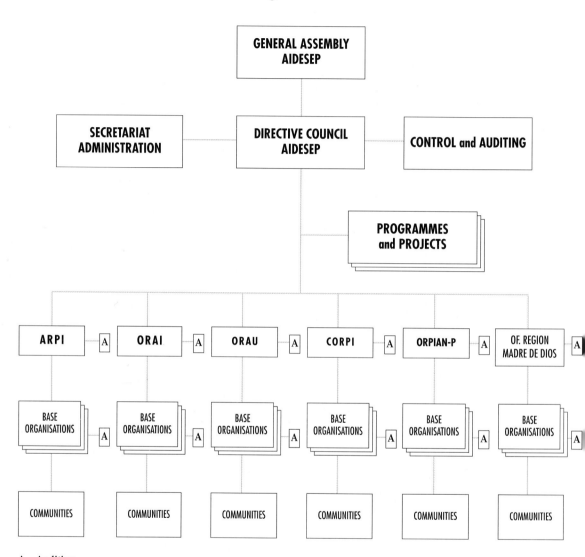

A = Auditing

- Demarcation and titling of the communal territories and establishment of communal reserves. As a result of this work, more than 8 million hectares of territories have been titled.
- Over one million hectares of territorial reserves benefiting the indigenous peoples in isolation.
- Creation of the communal Reserves of El Shira, Purús and Amarakaire.

- Legal training for indigenous promoters in the management and defence of their territory and natural resources.
- Proposals and initiatives regarding the condition of the territories and natural resource management in the Amazon forest.

Economics and alternative development

This area of work aims to promote an inter-ethnic exchange of traditional knowledge, both technical and strategic/conceptual, and of innovations relating to the use and management of plant and animal resources and subsistence activities. The objective is to recover indigenous natural resource management wisdom. This is reflected in economic practices and in social models and powers of co-existence and interrelating. The conservation and rational use of resources and the biodiversity is vital in this, for it guarantees indigenous life in the long term. It is also responsible for drawing up forest management plans and sustainable development projects, all aimed at improving indigenous peoples' quality of life. The work includes:

- Compiling, researching, promoting and training on tropical ecological agrarian technology, in accordance with indigenous knowledge and practice.
- Formulating management plans and projects for the sustainable economic development of natural resources.
- Conservation and regeneration programme for renewable natural resources.

Indigenous health

This area of work is aimed at recovering traditional indigenous medicine uses and practices through promotion of a healthy environment, cultural self-esteem and social harmony. It is also responsible for developing an indigenous health system appropriate to the reality of each region and area, recovering and developing indigenous health knowledge with the objective of providing the human resource training and self-training necessary to the system's progress.

At the same time, the Indigenous Health Programme (PSI) is aimed at improving the indigenous population's access to western health resources for treatment of illnesses that have "come from outside".

Over the last few years, after much hard technical and organisational work, it has been possible to establish indigenous health systems that work in harmony and coordination with the western system at the level of three grassroots organisations. The work includes:

- Recovering and developing indigenous medicine as a basic component of our culture, both its human and material resources and, fundamentally, its spiritual, magical and anthropological aspects.
- Gradual incorporation into an indigenous health system, as appropriate, of effective western medical contributions.
- Achievement and implementation of agreements with the

Ministry of Health in areas of support to the control of epidemics, research work into tropical and infectious diseases and the development of intercultural health polices.

- Proposal for the creation of an Amazonian Intercultural Health Institute (INSIA), in collaboration with the Ministry of Health and the Institute for Human Resource Development (IDREH).

Indigenous rights and civil rights

Grassroots leaders are being trained to be able to effectively carry out the tasks of representing their peoples and fulfilling the political offices they have assumed. Legal defence and advice are also provided by this area of work, on issues related to collective rights and regularisation of people's personal documentation.

Alongside this, consultancy work is being undertaken with the grassroots federations in relation to all administrative and legal steps required to obtain their legal status.

Education and culture

AIDESEP is particularly concerned to ensure that indigenous peoples enjoy their constitutionally-recognised right to bilingual intercultural education. From this perspective, indigenous languages are now, for the first time, no longer a transitory vehicle towards "hispanicisation", nor are they tools used to perpetuate the dominant ideology but tools created by a society to conceptualise and interpret its reality, tools that there is every reason to believe will continue to develop in order to incorporate new technical and scientific concepts.

With the Training and Professionalisation Programme for indigenous bilingual teachers, an educational proposal was for the first time developed. An educational proposal that was based not only on bilingualism but also on an intercultural methodology which, based on the knowledge of the indigenous peoples themselves, and free from prejudices, comes close to the knowledge formulated by western science.

This area also promotes access to grants programmes for professional or technical training on the part of indigenous youth. The work includes:

- Training of bilingual intercultural teachers.
- Endeavouring to get indigenous teachers into posts within the Regional Education Authorities, in order to ensure better orientation of the official system towards the communities.
- Co-implementation of the Programme of Bilingual Indigenous Teachers of the Peruvian Amazon (FORMABIAP), through an Agreement with the Ministry via the Loreto Institute of Higher Education.
- Formulation of curricula for primary schools and for teacher training programmes in relation to the bilingual intercultural education specialism.

- Programme of professionalisation of bilingual indigenous teachers.
- Promotion and affirmation of the cultural values of the peoples of the Amazon based on research undertaken into their culture, science, technology and art.

Relations with the Peruvian state and the international community

As the representative institution of the indigenous peoples of the Amazon, AIDESEP maintains relations with the various Peruvian state bodies, it also has relationships with national and international institutions that have an interest in establishing friendship and cooperation links with the Amazonian peoples.

We have established an agreement between the Ministry of Education, AIDESEP and the Loreto Institute of Higher Education, for the implementation of the Bilingual Teacher Training Programme (FORMABIAP). We have also established agreements between: the Ministry of Agriculture's, special project for land titling – PETT and AIDESEP for the titling of the native communities of the Peruvian Amazon; with the National Institute for Natural Resources (INRENA) for work on the sustainable management of the Amazon's natural resources; with the "Alexander von Humboldt" Institute for Tropical Medicine of the Cayetano Heredia Peruvian University for the joint design and management of projects and programmes to control the main diseases affecting Amazonian indigenous peoples and development of environmental defence actions and their impact on health; with the Ministry of Health through the General Epidemiological Office (OGE) to develop actions to assess the health situation of Amazonian indigenous peoples; and with the Institute for Human Resource Development (IDREH) to implement actions of human resource training and education for the Amazonian indigenous peoples.

We have signed agreements with the following international organisations:
- Technical Cooperation of the Government of Denmark (DANIDA), through IWGIA.
- Italian Technical Cooperation, through Tierra Nueva.
- The Norwegian government, through FAFO International.
- The Karen Elise Jensen Foundation, through NORDECO, to implement actions of Indigenous and Intercultural Health.
- GTZ – Germany, to implement workshops with indigenous women.

National and international recognition

In 1986, AIDESEP, the Aguaruna and Huambisa Council and the Coordinating Body of Indigenous Organisations of the Amazon Basin

(COICA) received the Alternative Nobel Peace Prize in Stockholm, Sweden.

In 1993, the National Institute for Statistics and Computing (INEI) in Peru awarded AIDESEP a certificate on behalf of the nation, in recognition of the support provided during implementation of the National Population and Housing Census.

Our shared vision of the future

We wish to be an organisation that is representative of all the indigenous peoples and communities of the Peruvian Amazon, recognised by the Peruvian state as the valid intermediary with whom to resolve all the problems of the Amazon, and by the international community as the genuine representative of the aspirations of Peruvian indigenous peoples, and the indigenous peoples of the world as a whole, in relation to their established rights in international legislation.

We aspire to building a multilingual, multicultural and democratic Peruvian national state that respects the human rights of our children and our children's children. Within the context of this national state, we seek the autonomous and sustainable human development of all indigenous peoples of the Amazon, within their recognised territory, and the building of a shared vision of the future with other peoples.

1. ATI: Achuar
2. ACONADIYSH: Asháninka - Amahuaca
3. ANAP: Asháninka
4. AIDECOP: Cocamilla
5. AIDECOS: Cocamilla
6. CAH: Aguaruna - Huambisa
7. CARE: Asháninka
8. CECONSEC: Asháninka
9. COHAR YIMA: Haramkbut, Yine, Mastigenka,
   Ese-Eja, Yora, Nahua, Kichuaruna
10. CHAPI-SIWAG: Aguaruna
11. FECONA: Bora - Huitoto
12. FESHAM: Shapra
13. FECONAU: Shipibo
14. FECONBU: Shipibo
15. FENAMAD: Haramkbut, Yine, Mastigenka,
    Ese-Eja, Yora, Nahua, Kichuaruna
16. FECONACO: Achuar, Urarina, Muratu
17. FECONAMN: Maijuna - Huitoto - Cocama
18. FEDECOCA: Cocamilla
19. FENACOCA: Cocataibo
20. FEDIQUEP: Quechua
21. FECONAYY: Yine, Yami
22. FECONADIC: Aguaruna - Chayahuita
23. FEPYIROA: Yagua
24. FECONACHA: Chayahuita
25. FECONACADIP: Candoshi
26. FECONAFROPU: Maijuna - Cecoya - Huitoto - Bora
27. FECONAJE: Jebero
28. FECONARINA: Huitoto
29. FECONAT: Quechua
30. FECOTIBA: Ticuna, Yagua
31. FECONADIP: Shipibo
32. FECONAPU: Cashinahua, Sharanahua, Amahuaca, Culina
33. FECONAPIA: Asháninka
34. FEPIKRESAM: Quechua
35. KANUJA: Asháninka, Nomatsiguenga
36. OIRA: Asháninka, Yine, Amahuaca, Yaminahua

37. ORIAM: Aguaruna
38. ORACH: Achuar
39. ORASI: Aguaruna
40. OAGP: Ashéninka
41. ONAPAA: Aguaruna
42. ASHDEM: Huambisa
43. OARA: Asháninka
44. ORKIWAN: Kichuaruna, Wnagurina
45. ORDECONADIT: Ashéninka, Shipibo, Conibo
46. ORDIM: Shipibo
47. ODECOFROC: Aguaruna
48. UNAY: Yánesha

Map 1. AIDESEP: Member organisations.

25

Map 2. Peru: Working areas of the PSI-AIDESEP.

Ashéninka design

1. Introduction

Project Summary

By Thomas Skielboe, Co-director of NORDECO[1]

The inception of the project

The pilot phase of the Indigenous Health Programme was initiated in mid-1993 as a form of co-operation between the funding agency, Karen Elise Jensen's Foundation, the development agency Nordic Agency for Development and Ecology (NORDECO) and the Peruvian umbrella organisation for indigenous peoples of the Peruvian lowland, *Associación Interétnica de Desarrollo de la Selva Peruana* (AIDESEP). The Project has undergone three phases of implementation from 1993 to the end of 2000, and has been marked by a strategy favouring a trial-and-error approach. This approach puts great emphasis on using experience gained along the way, changing strategies, where necessary, as the project progresses. The Programme was the first long-term project initiated by the development and environment agency, NORDECO, established in 1990. The NORDECO staff, however, already had many years experience working with indigenous peoples and organisations in lowland Peru, specifically with the nascent indigenous organisations of the Ucayali River region.

AIDESEP, which was established in 1980, had for the past decade been working intensively on indigenous peoples' rights, and much effort had been put into defining indigenous territories in the Peruvian legal context and securing land titles to indigenous communities, as well as developing the bilingual education concept into a bilingual inter-cultural education system to be implemented in the indigenous areas. Health aspects and aspects of environmental and local economic development had also been touched upon as part of the strategy of supporting the indigenous peoples' possibilities for influencing their own life and future. To move more intensively into the health sector with an integrated approach was, at this time, a natural step for AIDESEP in its work with the local indigenous organisations. The national health system does not cover the Amazon area in any sufficient way, and there is a serious lack of resources, clinics, medicine and health workers. Generally, there was at that time a total inability to address the local indigenous reality, including their language and their understanding of health. The indigenous health systems had, for centuries, been suppressed by the national society and, particularly, by the Christian missions, and AIDESEP wanted to focus on a revitalisation of indigenous health knowledge as part of the indigenous reality. As a consequence a project document for a two-year pilot phase was formulated, in collaboration between AIDESEP and NORDECO. Three smaller projects run by AIDESEP were merged into one and analysed, with the aim of developing a two-year pilot project in which different approaches could be tried out in order to lead to an actual programme for indigenous health, in line with specific indigenous needs and with AIDESEP's overall strategies.

In 1992 the project document was submitted to the Karen Elise Jensen Foundation, together with an application, and the project was approved in early 1993. The three projects implemented in the pilot phase were located in San Lorenzo in Alto Amazonas in the north of Peru (in association with three indigenous peoples' organisations), in Madre de Dios (with one organisation) and in the Atalaya province (with one organisation). Following the lessons learned through implementation of the pilot phase, it was decided to concentrate the work in Atalaya province, where the largest project had been implemented and which had had the highest success rate. The project area in Atalaya was expanded from some 50 communities to covering 119 communities in three districts, working with three organisations in these districts: OIRA (the Indigenous Organisation of the Atalaya Region), ORDECONADIT (the Regional Development Organisation of Indigenous Communities of the Tahuanía District) and OAGP (the Indigenous Organization of the Gran Pajonal).

Project structure

The organisational structure of the project comprises five levels of stakeholders, all with different responsibilities:

Table 1: Project stakeholders and main responsibilities

Orginasational level	Main Body Responsible
Financing	Karen Elise Jensen
Foundation overall supervision and quality assurance	NORDECO
Strategic development project administration and field supervision	AIDESEP-Central/PSI (Programa de Salud Indígena)
Local implementation	OAGP, OIRA, ORDECONADIT
Implementation	Health Teams and Native Communities

The Karen Elise Jensen Foundation, the project's funding agency, has also been involved in project supervision in the sense that they have participated in all review visits to Peru carried out by NORDECO. NORDECO has had overall responsibility for the project, providing supervision, backstopping and quality assurance in close collaboration with AIDESEP and the project administration in Peru.

In Peru, the project was initially implemented centrally by AIDESEP in association with the local organisations; the project had its main office in Lima. However, in phases II and III, the project was decentralized and more responsibility for implementation was handed over to the local organisations. A project office was established in the regional capital, Pucallpa, and a smaller extension field office in the provincial capital, Atalaya. AIDESEP still retained overall responsibility for implementation but a field coordinator was now based in Atalaya, with responsibility for planning and supervising the field work in collaboration with the local organisations. A Project Director based both in Pucallpa and Lima was responsible for supervising implementation and overall project performance. Each of the three regional indigenous organisations had their own budget and was responsible for implementation in their own area. The decentralization had an important impact in terms of developing local ownership of the project. In each of the project areas, *health teams* consisting of two indigenous *co-ordinators* and a nurse have played key roles in implementing the health system. The teams have continuously travelled throughout the area, visiting all communities two or three times a year. The teams have conducted awareness campaigns, supervision and training in basic western and traditional medicine for promoters and leaders, as well as training in the structure and functioning of the Indigenous Intercultural Health System. Moreover, the teams have established village-based health posts in all villages. The health teams have, together with the Project Co-ordinator and Director, been working on the capacity building of the organisations, specifically related to the administration and maintenance of the health system.

Collaboration with the Ministry of Health, MINSA, has been an important priority in the project's strategy for sustainability, and MINSA has been involved at many levels.

Participating organisations

The funding agency, the Karen Elise Jensen Foundation (KEJF), is one of the largest Danish foundations exclusively funding health research and related projects. The foundation mainly supports work in Denmark and, as the involvement with health and indigenous peoples in Peru was a totally new activity, the Board of the Foundation has actively been monitoring the development of the project, through all three phases. This has been a great advantage for the project.

Founded in 1990, NORDECO is a consultancy company wholly owned by the non-profit making Nordic Foundation for Development and

Ecology. NORDECO's main area of work is providing advice on development processes, integrating local development and nature conservation. The consultancy services offered are concerned with enhancing the quality of development efforts by approaching the interactions between society, culture and the environment as an integrated whole. NORDECO consists of experts from both the social and natural sciences and has, through this integrated approach to development, very broad experience in working with participatory methods. Through the senior anthropologists connected to the office, NORDECO also has solid experience of working with indigenous organisations and indigenous affairs.

As the umbrella organisation for indigenous peoples of the Peruvian Amazon, AIDESEP is an important stakeholder in the project. It has 44 member organisations and among these are the three local organisations OIRA, ORDECONADIT and OAGP. AIDESEP's main offices are in Lima and it has five regional offices around the country. In relation to this project, AIDESEP has developed a special section, *Programa de Salud Indígena, PSI*, that works with indigenous health problems. The Indigenous Organisation of the Atalaya Region, OIRA, consists of 50 communities from six ethnolinguistic groups situated along the main rivers, Rio Tambo, Rio Urubamba and Rio Ucayali, and their tributaries. The organisation was formed in 1988 and has an office in Atalaya. The Development Organisation of Indigenous Communities of the Tahuanía District, ORDE-CONADIT, covers 27 communities belonging to two ethnolinguistic groups: the Shipibo-Conibo and the Ashéninka. The communities are situated along the Rio Ucayali and its tributaries in the district of Tahuanía. The organisation has its office in the village of Bolognesi. The Ashéninka Organisation of the Gran Pajonal, OAGP, has its main office in Ponchoni in Gran Pajonal and another smaller office in the regional capital, Pucallpa, a necessity due to the remoteness of Gran Pajonal and resulting logistic difficulties. The area is very different from the riverine areas of OIRA and ORDECONADIT. It is situated at an altitude of some 3,500 feet (1,200 m) and all transportation takes place on foot or on horseback. All three local organisations had been working with projects before but this was the first time they had actually been responsible for the budget and administration. This responsibility turned out to be of great importance, both in relation to the involvement of the population and the development of a sense of project ownership, and in terms of strengthening the organisations per se.

Funding and supervision

For the funding agency, the Karen Elise Jensen Foundation, this was the first time it had been involved in a health project of this kind. The foundation has shown a remarkable interest in following the project's implementation, its development, and sharing the experience gained throughout the three phases of the project. Two members of the Foundation's board have visited the project at least twice a year, participating in the review missions carried out by NORDECO. The medical expertise of the board members has also played a significant role in the quality assurance of the western medical input into the project. This active involvement of the funding agency has proved to be of great importance for the development of and interaction within the project.

One co-ordinator from NORDECO has been responsible for the supervision and Danish administration of the project throughout all project phases, and a team of two anthropologists from NORDECO has carried out technical backstopping and quality assurance.

Project developments

As already mentioned, project implementation has been characterised by a *trial-and-error* approach with a specific focus and ongoing discussions on project outputs at all levels. Since the idea has been to develop a kind of prototype health system to be applied in different settings in the Amazon area, it has been important to test different strategies both in relation to capacity building, training, management and project sustainability. Based on the experience gained throughout the different phases, the Programme has made particular achievements in two fields: a) it has increased the focus on strategic flexibility in order to be able to adjust to the specific health understandings of a specific ethnic group; and b) the focus on sustainability of the health system has expanded towards development of a project for public inter-cultural training course for *indigenous health technicians*, who are seen as important promoters of the integrated indigenous health system.

Present situation

The integrated indigenous health system has now been developed and implemented in three districts in the Atalaya region. All participating communities have 2-3 trained health promoters. The three organisations have been trained in management and maintenance of the system, ensuring contact and supervision of all villages both in relation to maintenance of the village pharmacies and in relation to village human resources and contacts with the public health system. Manuals for applying the system to other areas of Peru have been developed and an office within AIDESEP's *Indigenous Health Programme* is functioning, focusing on dissemination of the system and development of the training course for health technicians. It is an important challenge for AIDESEP to follow up on these initiatives. A proposal for the establishment of a National Institute of Intercultural Amazonian Health, INSIA, has been finalised and approved by the Ministry of Health, and a four-year pilot project proposal has been formulated. The Karen Elise Jensen Foundation has agreed to finance the first year of INSIA's start-up phase. A well-functioning collaboration with the Peruvian Ministry of Health, MINSA, and with the regional health administration has been developed, and should be carefully cultivated in the coming years. The present situation is thus a crucial time for the Programme. This is the time when the project will demonstrate whether it can work in the hands of the organisations, and in association with the public system.

Note

1. Thomas Skielboe is a Danish anthropologist working as a socio-economic consultant. He is the co-director of NORDECO and a member of its board. He has broad experience from South-East Asia, Africa, Latin America and Russia. He has the administrative responsibility of the PSI-AIDESEP in relation to the funding Karen Elise Jensen Foundation, and has supervised the project during its entire operational period. Mr. Skielboe has actively contributed to the establishment of a National Institute of Intercultural Amazonian Health, INSIA.

Taking a break on the Ucayali River.   *Foto: Thomas Skielboe, 1998*

Waiting for the soda pop.

Photo: Cæcilie Mikkelsen, 2000

Yine design

2. The Context

Place, People and History

By Søren Hvalkof, anthropologist[1]

THE PLACE
Introduction

The Indigenous Health Programme is located in the Upper Amazon of eastern Peru. This area is characterised by a dramatic encounter between two major geographical features: the majestic mountain range of the Andes and the enormous Amazon basin. The meeting of these two features has created one of the most impressive, varied and logistically complicated geographical formations in the world, called the *Montaña*. In fact, the Montaña formation bounds the entire eastern edge of the greater Amazon basin in a long u-shaped transitional zone along the eastern slopes of the Andes, running all the way from Venezuela north of the equator, through Colombia, Ecuador and Peru, to merge with the great plains of eastern Bolivia far south of the equator. Obviously, there is great geographical and ecological variation within this zone, which holds the highest biodiversity in South America[2]. It is also the area with the highest cultural diversity, being the area in Latin America where the highest number of different indigenous peoples still lives. This, combined with a dramatic history of European expansion driven by the assumed potential of the extractivist economy, has created a framework that is essential for an understanding of the livelihoods and health of the present inhabitants of the area, and thus an understanding of the overall social situation.

The following chapter will sketch the geography, history and ethnography of the particular section of the Montaña and neighbouring floodplain in which the Indigenous Health Programme is operating, namely the Upper *Ucayali* river basin of eastern Peru and adjacent interfluvial areas, each of which presents particular characteristics integral to the development and implementation of the Indigenous Health Programme. We will then follow up on the recent political and social achievements of the indigenous population in the region and the social movement it has given rise to over the last two decades.

The Amazon and the Ucayali river systems

The Ucayali River is the most important tributary of the main Amazon river. It drains a major water catchment area of the south-eastern Andes of Peru, known to be the initial source of the Amazon. The Ucayali river changes its name during its course from the mountain source to the Amazon river's mouth in the Brazilian estuary of the Atlantic Ocean. Despite being augmented by hundreds of large tributaries on its way, it is still possible to trace the course of the main river from one end to the other. It covers a stretch of some 3,000 km in Peru, with a width varying between 400 m - 2,000 m. It originates in the Mismi glacier at a high altitude of 5,597 m (Peñaherrera del Águila 1986:151) and, as it is joined by other Andean glacial streams, it soon turns into the torrential Apurimac river, today a popular challenge for elite white-water kayakers and adventurers. Once it reaches the lower tropical forest zones, its name is changed to the river Ene when joined by the Mantaro river, and again to Tambo when it merges with the Perené river. A few hundred kilometres later, it is given the name of Ucayali when it merges with the Urubamba river running from Cuzco, the ancient centre of the Inca empire. This point is situated just below the small provincial town of Atalaya, where the PSI has its headquarters, giving excellent fluvial access to the upstream Urubamba watershed and the downstream Ucayali and affluents. Some 1,600 kilometres further downstream, when it is joined by another big affluent, the Marañon river, the name changes to Rio Amazonas, a name this majestic river maintains until it enters Brazil a little over 700 km further downstream, where its common Portuguese name is Rio Solimoes. The distance from the confluence of the Ucayali and the Marañon, where the main Amazon river takes its name and turns eastward to its mouth in the Atlantic in eastern Brazil, is 3,762 km (ibid. 169). If we add the total length of the Ucayali-Apurimac headwater we end up with a total length of the entire Amazon river of some 6,762 km, making it the longest river in the world, even longer than the Nile. However, it transports 50 times as much freshwater as the Nile, and the entire Amazon basin of an estimated 6,430,000 km2 (not including the Orinoco watershed) holds close to 25% of all surface freshwater in the world. During the Amazon river's course through its basin, it is joined by hundreds of affluents. More than 200 of these have a length of over 1,500 km each and the navigable fluvial network has an estimated total length of some 50,000 km (ibid.)

The river system of the Amazon is enormous and impressive and, as one can imagine, the variety of ecosystems, subsystems and local variations is equally immense. Water is the all dominating creative element, and the diversity in aquatic systems has moulded the most varied habitat for all kinds of life, and not least for the survival of man. Despite this great diversity, we can broadly distinguish between two main habitat types in the Amazon: the alluvial floodplains along the major rivers, and the interfluvial areas.

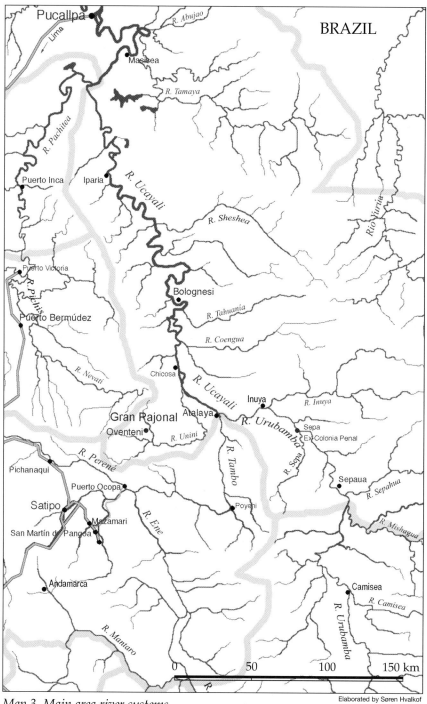

Map 3. Main area river systems.

Elaborated by Søren Hvalkof

The floodplains

The floodplains are created and constantly recreated by sedimentation from the changing water levels and seasonal inundation. The variation in water level can be up to 12 metres. These alluvial soils are very fertile but the annual inundation converts potential agricultural land into swamps for large parts of the year, making it impossible or very difficult to exploit for agricultural production or cattle ranching. Only small-scale horticulture and husbandry are well adapted modes of subsistence, which the local inhabitants, indigenous and non-indigenous, have developed and practised for centuries. An additional obstacle to modern agricultural production is the seasonal unpredictability. Fluctuations from one year to the next regarding the onset of dry and rainy seasons, besides great irregularity in the volume of precipitation, intensify the capricious nature of the floodplain, halting most attempts to establish larger agricultural enterprises where predictability and planning are a prerequisite for success.

The small-scale combined subsistence and market producer, on the other hand, can adapt to the structural characteristics of the floodplain landscape and its whimsical climatic behaviour. The levees along the meandering rivers form small rises and hills, which may be dry most of the season. Such knolls are called *restingas*, and are obviously favourite places for cultivation and settlement. Oxbow lakes formed by cut off river bends are called *cochas* or *tipishcas*, being habitats for special aquatic faunas and favourite fishing places. The hinterland behind the river levees is often flooded most of the year and forms complex swamp systems or *tahuampas*, criss-crossed by canals and smaller rivers. Such swamps in the Upper Amazon are usually characterized by extensive growths of *aguaje* palms[3], or *aguajales* in local Spanish. The aguaje fruit is a very popular snack and there is always a demand on the local markets. But small green parrots also favour the fruits and nest in the palm trunks. These small parrots are sold as pets on the local markets and the indigenous inhabitants are masters at domesticating them.

The climate is tropical in the floodplains, with average temperatures in the mid to upper twenties (degrees centigrade), and with a precipitation that varies locally between 1500-3000 mm annually. Seasonal variation in rainfall is dependent both on the distance from the equator and the closeness to the Andean mountain range but, although it rains all year round, there are generally marked differences between the rainy and dry seasons. The plains are covered with lush tropical forest of various compositions, depending on local soil qualities, with the canopy reaching over 30 m.

The interfluvial areas

The higher lying interfluvial areas between the floodplains of the major rivers can roughly be subdivided into two areas: the interfluvial areas of the larger Amazon basin, and the interfluvial areas merged with the foothills of the eastern Andes, known as the Montaña. The Lower Amazon's higher lying zones between the rivers generally have poorer soil quality than the silt fertilized floodplain and fewer people live here. It is not suited to most agricultural production but is still the basis for the most impressive tropical rainforest. There are good ecological reasons for this balanced system but it is beyond the scope of this chapter to discuss it in detail. There is no sharp boundary between the floodplain and the higher lying hinterland between tributaries, and there are many transitional areas that combine characteristics of both zones, particularly along the many smaller and medium-sized tributaries.

The other type of interfluvial zone is the montane forest of the foothills, the *montaña* or *selva alta*, with quite different features. It is characterised by a combination of steep mountains up to above 2000 m, relatively narrow and deep valleys with fast running rivers, all tributaries of the Amazon system, plateaus and forest plains with rolling hills, crisscrossed by smaller rivers and streams running through gullies and gorges. The rivers are fast white water types, with rocks and many rapids, making navigation only possible in parts, particularly the lower sections. Precipitation in this montane tropical forest is the highest in the Amazon, in certain places reaching well over 4000 mm annually which, combined with marked seasonal differences, means a lot of rain in a few months of wet season. Generally the area has better soil quality, particularly in the intermontane valleys, than in the interfluvial areas of the lower Amazon basin. However, only the valley bottom lands are suited to intensive agriculture, due to imminent erosion problems on the steep slopes that constitute most of the landscape. It is covered with dense tropical and subtropical rainforest, which may not develop a canopy as high as in the low lying floodplains but which, nonetheless, is much denser and more diverse. Because of the ruggedness of the landscape and logistic difficulties in access, it has through pre-history and history constituted a favourite refuge for both man and beast. The combination of better productive potential for swidden horticulture, good hunting potential, protection and a pleasant climate and, not least, access to trade with the Andean civilizations, has altogether contributed to making this area attractive to the greatest number of different indigenous groups in the Amazon area in historic times. We will examine the history of human settlement and development in a later section.

The Upper Ucayali project area

The part of this system that constitutes the project areas of the PSI is the Upper Ucayali river and its tributaries, the Lower Urubamba river and tributaries as well as the interfluvial *meseta* of Gran Pajonal, which forms a natural mountainous barrier to the west of the Upper Ucayali. The partition of rivers into "upper" and "lower" sections is a typical way of organising direction and space in the Peruvian Amazon. In Peru, it is common to speak about the "upper" and "lower" rainforests (*selva alta* and *selva baja*), the "upper" being the tropical forest areas of the eastern foothills of the Andes and the "lower" referring to the Amazon floodplain rainforests.

The target area of the Indigenous Health Programme basically embraces all three types of landscape: 1) The immediate floodplains of the Upper Ucayali and the Lower Urubamba and tributaries joining at the right river-side, 2) interfluvial areas of the headwaters of the tributaries east of the main rivers and the narrow interfluvial brim area on the left bank of the Upper Ucayali bordering the Gran Pajonal rocky barrier to the west, and 3) the Montaña plateau of Gran Pajonal to the west. The different geographical features of the three zones demand quite different logistic approaches through which to access the communities. The communities situated on the levees along the main rivers and in the immediate hinterland can be accessed by speedboat with powerful outboard motors and by foot when within reasonable walking distance from the river. "Reasonable" in this context may imply up to a day's walk.

Communities situated in the interfluvial areas are more difficult to access. The communities on the headwaters of the tributaries east of the Ucayali and the Urubamba can only be visited by canoes or canoe-like boats with smaller outboards, which are able to go upriver on the extremely meandering tributaries, provided that there is enough water. This basically means that project teams cannot visit these areas in the dry season. It may take up to ten days to reach the farthest communities, a journey always combined with long treks from the river to the hinterland settlements. The hinterland communities of the left bank to the west of the Ucayali and Urubamba are normally accessed by foot without major difficulties.

The third geographical zone, the Gran Pajonal, presents quite different characteristics. It is a vast interfluvial tableland between the rivers Ucayali to the east, the Tambo to the south, and the Perené and the Pichis-Pachitea to the west. The plateau rises up to an average of 1,000-1,200 m with higher peaks on the edges up to some 2,000 m. It is criss-crossed by numerous streams and smaller rivers cutting deep ravines and gorges, giving the area a very rugged appearance although it is still regarded a plateau in geographical terms. The name Gran Pajonal means the Great Grassland, a designation it gained because of the many open grass areas ranging from larger savannas of several hundred hectares each to smaller open glades in the forest. Still, less than 10% of the area is covered with natural grass, although the grassland is increasing due to settlers clearing forests in order to expand their cattle raising. There are no navigable rivers in Gran Pajonal and, although the largest system, the Unini river, flows into the Ucayali at its upper end, it is only navigable for a couple of miles close to the mouth. There are still no roads in, and the only way to enter "the Great Grassland" is by foot, horseback or small plane. The health teams stationed here travel around on foot and horse when visiting the communities.

Regional divisions

The main political and administrative division is the Region (and Department) of Ucayali, and the PSI has focussed its work in one of the region's provinces: the huge Province of Atalaya, which is subdivided into several districts. The PSI works in the District of Tahuanía, the District of Atalaya (same name as the Province) and the district of Gran Pajonal[4].

The District of Tahuanía has its administrative centre in the small riverine settlement of Bolognesi, on the right bank of the Ucayali. Bolognesi was initially founded as a trading post during the rubber boom at the turn of the last century. Now it has a small health clinic, a harbour and an airstrip for small planes. Today, both the mayor and vice-mayor are indigenous Amazonians, a major shift in power relations that will be discussed later in this chapter. The PSI is working with the two major indigenous groups in the district: 1) the riverine Shipibo-Conibo living along the major rivers and on the banks of some of the larger lakes in the district, and 2) the interfluvial Ashéninka living in the hinterland and along the tributary headwaters. The indigenous organisation in the District of Tahuanía is ORDECONADIT, which is the partner and counterpart of the PSI there, and responsible for implementing the programme.

The next division up the Ucayali river is the Province of Atalaya. The provincial capital is the small riverine town of Atalaya situated a little upstream from the mouth of the Tambo River in the Ucayali-Urubamba junction. Its strategic location, with access to all three rivers, is obvious, hence its name, which means "watchtower". Atalaya is a former rubber trading post that the local patron donated to the Franciscan mission in the late 1920s. Around the mission grew a tiny colony which, today, has reached well over 3,500 inhabitants of mixed heritage. Atalaya is the service centre for several districts contained within the province. The province reaches all the way to the Brazilian border along the Rio Breu and points far into Brazil along the upper reaches of the famous Purús river to the extreme east. To the west it encompasses most of Gran Pajonal, which has applied for district status but officially still only holds the status of an annex to the District of Atalaya itself. However, it has its own Ashéninka mayor.

Most of the project activities of the PSI take place in the Atalaya Province, working with five of its major indigenous groups: the Ashéninka, the Asháninka, the Yine (former Piro), the Amahuaca and the Yaminahua. There are other smaller groups as well, in the province, some of them nomadic and having only casually been in contact with the PSI. The town of Atalaya has a small hospital, a harbour, and a small airport with a new large asphalt runway, which even larger-sized planes can use. The PSI's base is in Atalaya where it has a small office, and where the project physician was stationed. Most of the activities have been developed with the Asháninka, the Ashéninka and the Yine and only infrequently has it been possible to help the Yaminahua and Amahuaca due to logistical constraints. The regional indigenous organisation of Atalaya, OIRA, is the organisation responsible for managing the PSI programme in the province.

Only one indigenous group lives in the Gran Pajonal, the Ashéninka, who constitute the vast majority of its population, numbering some 6,000. The zone has a small colonist settlement, Oventeni, in the centre, with a landing strip for small planes, a municipal council, a health clinic with a few nurses and, occasionally, a doctor. The colony recently had potable water installed thanks to the indigenous organization, OAGP. This organization is responsible for the PSI in the Gran Pajonal. The headquarters of the organisation is in the indigenous community of Ponchoni, close to Oventeni, where two project teams also have their base. Ponchoni also has its own landing strip. The PSI serves all 36 communities of Gran Pajonal, where all transportation takes place on foot and horseback. The PSI owns a few horses and donkeys for that purpose.

The three project areas serviced by the PSI, each with its autonomous project management and decentralized funding, are linked together and coordinated by the PSI offices of AIDESEP in Pucallpa and Lima. The public Peruvian health service has been involved through a cooperation agreement with the regional health sector and the hospital in Pucallpa, providing emergency services, cooperation on specific campaigns, such as minor surgery campaigns, and providing laboratory analysis of TB samples and others. The public political divisions have constituted no hindrance to the activities of the PSI, since the indigenous organisations have adapted to this Peruvian administrative structure.

THE PEOPLE

The ethnic scenario

The indigenous population in the project areas belong to two major ethno-linguistic families: the Arawakan language speakers and the Pano speakers. The Arawakan branch is one of the oldest language families in the Amazon and, according to available archaeological evidence, the first proto-Arawakan people settled in the area over 4,000 years ago (cf. Lathrap 1970). Unfortunately, very few systematic archaeological investigations have ever taken place in the Upper Ucayali, and never in the Gran Pajonal, and it may very well be the case that the Arawakan presence in the zone dates back much further. The Arawakan family in the area comprises the Asháninka, the Ashéninka and the Yine. The Matsigenka and Yánesha who live outside the project areas of the PSI are also related. The Pano speakers migrated into the area up the Ucayali river later than the Arawakan speakers, probably during the first century A.D., pushing the indigenous groups already there further upstream and into the hinterland. This is, at least, the governing theory based on the joint evidence at hand (ibid.). Of course, this process of indigenous migration over thousands of years is much more complex than outlined here but again we have only scattered evidence from the area. The Pano-speaking branch comprises the

numerous Shipibo and Conibo, today almost merged into one group, and several smaller groups such as the Uni (Cashibo), the Amahuaca, the Yaminahua, the Cashinahua, the Sharanahua and the Mayoruna. In recent years, several smaller nomadic bands, always Pano speakers, with very sporadic contact with other people, have turned up at oil exploration sites and lumber camps, asking for merchandise or medicine. In some cases, the encounter has been confrontational and conflictive. The results of such contact are always the same: contagion with common diseases like colds, influenzas and similar viral infections, which turn out to be fatal for these small family bands. The PSI has been in contact with one such band, which had joined the Yaminahua at the former oil colony of Sepahua, needing health care and asking to be relocated to an Amahuaca area due to discontent with their Yaminahua hosts. But this is the only case the PSI has been involved in. The bulk of project activities are undertaken with the Asháninka and Ashéninka, the Yine, and the Shipibo-Conibo. In the following pages, we will give a brief ethnographic description of each of these major groups, leaving, however, the Amahuaca, Yaminahua and other interfluvial Pano speakers aside, since they have played only a minor part in the project, having received but a few sporadic visits. The Indigenous Health Programme has had to restrict its work to the major groups, mainly due to limitations in organisational capacity and budgets given the logistical complications and transportation costs.

Besides the indigenous population, the Upper Ucayali is also inhabited by a very visible non-indigenous population of mixed origin. The majority of this population are mestizos, either local Amazonians of mixed indigenous-colonist descent, so called *ribereños*, i.e. "river dwellers", or settlers with a mixed peasant background from the Andean highlands, *serranos*, often with *Quechua* roots[5]. Whereas the *ribereños* are considered legitimate Amazonians locally, being a self-reproducing group living in small riverine settlements, the Andean immigrants are regarded as newcomers and most often referred to as *colonos*. As we shall learn later, most of the conflicts of indigenous communities over land are with this growing group of colonists. These Andean settlers, however, tend over time to assimilate with the *ribereño* populations. The last distinct population in the area is the group of old colonists of European background, although intermarried for generations with Peruvian mestizos. These are descendants of merchants and rubber barons, who settled in the area around the turn of the last century, during the rubber boom, which lasted until the 1920s. Some of them stayed on, attempting to make a living out of agriculture, cattle or timber extraction. They settled on small homesteads, "fundos" or "haciendas" if they could invest, and soon became the local power elite

Ashéninka basket-weaving, Gran Pajonal.   *Photo: Søren Hvalkof, 1996*

and patrons of indigenous labour. This is a small but still powerful elite of entrepreneurs in lumber, transportation and services; an ethnic group that also tends to reproduce itself within its own circles and identifies itself as white.

The Ashéninka and the Asháninka

The Ashéninka and Asháninka are two distinct dialect groups who yet share most cultural characteristics. They are by far the most numerous indigenous groups involved in the health programme. They belong to a larger conglomerate of Arawakan-speaking indigenous groups in Peru, which also includes the Matsigenka and the Nomatsigenka. Sometimes Yinetheir Yine (formerly Piro) and Yánesha neighbours are included, but linguistically they are regarded apart, although still Arawak speakers. Today the conglomerate numbers an estimated 85,000 persons (1990) but given a relatively high natural population growth rate they may number considerably more. In earlier ethnographic and historical literature, members of this ethno-linguistic conglomerate were commonly referred to as Campa Indians, with the exception of the Yine, who were referred to as "Piro" and the Yánesha as "Amuesha". The term Campa is today considered disparaging and is practically out of use. An even more derogatory term used in older literature and synonymous with Campa is *"chuncho"*, a Quechua derivate meaning "savage". The Ashéninka and Asháninka alone number over 60,000, dispersed over a vast area of the central Peruvian Amazon (Selva Central), an area of more than 100,000 km². The area covers all the intermontane valleys of the eastern Andean foothill forests and stretches out into the Ucayali basin and beyond, all the way to the Brazilian border in the district of Breu of the Upper Yuruá river. However, it is in the Montaña that the highest concentration of Asháninka and Ashéninka is found, whereas they are more scattered in smaller communities in the interfluvial areas of the Ucayali basin, living as islands in an otherwise Pano-dominated area.

The difference between the Ashéninka and Asháninka is mainly of a linguistic nature. The two languages may be defined as different dialects of the same language and are mutually understandable, although there are great differences - so great that Ashéninka parents in Gran Pajonal once filed an official complaint about the assignment of an Asháninka-speaking schoolteacher to one of their bi-lingual schools, as the Pajonal children did not understand him. The Asháninka mainly live in the southern part of their territory and predominantly along the larger tributaries, whereas the Ashéninka are mostly distributed in the northern zones and in the interfluvial areas such as the Gran Pajonal. This division is also reflected in the Ucayali where the indigenous inhabitants from the mouth of the Unini downriver on both sides speak Ashéninka, and the communities upriver (south) around Atalaya and up the Urubamba and Tambo rivers speak Asháninka. However, their material culture, cosmology, religious practices, economy and social organisation are basically the same.

For the sake of simplicity, we will refer generically to those involved with the PSI as Ashéninka, except in specific contexts where either Asháninka or Ashéninka (or other denominations for other groups) will be used, depending on the specific location.

These peoples typically live in small communities with scattered houses. Those living in a riverine environment often have a more village-like structure and often number more families than those living in the hinterland and in the higher altitudes. These truly interfluvial residents live in small family dwellings of some three to five household units, some distance from the next small settlement. They are all linked together through kinship ties and often clustered around a headman's family unit. A headman is a charismatic leader of a group of such household clusters. He may be referred to as "the chief" by outsiders, but has no other formal powers than those his followers and supporters assign him. Such a headman of a local Ashéninka group has responsibility for organising the community, representing it to outsiders and guests, and building and maintaining a social network that guarantees good trading relations and exchange systems. The Ashéninka and Asháninka are famous for their long distance trading and exchange networks, the *ayompari* system, which causes favoured articles and goods to circulate and at the same time upholds a social network of personal trading relationships, which connect the different dialect groups over a vast territory with dispersed settlements. The system is operated by specialized exchange partners and, by attracting such *ayompari* partners to come to the local settlement, the headman provides for his supporters.

The Ashéninka houses are typical of the indigenous Amazonian architecture, all constructed from local materials, posts and beams tied together with special vines, not nails, and roofs thatched with palm, where the palm leaves are woven and braided together. The Ashéninka live in all kinds of local environments, from the highest lying settlements in the Pajonal above 1,300 metres to the lowest riverside dwellings on the Ucayali riverbed, and their architecture reflects all these different conditions. Houses in the warmest spots are usually open houses with a roof and house posts only and no walls. In the case of riverside locations, the inhabitants generally use raised floors above the ground to protect against seasonal flooding from the rivers. Contrary to this, in the most high lying settlements on some grass covered ridge tops in the Gran Pajonal, the temperature in the dry season may drop as low as 10 degrees centigrade at night, sometimes lower, making closed houses with walls and a door preferred, and normally with the immediate ground as floor. All kinds of hybrid architecture between the two extremes can be found.

The Ashéninka do not favour a village or hamlet structure as such. Even where there are larger clusters in the river environment, the houses are organised in family clusters. Each family normally has two houses, a family house where the women and children sleep and where you cook, and a guest house where visitors can stay overnight and where visiting men drink their manioc beer together. In areas close to mestizo, colonist or ribereño settlements the Ashéninka have increasingly adopted their architecture, which means houses built of boards and corrugated iron using nails. They are easier to build and signal that the owner is a modern person, but it is definitely a less elegant architecture and not nearly as good a shelter as the traditional houses.

The Ashéninka are not riverine people to the same degree as, for example, the Conibo. They live mostly in the upper sections of the fast running tributaries, and although canoes are part of the river Ashéninka's means of transportation, they most often transport themselves downriver on rafts, to walk back later. They are typical hinterland horticulturalists and hunters. They have one of the most well-developed swidden agricultures in the Amazon, a system known as "indigenous agro forestry". They grow hundreds of edible and useful plants in their garden plots, the *chacra*, which gradually return to secondary forest in a controlled system of succession. Thus such gardens can still be harvested for years while the land lies fallow. The fallow period depends on location and soil quality, and it may take as long as 25 years to complete the cycle. Their staple crop is sweet manioc (manihot esculenta) called *yuca* in Spanish, of which they have close to 70 varieties, but sweet potato, yam, taro, arrowroot and yambean all form part of the daily tuber diet. They also grow several varieties of corn, bananas, peanuts, fruits and vegetables. Add to this perennial tree crops like avocado, brazil nuts and citrus and you have a very varied diet. Each stage has its composition of crops and species. Even when a plot has been abandoned and has returned to secondary forest, some of these tree species will survive and can be harvested in the fallow forest for years. Such fallow forests are called *purmas* in Spanish and are owned by someone, although they appear to be jungle regrowth. Like all other indigenous groups of the Peruvian Amazon, the Ashéninka ferment the yuca and brew an alcoholic drink, *masato* in Spanish, a kind of milky manioc beer. It can be mixed with other tubers and even sugar-containing palm fruits to add extra strength. They drink *masato* daily in a diluted version and reserve the stronger brew for parties, which often develop into drinking bouts of Dionysian proportions. And they love it.

Their need for high quality protein is covered by game hunted in the forest, small animals collected such as grubs, insects and amphibians, as well as through eating fatty palm fruits. The Ashéninka are hunters par excellence, whereas their fishing abilities are somewhat more limited. Today, this subsistence economy is extended with some cash-cropping and wage labour. This is particularly true where the Ashéninka are living close to colono and other mestizo settlements. The favourite cash crop of the Ashéninka living in the higher lying zones of the Montaña is coffee which, particularly in the Gran Pajonal, is of very high quality. Coffee is well integrated into their multi-cropped garden plots and rotational cropping/fallow system. But also other products like cocoa, beans and peanuts are marketed, albeit with varying results. Wage labour is almost exclusively in the form of hired hands for colonists or lumber patrons. Usually they are very poorly paid and most often in kind rather than in cash. Working conditions are abysmal and debt bondage and chattel slavery was widespread until very recently. The colono use of indentured labour still occurs, but is much more limited than even a few years ago. The reason for this change in the situation will be dealt with below in the section on the history. (cf. Hvalkof 2002b).

The material culture of the Ashéninka is simple. People do not own much and can easily move if desired. The men hunt with longbows and arrows, a must in a man's paraphernalia and, if they can afford it, with shotguns. They always wear a small woven shoulder bag, which may hold a mirror, cockle shell tweezers to remove facial hair, a comb, a bag of coca leaves for chewing, a tiny calabash with lime powder for the coca chewing, a tube of tobacco syrup also for chewing, a bamboo tube with red facial make-up made of annatto, a black or lilac pencil for underlining facial tattoos, amulets and other magical artefacts, a knife, shot gun shells and a small box of matches.

The typical dress, which is virtually their ethnic hallmark today, is the "cushma"[6], an ankle long cotton tunic, which both men and women wear. The best quality is hand spun and home woven. The colour comes in different shades of natural light cotton with woven darker died stripes, most often brown, greyish or black. Some also use coloured stripes of factory spun yarns. In the men's version, the cushma is stitched together out of two long pieces of fabric, worn lengthwise and doubled, leaving out the stitching in the centre and making a hole for the head, and likewise making holes for the arms at the shoulders. It is like a poncho stitched together at the sides. The women wear their cushma across transversely, which requires an alteration in the design since holes left open for the arms are in the same stitch line as the head opening. The head opening in a woman's cushma is also wider, to allow for breastfeeding babies. If one is ever is in doubt of a person's sex, looking at old photos of Ashéninka or Asháninka, a man's cushma always has the stripes vertically and a woman's horizontally. It is unthinkable that they would swap them. Large new white cushmas are the men's favourite trading object in the ayumpari exchange network. When a cushma becomes worn it is usually dyed reddish brown, a process which will be repeated through its lifetime until it turns almost black. Today, cushmas are also made out of factory woven cloth, still not regarded as being as prestigious as an original hand woven one. (cf., Veber 1992, 1996)

To the women's attire must be added the baby sling, worn across the body hanging from one shoulder. The finest ones have a number of small engraved bones dangling, which sound like small bells or fine rattles when walking. The female symbol, paralleling the bow and arrows, is the basket, which is carried on the back hanging from a headband on the forehead. The women can carry an impressive weight this way and often over long distances. Besides the facial painting with red annatto make-up paste, they have few adornments apart from some shoulder and neck pendants, amulets and feathers. Men often wear large plumages on their backs. As a headdress, the women sometimes wear loose red headscarves, while the men use a wide headband made of the inner cortex of a type of large bamboo cane. The Asháninka seem to favour a crown of fine plaited cortex, a fine wickerwork in keeping with typical Asháninka designs, as reproduced in the vignettes of this book. At the back of the headband or crown they often attach a few feathers in an upright position, looking very decorative. Although they may sound exotic, the Ashéninka are quite modest in appearance, with no conspicuous ornaments, handicrafts or artwork, no colourful rituals. They basically have the colour of the earth and merge with the forest. We will later discuss aspects of their beliefs, religion and shamanic practices, while comparing all three ethnic groups.

The Shipibo-Conibo

The Shipibo and Conibo form the largest Pano-speaking complex in the Amazon which, together with the rest of the Panoan conglomerate of some 42 ethno-linguistic groups, number an estimated 40,000. (Erikson et al. 1994). The Shipibo-Conibo total some 25,000 of these. (Morin 1998:286). Contrary to the Ashéninka, they are a decidedly riverine people. They live along the main Ucayali river from the upper end all the way downstream to the lower middle Ucayali, where they are replaced by the descendants of the Tupi-speaking Cocama and Spanish-speaking ribereño communities. According to the German explorer and geographer, Günter Tessmann, who visited the Ucayali in the 1920s, "Ucayali" means the "mosquito river" in Shipibo. This may not be completely true, but it could just as well be since their habitat is the lower floodplains of the Ucayali riverbed with its aguaje swamps, oxbow lakes and other larger lake systems of the seasonally flooded alluvial landscape. There are indeed a terrifying multitude of mosquitoes. We will refer to the people as Conibo, as the upriver people are Conibo descendants and the downriver people are Shipibo. There are still dialectal differences although they have basically merged into one ethno-linguistic group. A Shipibo shaman trainee, Tomás Arévalo, explains the different subgroups:

"...a shipi is a little monkey...Shipibo means 'little monkey men'...in actual fact, in the past, there were different groups of people: the tigers, birds, monkeys...there were many of them...but they were all from the same tribe. With time, and because of their common exploitation, they joined together, the Shipibo came together with the Setebo and the Cunibo to defend themselves..." (Cárdenas 1989:29).

The historical processes causing the ethnic differentiation between the different subgroups of Pano speakers are very complex, and the unification mentioned by the Shipibo student is very recent, whereas most of the history of contact is rather characterized by escalating interethnic conflict and slave raids induced by the colonist economy, a phenomenon that will be dealt with below.

Weaving a basket, Gran Pajonal. *Photo: Søren Hvalkof, 1996*

Weaving a cushma, Gran Pajonal. *Photo: Søren Hvalkof, 1996*

The Conibo have always been attached to the riverine environment, developing excellent skills in canoeing, fishing, and floodplain and riverbed horticulture. Fishing is unquestionably their most important economic activity in the context of subsistence. It is their main source of high quality protein but also plays a role in terms of income generation. Fishing is essentially a male activity, and the Conibo use a number of different techniques and types of fishing. When fishing traditionally with poison in small streams, creeks and brooks, however, both women and children may take part in catching and collecting the paralysed fish. This is common practice among all interfluvial groups, including the Ashéninka and other Arawakans. Hunting is only a secondary source of protein for the Conibo, and mostly practised during the seasonal flooding when game is concentrated, seeking refuge on the *restinga* knolls.

The Conibo practice the typical Amazonian swidden horticulture described for the Ashéninka above. It is, however, less diverse than the Ashéninka interfluvial system in terms of different cultigens. The Conibo benefit from the rich silt-covered alluvial soils along the Ucayali, which permit mono-cropping such as bananas and plantains combined with beans. But they also cultivate the typical manioc gardens with mixed crops for their daily food consumption and for *masato* brewing. Cash cropping is part of the economy, with plantains, beans, maize and rice being marketed on a regular basis. Unlike the interfluvial groups, the riverine Conibo are extremely dependent on the seasonal variation in the river's water level. The cyclical variation in the river's level and course creates a very special environment. It renews the nutrients in the soil creating special conditions and productive opportunities, which are only found here. One example is the rice cultivation that takes place in the dry season on the mud banks, the so-called *barreales*. Also, water melons are favoured cash crops on the dry sandy beaches, arenales, in the "summer"[7]. Turtle eggs are another very popular product that can be collected on the sandy beaches and banks and marketed. Boiled turtle eggs are very popular in the Amazonian towns and cities. When the river starts rising again, many different species of Amazonian fish begin their seasonal migration upriver to their spawning grounds in tributaries, lakes and swamps, sometimes creating a fishing El Dorado for the local people, increasingly under competition, however, from outside commercial fishing vessels. Still, the blessings from the river's fluctuations are mixed, and the other side of the picture is a seasonal lack of food. The rainy season floods inundate the villages and lower lying gardens, destroying most of the remaining crops. Only cultivation on high lying *restingas* is still possible in this season. In recent years, these floods have seemed to be increasingly violent, probably due to the combined effect of global warming, which has caused the Andean glaciers to melt, and the expanding deforestation in the colonist frontier, which causes the rainfall to run off much faster than before. In certain stretches of the Ucayali, extreme flash flooding has reached catastrophic proportions, sweeping away entire villages, drowning people and destroying all crops, even on the higher knolls. The Conibo communities of the Upper Ucayali suffered such a disaster during the rainy season of 2001.

Most of the Conibo communities that form parts of the Indigenous Health Programme have their villages situated on the river levee, usually with the main settlement a little back from the immediate river bank, where they have their harbour for canoes and boats, and where river barges can land to load and unload merchandise or passengers. Unlike the Ashéninka communities, which are characterised by dispersed settlement clusters, the Shipibo-Conibo favour a hamlet-like structure for their settlements. The houses in the central hamlets are typically organized in two rows of houses with a wide cleared "boulevard" between the two rows. The centre may broaden into a plaza-like place, the prolongation of which again takes the form of a wide street. The school building, community office (a recent innovation) and health post are usually situated close to the central plaza. In larger Conibo communities, which house up to a thousand persons, the village lay-out may be extended, with other "streets" crossing or running parallel to the main "boulevard". This adaptation of the Spanish colonial village structure is the result of years of contact with the Catholic missions and mestizo nationals. Most communities have a few hundred inhabitants but the Conibo villages along the Ucayali river banks were known to have up to 1,800 inhabitants at the time of European contact, between the 16th and 17th century. (Santos and Barclay 1998: xxii) Thus the nuclear village as such is not a new phenomenon among the Conibo. The architecture is typical for most river dwellers today, indigenous or not, with palm leaf thatched houses as described for the Ashéninka, but always with a raised floor of either split palm cortex or sawn planks for the wealthiest families. The raised floor is a must in an environment that floods seasonally. The house is basically a single family unit but may also function as home for the matrilocal extended family. Today, it is increasingly common to see houses with partition walls to create several small rooms, making privacy for the extended family members and visitors. Otherwise, mosquito nets serve the same purpose in more traditional one-room houses with no or few walls. Besides the main family unit, they have a cooking unit with a hearth, also on a raised platform. The two houses are sometimes connected by a little bridge, making it possible to pass dry-shod between them. This is quite common to many riverine people adapted to the floodplain.

What really distinguishes the Shipibo-Conibo today from other indigenous groups in the Peruvian Amazon is their ceramics, their dress and adornment, and their exclusive ornamentation and design. Their dress has obviously developed and changed over time as fashion changes and they come into contact with other peoples, including the European and Peruvian colonists. Yet there is a strong continuity in dress and ornamentation among the people of the Ucayali floodplain from the time of contact until the present day (cf. Thomas P. Myers n.d.:17). Today the

Conibo men ordinarily wear western clothing, such as shirts and trousers or sport shorts, but they do have white or reddish dyed knee length cushmas like the Ashéninka. Instead of the longitudinal stripes, they paint black elaborate Conibo geometric patterns, as can be seen in the vignettes of this book. These cushmas are their festival dress together with crown-like headdresses, and blue-black genipap body paint with the same ornaments and different bead necklaces, bracelets and bandoliers. Unlike the Ashéninka, only the men wear cushmas and not as their usual dress, whereas the Conibo women use a very conspicuous and colourful everyday dress, a fashion that was initially developed at the Franciscan mission of Sarayacu in the early 19th century (ibid. 8). Today it consists of a short sleeved blouse and a knee length decorated cotton skirt, a *pampanilla*, consisting of a tubular piece of material wrapped around and rolled down the waist to the hips. The blouse is made of fine cotton in bright colours like clear blue, red, yellow or purple with or without figured patterns, a large collar and front with different coloured edging. The skirt is usually either black, white or brown with the typical elaborate geometrical design embroidered or painted on. To this attire is added a slack belt, made of many loose strands of small white beads worn around the waist, and multicoloured beadwork bracelets. Some also wear a necklace made of old silver coins or seed beads. To the festival dress is added a small silvery metal disc fastened through the septum and hanging under the nose. Sometimes they also insert another thin metal piece a couple of inches long through the pierced lower lip. A necklace of tiny coloured glass or plastic beads in a multi-strand design wrapped tightly around the neck, and a string with pendants of seeds that produce a rattling sound when walking attached to the instep, complete their dress.

The Shipibo-Conibo are particularly famous for their very fine polychrome ceramics. They produce a number of sizes and forms, including anthropomorphic pots. The largest vessels produced for the masato manioc beer may contain up to 500 litres. The ceramics are usually white, decorated with characteristic geometric patterns in black, but ochre and red with white or black patterns are also common. However, plastic buckets and aluminium pots and pans are increasingly substituting the ceramic ware in daily use. A determining factor for the production of this beautiful ceramic seems to be the possibilities of selling it to tourists. Only a few years ago, the Shipibo and Conibo operated an arts and crafts cooperative shop near Pucallpa, the *Maroti Shobo*, exporting quite a lot of their ceramics, and supporting the local communities' potters and economies. It is an exclusively female occupation to make and design ceramics and the knowledge of their elaborate geometric patterns is a woman's "secret". The women thus control the most important income-generating potential in Conibo society: pottery. Their geometric patterns are also very important identity markers for the Conibo and they apply the designs to any blank "space" including their own skin. As only women are able to acquire the knowledge of how to paint the patterns, the Conibo men are dependent on the women's design skills, which give the women a central position in their society. No other indigenous Amazonians have similar designs, except their immediate neighbours upriver, the Yine.

The Yine

The Yine were, until very recently, referred to as *Piro* both in ethnographic literature and in common speech[8]. Yine working with the PSI explain that "Piro" is the name of "a little fat and ugly fish", and that it is an unfortunate misunderstanding to use this designation for their people. The Yine are the other indigenous group of the Arawakan linguistic family branch participating in the Programme. They are truly riverine like the Conibo, and are equally excellent river navigators, canoers and outboard motor pilots. Although of the same linguistic stock, their language is rather distant from the Ashéninka/Asháninka and not mutually intelligible[9]. The Yine live in a few communities on the Lower Urubamba river and at the upper end of the Ucayali, from the Unini river mouth and southwards to the Sepahua and Mishagua rivers mouths in the lower and middle Urubamba. The provincial administrative town of Atalaya is in some way situated in the middle of Yine territory, if such a concept exists. They number an estimated 2,500 - 3,000 today but it is difficult to give an exact figure. Who among them should be considered Yine and who not is hard to determine since they frequently intermarry with their indigenous neighbours. Their communities are dispersed along the main rivers, and they neighbour numerous Asháninka communities on both rivers. But inside the Yine communities there are also several Asháninka families and individuals present. The Yine could be characterized as an interethnic group which, in many ways, resembles the Cocama ribereños of the Lower Ucayali. Mixed marriages between Yine and Asháninka are very common but marriages with mestizos and Matsigenka are also frequent. (cf. Gow 1991) The Yine have, throughout modern history, developed a particular trade and war relationship with the Asháninka, the Conibo, mestizos and other neighbouring groups. They have been involved in slave raiding against neighbours but also in extensive river trade up and down the Urubamba and the Ucayali. They have often been used as labour contractors and brokers for the mestizo colonists and larger patrons around Atalaya. The Yine regard themselves as the most civilized of the ethnic groups of the Ucayali-Urubamba nexus, specialized in entrepreneurship, middlemanship and inter-ethnic trade. To be "civilized" in the indigenous context in no way means that they are losing their identity as members of indigenous groups. On the contrary, it rather signifies that they have now developed a kind of autonomy and status as Yine inside modern Peruvian society, and that they are able to deal with the requirements of modern society, a development that will be described in the next section. Part of their civilised imagery is expressed in their excellent Spanish language skills, and their deep interest in education and the bilingual community schools. The Yine share several cultural characteristics with the Conibo, including their ceramic tradition and design patterns. It has been suggested that it was, in fact, the Yine who introduced several of the features of material culture that are today regarded as typically Shipibo-Conibo. Although the Yine in daily life use standard Peruvian clothes, the men wearing shorts, trousers and shirts and the women a plain summer dress of cotton or nylon, they do express their ethnic position when putting on their festival attire. This comprises white cushmas with black Yine designs and decorated crowns with feathers for the men, and for the women the wrap around skirt, the pampanilla, and a blouse or bare torso decorated with geometrical designs and figures, besides crossed bandoliers and strings of seed beads hanging from their necks. Their architecture and housing structure is very similar to both the Conibo and the river dwelling Asháninka of the Urubamba. The community layout is indistinguishable from the latter. Their production is a combination of the advanced swidden horticultural system of the Asháninka and the fishing excellence of the Conibo. They have many ties to the mestizo society in the area and are apparently more involved in cash cropping and commercialization of products than any other indigenous group around Atalaya. They also regularly work in timber extraction for the local patrons. Although numerically few in comparison to the Ashéninka, the Yine always occupy a number of high positions in the Regional Indigenous Organisation of Atalaya, OIRA, an organisation meant to represent all indigenous groups in the province.

Shamanism and healing

Each of the indigenous people involved with the PSI have their own impressive cosmological system, with complex structures of time and space. These world orders are kept alive and in place through an elaborate mythology that rationalizes and regulates the place and meaning of all things and events. The landscape is obviously part of this construct and all important features refer to some mythological event. In consequence, places are intrinsic parts of people's self-identification. These cosmologies are not the same for each group, although they are structurally comparable. The modern western world and rationality is articulated and often rationalised in the indigenous ideological process, thus avoiding the alienation that concerned non-indigenous visitors are often worried about. Peruvian national society, its logic and its rules, are very much seen as a resource potential to be exploited rather than as a threat to indigenous culture and survival. Thus, although the modern state's economy and culture is expanding, there is also the opposite process evolving, an appropriation and indigenisation of the "white world". This became quite clear as the PSI developed, in the sense that non-western healing practices and the rationale they are based upon came to impact on the entire Programme and even the public health system in a surprisingly constructive way.

We cannot in this chapter review the different indigenous cosmological orders represented in the Indigenous Health Programme, but we can try to sketch a few basic structures of indigenous illness and healing. Common to all groups is a world in which basically all things have a life of their own and a history of creation reflected in mythology. No single person knows all the stories, myths and narratives but all know something and at least have a core knowledge. Illness is, in most cases, believed to be a result of a conflict between the human world and the spiritual world. In this context illness is understood to be a malignant spirit who has entered the body to do you harm for some reason. As a matter of principle, all living things, including objects that we usually regard as dead like rocks and lakes, may inflict damage on you. For example, certain trees may not like pregnant women for a primordial reason explained in their mythology, and may inflict harm on the foetus if the pregnant woman touches the trunk when she walks by. This may prevent pregnant women from walking in the forest. Humans can also call upon certain evil spirits, through rituals, to do harm to specific individuals for revenge or envy. This is witchcraft and believed to be one of the major causes of illness and death. Witches and sorcerers can be both men and women, but also children and even domestic animals may be accused of sorcery. The problem is that weak and vulnerable souls (e.g. those of children and adolescent girls) may be invaded by evil spirits that may "hypnotise" them to do sorcery while they are asleep. Accordingly sorcery is very often seen as a type of illness in and of itself. It is severely punished if proven and cannot always be cured. However, some very common diseases such as colds and simple infections are most often not seen as the result of witchcraft but rather regarded as contagion, which is self-propagating, or regarded as a general punishment from God and, as such, just a condition of everyday life.

Although each indigenous culture has its own system, there are certain common features, and they all have specialists in repairing imbalances in their animist universe. The most important is the shaman, the spiritual master, who can interpret signs and events, as well as investigate and explain cause and effect relationships. The shaman also has the ability to communicate with the spiritual world, thus building bridges between the earthly human beings and the spirits and God(s), with whom humans lost direct contact when the secular and the spiritual worlds separated. For example, the shaman may renew "contracts" with animal master spirits for hunting a specific animal species or even enter into a fight with threatening genies at night. Sickness and disease can also be cured by the shamans through a series of different rituals and methods. The Conibo, Ashéninka and Yine all have different ways of curing. In order to enter into a mental state that permits the shaman to interact with the spiritual world, different herbal medicines and drugs may be taken to alter the mind. One of the best known and commonly used by shamans from all ethnic groups in the Upper Amazon is a powerful hallucinogenic concoction made from the *ayahuasca* vine (*Banisteriopsis sp.*) in combination with *chacruna* leaves (*Psychotria sp.*). Ayahuasca is a Quechua word meaning "death vine" and is the common term in Spanish, but each indigenous language obviously has its own term. Ayahuasca produces a mental state in which the shaman can look into the past and the future, while identifying possible sorcerers and other reasons for illnesses. Although all indigenous groups know and use ayahuasca, it is much more dominant among riverine groups such as the Conibo, Yine and even mestizos than among the Ashéninka. Indigenous shamans often claim that real knowledge and insight into the world order and its condition come from the ayahuasca. The Ashéninka shamans are much more associated with the curing effect of tobacco. They produce a very strong tobacco syrup by making a concoction from tobacco leaves and boiling it down to a viscous black substance that is kept in a bamboo tube. The syrup is then licked in very small portions at a time, from a stick dipped in the syrup. It is mixed with coca leaves, which the Ashéninka chew with lime, together with a bit of another dried liana that makes it taste sweet. The nicotine intoxication in combination with the coca also alters the mind, resulting in insight and visions. The tobacco plant spirit is central to Ashéninka and Asháninka shamanism and healing practices, hence the name of the shaman is *Sheripiari*, i.e. the "tobacco spirit master". They sometimes mix ayahuasca into the tobacco syrup as well as other herbal medicinal substances. The Sheripiari cures almost everything with tobacco and is, in his intoxicated state, able to suck the evil causing the sickness out of the afflicted body.

Yine family in the Urubamba.   *Photo: Dorte M. Jensen, 1994*

This evil agent may even be identified as a small object he will be able to hawk and spit into his hand. Another commonly used and very powerful drug is *toé* (*Datura sp.*), often applied in cases where other remedies do not function. Some shamans see the toé as antagonistic to the ayahuasca spirit.

It requires years of training and guidance by an experienced master to be able to gain sufficient insight and knowledge to be a shaman. Several taboos, including sexual abstinence, must be meticulously observed and a strict diet kept for years, and sacred shamanic chants, *ícaros*, must be learned and practised with the master. The shaman, *Unanya* in Conibo, *Sheripiari* in Ashéninka, and *Kamchí* or the Spanish word *curandero* in Yine, not only serves the important function of a psychotherapist, curing the somatic and mental diseases of individuals, he (or she sometimes) also works as the society's guarantor of collective mental health, the one who maintains the moral values and balance of the society within the indigenous cosmos. This is indispensable for the collective well being of humans and, in the last resort, for the survival of the indigenous group.

Besides the shamans, there are several other medical specialists in indigenous society. One is the herbal healer, who may also be the shaman, but not necessarily. Knowledge of herbal medicine requires long-term commitment. All plants are living and have spirits, and it is the spirit of each medicinal plant species that cures specific diseases. The knowledge of the curative powers of plants, and how to deploy them, is particularly developed with the Yine and Conibo, where it is part of the shamanic curriculum; whereas among the Ashéninka it is particularly knowledge that older women have accumulated but otherwise is common knowledge in any family. Herbalism is also well developed among mestizo ribereños, a population who adopted the practice from their indigenous neighbours but were in a position that allowed them to mix practices and knowledge from several different ethnic groups.

A special type of herbal healing is practiced by the "vapour healer", the *vaporadora*, who almost always is a woman. The *vaporadora* is, in many ways, the female counterpart to the male shaman. However, her activities are particularly focussed on personal healing and do not reach into the shamanic sphere of wider cosmological commitment. Vapour therapy is applied by putting red-hot stones in a pot with water and herbs with particular curing properties, and then letting the patients squat over the pot wearing a *cushma*, which will keep the vapour inside like a tent. Afterwards, the remaining herbs in the pot will be examined and a small object, exorcised from the body, identified among the residue. The *vaporadora* is often also the midwife, the *partera*. Midwives are generally highly respected in indigenous communities, and the midwife is expected to be a person with extensive knowledge of healing, her role being that of the "chief nurse" of the community. The last category of medical specialists we should mention is the *huesero*, the osteopath, who is specialised in healing bone fractures and repositioning dislocated joints. Some of them are very skilled and combine their osteopathic capacity with anaesthetic herbal treatment. All types of indigenous healers and medical specialists are frequently visited by non-indigenous inhabitants from the area, however discreetly.

Shamans are greatly respected but also feared, as their spiritual powers and psychological skills may be turned against any person if so wished. Shamanism and other healing practices have been repressed by the Church and by missionaries from all religious communities, Catholic or not, through the centuries. It has been a major objective of the Indigenous Health Programme to revalue, regain, legalise and reinstitute these specialists, as they are crucial for the acceptance, support and building of any sustainable indigenous rural health system. Their knowledge and cooperation is indispensable for success.

HISTORICAL OVERVIEW
Introducing the colonist frontiers

As mentioned previously, the Upper Amazon of Peru can be roughly divided into two main geographical zones: one is the *selva alta*, the highly-lying rainforest constituted by the rugged eastern slopes of the Andes, stretching into the Amazon basin. The other is the low rainforest, the *selva baja* comprised of the river basins of the Ucayali River and other major rivers and tributaries[10]. These two different geographical formations have determined the distinctive way in which the colonisation and expansion of national society has developed in the two zones. The high forest is immediately connected to the Andes which, despite their difficult topography, have had certain logistic advantages as they are relatively close to markets and labour. All rivers in this area are fast running white water tributaries with no potential for fluvial transportation. Penetrating the area requires road construction. Because of these characteristics, the higher rainforest areas have primarily been targeted for their potential for agriculture and cattle ranching, connecting to the national commercial centres by means of roads.

The lower lying tropical forest belongs to the great Amazon basin, characterized by slower running rivers flowing towards Brazil, far away from the Peruvian commercial centres of the Pacific coast. Despite rich alluvial soils along the main rivers, this area has not been dominated by agricultural expansion, due to the combination of unpredictable fluctuations in seasonal flooding and the distance to markets. All transportation is carried out by river, forming a complex logistic network traditionally oriented toward the markets of Brazil. The Lower Amazon of Peru has, since the first European contact, been an appendix to the rest of the country, living an economic life of its own dominated by extractivist activities, such as *Chincona* bark for quinine, rubber tapping, extraction of tropical hardwood, gold and crude oil deposits, to mention a few typical products.

Thus we have two frontiers of national economic expansion pushing into indigenous territories, framing the development of the indigenous societies in the area: the agricultural frontier moving down and eastwards from the Andes, imposing permanent colonisation and infrastructure; and the extractivist frontier moving upriver and westwards, implying fewer permanent settlements initially but great demands for indigenous knowledge and labour. In the following, we will briefly review the history of colonisation in Gran Pajonal and the Ucayali simultaneously, in chronological order.

Missionaries and rebellions

The European expansion and colonisation of the Peruvian Amazon began, as in so many other places in the world, with a pacification process launched by Catholic missionaries, who pioneered the penetration and exploration of unknown lands and established mission stations and outposts in the forest of "infidels", as they regarded the unbaptised indigenous inhabitants.

However, the first ascent of the Ucayali took place long before the missionaries ever set foot here. It was the expedition of Juan Salinas de Loyola who, as early as 1557, departed from Ecuador in search of the famous El Dorado and new lands to claim for the Spanish crown. He travelled upstream of the Ucayali and wrote several reports about his findings. According to his description, three indigenous groups dominated the Ucayali: the Cocama on the lower river, the Conibo in the middle and upper section, and what could be identified as the Yine in the area around the conjunction of the rivers Urubamba, Ucayali and Tambo. Salinas tells us that they lived in large riverine settlements, that they used cotton clothing with elaborate embroidered and painted designs, and that they wore gold and silver jewellery as nose pendants, earrings, necklaces and waist chains, along with head-dresses. As such metals cannot be found downstream of the Ucayali, they must have been trade items, presumably one of the specialities of the Yine, having contacts upstream of the Urubamba to the heart of the Inca empire in the Cuzco region of the Andes (Morin 1998:199-200). Another century was to pass before serious attempts were made to settle there.

Missionary activities accelerated rapidly during the 17th century, once the Spanish colonial order was well established. Both the Jesuit and the Franciscan orders obtained the concessional right from the Spanish viceroyalty in Peru to colonize and civilize the indigenous populations in our area of interest. The Jesuits were based in Quito, in what is now Ecuador, and the Franciscans were based in Lima, the capital of the Spanish viceroyalty. In the Ucayali, the two orders were competing for influence and proselytes, a dispute that ended with the expulsion of the Jesuits in 1767. Thereafter, the Franciscan order was left alone on the scene, and was to have a decisive impact on the history of the Central Peruvian Amazon and Ucayali over the next two centuries. The preferred strategy of these first missionaries was to establish positive relations with the lead-

Men cooking, Gran Pajonal.   *Photo: Bente Korsgaard, 1994*

ers of particular indigenous groups or sections thereof, through gifts of metal tools and other desired items, in exchange for conversion and loyalty. Once such a missionary outpost was established, the next step was to concentrate as many "Indians" as possible around the post and gradually develop a mission-controlled community. Such idealistic colonies were called *"reducciones"*, and were established all over South America during the first couple of centuries of missionary activities.

The Franciscans had penetrated the eastern Peruvian Montaña and established their mission stations among the Asháninka and Yánesha in the mid-17th century, with the support of the colonial army. They attempted to continue eastwards to reach the Ucayali in 1641 but the initial attempt failed, halted by an attack from the Shipibo who, at that time, lived upriver of the Aguaytia, one of the tributaries of the Ucayali. The next attempt by the Franciscans to proselytize in the Ucayali took place eleven years later when they succeeded in founding two mission posts that were, however, soon to be destroyed by indigenous rebellions. In fact, most of the initial mission stations had a short life span, finishing up destroyed or abandoned due to indigenous uprisings. This was certainly the case both in the Selva Central and in the Ucayali. The reason for the rebellions seems to be the same during the first period of contact: virulent epidemics in and around the missions and *"reducciones"* devastating the indigenous society, abuses committed by the accompanying soldiers and colonists, and Christian prohibitions and repression. The recurrent epidemics of smallpox, measles and other viral diseases introduced by the missionaries and soldiers, in particular, caused a fierce reaction against further contact from both the Asháninka and the Conibo (cf. Santos-Granero 1987, 1992). These epidemics had a dramatic effect on indigenous society and the demographic structure of the entire region. A devastating epidemic of smallpox ravaged large populations of Cocamas in the Lower Ucayali around 1644, causing a decline in population of some 85% in a very short space of time (cf. Myers 1988). The Jesuits established other "reducciones" in the north, along other tributaries of the Ucayali, the Huallaga and Marañon rivers, relocating a great number of the surviving Cocamas from the Ucayali to Huallaga. (Morin 1998: 302-302) The social order of the Cocama practically collapsed, opening up trade for the Conibo downriver into a territory that had previously been inaccessible for them. Some of the missions succeeded in their efforts and became local trade centres where indigenous traders could exchange their different goods, including food items, for iron, tools and salt. This was the case in the central rainforest, where the Franciscans established a mission in the vicinity of the famous Cerro de la Sal, i.e. the salt mountain, (cf. Varese 1973, Santos-Granero 1992), and it was also the case with the Jesuit mission in the Lower Huallaga. The epidemics had cleared the way for the Conibos, who began trading all the way downriver to the Jesuit missions in the Huallaga, a round trip of some 2,300 km by canoe! The trade journeys gradually developed into piracy ventures and the Conibo became notorious for ransacking indigenous settlements and capturing slaves. The booty and the slaves were brought to the Jesuits, who bought the slaves, taught them Quechua and used them as interpreters and guides for further evangelising in the Upper Ucayali (Morin 1998:303). Soon a new economy and social order developed in the Ucayali and vicinity, based on indigenous trade, piracy and slave raiding. The indigenous societies became destabilized, more epidemics followed and a rapid population decline ensued. The indigenous groups had an ambiguous attitude towards the Catholic missionaries. On the one hand, they were highly appreciated as sources of metal tools, salt and other rare trading items and, on the other, they were a nuisance bringing oppression, death and disorder with them.

Both the Jesuits and the Franciscans attempted to establish a mission in the Central Ucayali and eventually entered into a conflict over a mission station they both claimed the right to. Intense travel up and down river from both sides caused the Yine to intervene by attacking a Jesuit commission on its way to Lima via Ucayali-Tambo. The situation came to a head in 1686-87 when the Spanish Viceroy in Lima decided to divide the territory in two: the Lower Ucayali and Northern Amazon for the Jesuits and the middle and Upper Ucayali and central forest for the Franciscans. Consequently the famous Franciscan, Father Biedma, who had years of experience with the Asháninka in the Selva Central, established a new mission close to where Atalaya is situated today as a base for a renewed effort among the Conibo. Unfortunately he was killed in 1687 by the Yine in an ambush on the Rio Tambo, which caused the Franciscans to give up their mission in Ucayali. This spurred renewed efforts by the Jesuits to relocate as many Pano-speaking groups as possible into their "reducciones". The general turbulence in interethnic relations caused by a combination of epidemics and missionary imposition finally allied the Conibo and Piro in a common rebellion against the Jesuits in 1695-1698, with the outcome of destroying the mission stations in the Ucayali. The rebellion brought an end to both Jesuit and Franciscan travel and influence in the Upper Ucayali for the next 15 years. Several uprisings among the Pano speakers subsequently followed. But the Asháninka, the Yánesha and the Ashéninka in the higher lying areas of the Montaña also repeatedly rebelled against the Franciscan influence.

At the time of the Ucayali Pano-Piro rebellions, the Franciscans had still not visited Gran Pajonal but the area became increasingly interesting, partly because of the rumours of the grasslands, which evoked Franciscan dreams of great cattle ranching and agricultural production. Beside this economic potential and the potential Ashéninka proselytes, Gran Pajonal also opened up the possibility of over-land travel to the Ucayali from the central forest, thus avoiding travel down the Rio Tambo and passing through hostile Yine territory on the way to the Conibo. After careful planning several years ahead, the Franciscans made their first entry into Gran Pajonal in 1734. They were initially well received by the local

Ashéninka, who were very interested in their iron tools, liquor and weapons. It was apparently a great success and, over the following years, several mission posts, cattle stations and small colonies were established in the Gran Pajonal. The Franciscans were very satisfied, until 1742 when a large and coordinated rebellion was surprisingly started in the Gran Pajonal. The moving spirit in this was the now legendary figure, Juan Santos Atahualpa, who held the opulent title of *Apu Inca* "Chief Inca". Juan Santos was a mestizo claiming to be of Inca descent, educated with the Jesuits in Cuzco and with a background of travel in Europe and Angola. Fleeing a murder charge and descending the Apurimac-Ene river, he ended up with the Ashéninka in Gran Pajonal in 1742. From here, he staged a mass rally with a thousand Asháninka, Ashéninka and Yine participants, against the Franciscan mission. During the meeting, they declared the zone liberated and issued a ban an all missionary activities, giving the missionaries and followers two weeks in which to leave the area, which they did. Juan Santos also declared war on the Spanish colonial powers and promised to liberate all the indigenous inhabitants of the entire Montaña from the Spanish colonizers. Together with powerful headmen, he organized a standing militia of several thousand men. Soon after the first meeting, they moved their headquarter out of the Gran Pajonal to the Salt Mountain area, controlling the main trail and trade between the Andean highland and the Amazon. The rebellion rapidly spread and he attracted growing support from all indigenous groups and divisions in the central Peruvian Amazon, including the Shipibo and Conibo. The rebellious Asháninka, Ashéninka and neighbouring groups completely cleared the central Peruvian Amazon of Franciscan missions and colonisations, and maintained a standing Asháninka militia for more than 15 years. The rebellion ended in 1756, after which Juan Santos disappeared from the scene. This was the largest and most significant of all indigenous insurrections in the Peruvian Amazon, with far-reaching effects on the development of the region, which remained largely uncolonised until the late 19th century (Hvalkof 1998, Metraux 1942, Santos-Granero 1987, Varese 1973, Veber 1998).

The Spanish viceroyalty and colonial administration in Lima did not take great economic interest in the central Peruvian Amazon. Their main preoccupation was with the Andean highlands and the Pacific coast, with their economic centres of mining, agriculture and trade. Only the eastern Andean slopes on the edge of the Amazon basin were of some limited interest for its mining and agricultural potential. As mentioned, all attempts to establish permanent missions and colonies eventually failed. Still, the Franciscans, alone on the scene after the expulsion of the Jesuits, had a vision of a Catholic development utopia with the conversion of the Montaña into the bread basket of Peru. Besides the goal of proselytizing and saving souls, the mission's interest in the Lower Amazon was mostly logistic: finding a way of connecting the Pacific coast to the Ucayali and main Amazon river and waterways. Establishing such a connection across the Andes was soon seen as being the trigger for tremendous developmental potential, and this has remained a recurrent motivation for colonizing the area (cf., Hvalkof 1989, 1998, 2002a; Santos-Granero y Barclay 1998).

In the Ucayali River basin, an extractivist economy was taking form during the 18th century. Extraction of the *zarzaparilla* root (*Smilax sp.*), an export item to Europe as favourite anti-syphilitic medicine, and bark from the *quina* tree (*Cinchona officinalis*), also known as *cinchona* or *cascarilla*, to produce quinine for antipyretic purposes, was rapidly expanding. This was not driven by missionary zeal but by private investors and merchants. Logistic limitations still made canoeing Indians the masters of this area. However, it also made them obvious targets for being forced into indentured labour in the emerging extractivist economy, which was totally dependent on indigenous knowledge and labour. As we have seen, slavery and long distance trade were already well integrated into the indigenous economy, and the quest for metal tools, fire-arms and European merchandise was growing. The basis of a new and brutal economy and interethnic relations was being laid. Modernity was encroaching.

Rubber and slaves

Peru's independence from Spain in 1821 left the country in turmoil, and it took almost fifty years for the new Peruvian Republic to reasonably consolidate and begin functioning as a contemporary state. Meanwhile, the Franciscan were inactive, expelled from the country for a while, awaiting better times to come, and both the Montaña and the Ucayali were left without the proselytizing Catholic entrepreneurs for half a century. But one man's loss is another man's gain and, in the Amazon region, a new extractivist enterprise was rapidly developing - the extraction of rubber. Three European inventions were decisive in this new development: the invention of the steam engine, leading to the introduction of steam boats onto the rivers in the mid-19th century; the invention of the process of vulcanization of crude rubber; and the pneumatic tube and tyre. The demand for rubber in Europe and North America was exploding and a veritable rubber bonanza was unfolding in the Upper Amazon and the Ucayali from the 1860s to 1915. European commercial houses and capital ventured into this very profitable business, and scores of "wannabe" rubber patrons, so called *caucheros* and other soldiers of fortune, invaded the Amazon in a reckless search for instant wealth.

There are several species of latex-producing trees, and several ways of extracting the rubber. Some methods tap the trees in such a way that allows them to survive, others damage them severely or destroy them entirely by cutting them down. The common way to produce wild rubber in the Upper Ucayali is to find the rubber tree stands in the rainforest, make a cut in the trees and drain them completely for the milky latex sap, which is then coagulated, smoked and rolled up into giant balls or shaped into giant slabs, which may weigh well over 50 kilos each. The rubber is then carried to the nearest navigable tributary, loaded onto canoes or primitive rafts, and floated down to the Ucayali to a rubber collection post, later to be shipped to the nearest trading station or colony on the main river. If the tapping took place at the upper headwaters of the eastern tributaries, it was easier to carry it overland to one of the rivers running eastwards, such as the Yurua or Purus, and sell it downriver in Brazil (cf. Santos-Granero and Barclay 2000 for an excellent presentation and analysis of the Peruvian rubber economy).

Most of the labour involved in the tough rubber collection was indigenous, procured through debt bondage systems known as *enganche* and *habilitación*. The patron contracted his workers through advance payment in kind, which they then paid off through deliverance of a certain amount of rubber. The trick was to keep the worker indebted through constant advance payments or by claiming that the value of the merchandise advanced had risen, thus requiring ever more labour to balance "the account". The habilitación system and the debt bondage and chattel slavery system were systematized in a chain of exploitation, with contractors and subcontractors reaching the lowest level of the indigenous rubber tapper, who was carrying the bulk of the burden. In this system, the commercial agent or outfitter subcontracted one or more labour recruiters, "habilitating" them with sufficient merchandise, which might reproduce the habilitación at the next lower level, contracting workers or local indigenous headmen, who again controlled the local workers through advance payments etc. The productivity was kept in place through violent reprisals or killings if the peons did not comply with their contracts. Along with the caucheros, who penetrated all corners of the Upper Amazon, there followed violent epidemics of viral diseases, decimating many hinterland indigenous groups with no immunological resistance.

Parallel to the rubber economy itself, another much more destructive economy was rapidly evolving: that of the slave trade in indigenous women and children. As mentioned above, the slave trade had already been practised by the Conibo and Yine in the 17th century but, with the influx of outfitters, rubber patrons and merchants, the demand for domestic and sex slaves grew rapidly, creating a fast growing market for slaves. The common way to get these was to outfit indigenous raiding parties who, together with a mestizo or white foreman, assaulted and raided the hinterland indigenous settlements, killing adult men, and carrying off the younger women and children. The Franciscan father, Luís Sabaté, who made an expedition to Urubamba and Ucayali in 1874, described such a situation as follows:

"*That day the Piro [Yine] went on a correría against the Campa and stole many things. It was one of those surprise attacks which the savage tribes make against each other, when they are at war with one another. Women and children were taken and sold to the whites, being traded as if they were some kind of commodity. As can be seen, the whites in the area act as the stimulus for these inhumane incursions, for if they did not maintain this detestable traffic in human flesh, the Indians would lose the incentive for their barbarous excursion."* (Sabaté quoted from Izaguirre 1925: 99. Translated into English by the author).

Such slave raids are commonly known as *correrías*, and remained a widespread practice in the Upper Ucayali watershed and the Gran Pajonal. They involved all indigenous groups in the area, and several indigenous headmen among the Conibo, Asháninka and Yine were notorious for their raiding expeditions up the tributaries to the east or into the Gran Pajonal to the West[11]. The rubber economy declined rapidly after 1914, when new commercial plantations in Malaysia, Indonesia and Africa began to produce at a much lower cost. Rubber collecting was eventually abandoned completely in the 1920s. Notwithstanding this, the slave trade continued to develop, and correrías were practised well into the 20th century, the latest was reported to the author as having taken place in the late 1960s in Gran Pajonal up the Unini river (cf. Hvalkof 1998: 134-140).

The rubber period from the 1860s to 1915 turned out to be highly disastrous for the indigenous population. The demographic pattern changed drastically, with steep population declines. People were moved around and settled in new territories, the traditional economies of the hinterland groups were almost destroyed, and fierce epidemics, particularly of measles, ravaged entire areas. The indigenous societies were completely broken and divided, and it took decades to overcome the catastrophic effect of the correrías both in terms of depopulation but also in terms of mutual distrust and enmity among local groups. The areas were laid open to colonisation, and many of the rubber patrons now turned to more sedentary economic activities, such as agriculture and timber extraction. In the Upper Ucayali, haciendas and small colonist settlements were established in the place of the former rubber trading posts, creating a new need for loyal indigenous labour. The system of enganche and habilitación continued to provide contractual workers for the local patrons, and has continued to do so up to this very day. But alongside the quest for loyal male peons there also grew a need for domestic servants, which the new patrons secured by bringing up abducted Ashéninka children at their haciendas. Atalaya was founded in 1928, obtaining status as an independent district. A former rubber baron of the area, Sr. Francisco Vargas, donated land from his hacienda, La Colonia, to the Franciscans at Atalaya, and with help from the local colonists and their indigenous workers, the Franciscan mission was built. It was inaugurated in 1932 and the new town of Atalaya became a reality (ibid. 140).

Photo: Søren Hvalkof, 2000   *Early morning, Gran Pajonal.*

The agricultural frontier

While the new extractivist economy and new social order in the Ucayali and Urubamba areas were developing, the decolonisation of the higher lying forest areas lost before independence to the indigenous rebel militia of Juan Santos Atahualpa, was taking shape. The Franciscan mission had resumed its colonisation of the *Selva Central* in the 1860s and the new Peruvian State was highly motivated to back this process up. The upper and lower Amazon forests were believed to hold tremendous agricultural potential, and large colonisation schemes were planned. In 1891 a vast area of the central Peruvian forest of some 2 million hectares was given in concession to a British owned company, the Peruvian Corporation, in order to colonize and develop the Montaña. It was part of a compensation deal to foreign creditors following a Peruvian State bankruptcy. The concession area embraced a large part of the Yánesha, Asháninka, Ashéninka and Nomatsigenka territories. The Peruvian Corporation "only" succeeded in exploiting 500.000 hectares in the Chanchamayo valley, establishing big plantations of coffee, cocoa and citrus, but they maintained control of the area up until the agrarian reforms of the 1960s (Santos-Granero and Barclay 1998).

It is worth mentioning that the company also contracted a Seventh Day Adventist missionary from the USA, Ferdinand Stahl, to pacify and discipline the Asháninka and make them work for the company in exchange for easy access to converts. After nearly 30 years of work in the Chanchamayo, Ferdinand Stahl was eventually expelled by the company in 1948 and decided to leave the area and establish new Adventist missions further east. This caused an Asháninka exodus from the central Peruvian forest towards the rivers Tambo, Urubamba, Ucayali and Pichis. Stahl had many indigenous followers and, when he decided to leave the area, a veritable cult with Messianic overtones grew up around him. He succeeded in establishing several Adventist mission in the areas mentioned, and had particular success among the Yine and Asháninka in the Ucayali-Urubamba nexus. The Adventist missionaries worked in the area for many years, and the missions are still there with their Adventist followers to this day. Several of the indigenous leaders in the PSI project area are trained by the Adventists and support the programme.

The indigenous population suffered a sharp decline due to epidemics, and the frequent slaveraids, which extended all the way to the foothills of the Andes, had broken the solidarity between local groups. So, although skirmishes and local resistance to recolonisation occurred intermittently, new mule trails were opened, connecting Lima via the Andean highlands to the navigable tributaries of the Ucayali. The Franciscans made several expeditions to find out if it was safe to settle and they succeeded in establishing several mission stations west of Gran Pajonal and, as mentioned, also in Atalaya. Gran Pajonal was not recolonised until 1934, when the three mission posts were established, of which only one, the small colony of Oventeni in the centre of Gran Pajonal, survived. The

Franciscans contracted Andean settlers, mostly Quechua-speaking peasants, to help develop the new colonisation. Fear of the local Ashéninka, and the need for logistic support from the Peruvian Air force, caused them to construct a 1,600 m long airstrip, which has kept the colony alive until today. But it was not easy to colonize the grasslands. The distance from the markets, the high cost of transportation, the different ecology and the relative isolation from the rest of the Peruvian society caused many of the contracted Andean settlers to give up. Still, the Franciscans insisted on establishing a real mission and succeeded in constructing a brick church, a boarding school for Ashéninka children and living quarters for the Catholic fathers and sisters working there. However, they were well aware that the long-term survival of the Oventeni colony depended on access and so, in 1940, the Franciscans began the arduous task of constructing a small 80 km road from the Puerto Ocopa mission on the Perené river into Gran Pajonal and along the Unini River all the way to Ucayali and Atalaya. The road, including a suspension bridge, was finished in 1946, the same year that a new landing strip was opened in Atalaya. The landing strip was a sensible initiative because later that year an intense earthquake destroyed the road completely.

The colonisation of Gran Pajonal was not a success and the colony grew very slowly, until a group of investors from Lima was granted a concession to establish a modern cattle ranch on the interior grasslands in 1950. Aerial photo surveys were undertaken of the zone, and good cattle brought in, together with horses, mules and donkeys. Veterinarians and specialists were hired, and skilled workers from Lima and the highlands contracted. Fencing was set up, coffee was planted and the local Ashéninka contracted to produce food for the workers. It looked promising but it eventually turned into a fiasco. A combination of extremely high production costs, problems in marketing beef or live cattle, huge logistic problems and sky-high transportation costs, the poor nutritional value of the natural grass and cattle diseases and, last but not least, bad management - all contributed to the failure of the project. The cattle ranching adventure received its deathblow in January 1966 when the MIR guerrilla front, headed by the legendary Guillermo Lobatón, entered Gran Pajonal and, for a couple of weeks, occupied Oventeni and the hacienda in Shumahuani (cf. Brown and Fernández 1991). The *guerrilleros* killed and ate the best of the cattle breeding stock, held ideological talks for the settlers and hacienda workers, threatened and scared the Franciscan missionaries and eventually left the area. Apparently they had expected support from the Ashéninka, but they did not support the guerrilleros - nor did they oppose them. Immediately after the guerrilleros had left Oventeni, special counter-insurgency forces, the "Rangers" with American training, landed in Oventeni, chasing Lobatón and his men. With the help of an Ashéninka guide from the Adventist mission in Unini, they encountered them close to the Ashéninka community of Mapitzeviari, where most of the men were killed. Lobatón and his second in command, Jaime

Martínez, were captured and later executed and buried on a *pajonal* – grassland, not far from Oventeni. The incident spelled the end of the cattle ranching project and also of the Franciscan mission in Oventeni. The mission was evacuated and their boarding school closed, and three years later, in 1968, the hacienda eventually gave up too.

Some of the hacienda workers stayed on in the Gran Pajonal, trying on their own to make a livelihood as individual colonists. Others moved to Atalaya and Ucayali, which looked more promising with a new timber economy emerging. For the next decade, spontaneous colonisation was the only movement in the area and the influx of newcomers was limited. The colonists used the old system of *enganche* to secure Ashéninka labour to cultivate their fields, look after their cattle and pick their coffee.

Protestant American missionaries from the Summer Institute of Linguistics, the SIL, also appeared on the scene in 1968, when they undertook translating the Bible into Ashéninka. They settled in the vicinity of the abandoned hacienda in the interior and began working with young ashéninka as linguistic informants as well as engaging in discreet proselytising. This later came to have a decisive impact on the indigenous movement in the area. The indigenous population in Gran Pajonal had probably reached its lowest point in decades due to the devastating measles epidemics that the many farm workers at the cattle hacienda had brought with them. There were probably only around 1,500 Ashéninka living in the entire Gran Pajonal at that time (Bodley 1972). But along with the protestant missionaries came vaccination campaigns and limited health care. The collapse of the cattle venture also opened the zone up to indigenous resettlement, and Ashéninka families that had fled the area due to a combination of *correrías*, epidemics, cattle and new colonists began to return to their old territory. The indigenous population of Gran Pajonal grew rapidly throughout the 1970s. The colonists were happy as this initially meant more cheap labour to contract for their agricultural and cattle production. It became even more relevant when, around 1975, the Oventeni colonists successfully began planting good nutritional grass on cleared forest land, instead of grazing the natural savannas, of low value for cattle. The economic and social scenario in Gran Pajonal was beginning to change. A new government and new international development loan in 1980 radically boosted this process. Large, integrated development and colonisation schemes were launched during the 1980s in the Selva Central, financed and backed by international development agencies such as the World Bank, the Inter-American Development Bank, USAID and the German international development agency, GTZ. These expensive programmes, called the Special Projects, mainly built roads, and thousand of landless peasants from the Andes flooded the area, invading indigenous land, destroying the ecology of the zone by indiscriminately cutting down the forest, criminalizing the area through organized coca production for the Colombian drug lords, and finally introducing the Shining Path and MRTA guerrillas into the area, later to be followed by the Peruvian military. The Special Projects were a complete failure, and the international agencies promoting and financing them backed out when conditions began to deteriorate, leaving social chaos and an indebted Peruvian state behind. Although they fortunately never succeeded in continuing their efforts into Gran Pajonal, despite this being within their mandate, the development had a conspicuous effect on Gran Pajonal where new settlers began to appear and where new credits for the smallholders' cattle raising began to impact on the social scene. The colonists in the Atalaya area also noticed new winds blowing, making it advantageous to expand their economic activities both in cattle raising, timber extraction and illegal cocaine production.

Encroachment and conflict

The situation changed drastically during the 1980s. The new international development programmes, the Special Projects, pushed new settlers into both Gran Pajonal and the Atalaya region, and the pressure on land and resources increased. The indigenous inhabitants of Gran Pajonal and Atalaya in particular felt squeezed between the old patrons and the new colonists expanding from the riverside and the agricultural frontier moving in from the Andes. New credit possibilities for cattle raisers motivated an aggressive expansion of new grazing areas with planted fodder grass. Thousands of hectares of tropical forest were cleared to make room for the new cattle boom. The work of cutting and burning the forest, planting the grass and looking after the cattle was as usual done by the Ashéninka through traditional debt bondage relations to their patrons. The exploitation of indigenous labour from 1980-85 escalated to such a point that it threatened the economy of both the Ashéninka and the colonists. The Ashéninka had little time left for taking care of their own production and certainly had no surplus to sell to the settlers. The prices of daily necessities increased sharply in a very short space of time. The colonists responded by increasing their exploitation of indigenous labour and their repression of those who refused to comply. In the colony of Gran Pajonal, this was done by whipping and beating contrary Ashéninka peons on Sundays in the primitive jail of Oventeni. The humiliation led to several suicides, including one mass suicide of an entire Ashéninka family with small children, who had been threatened by the colono authorities. Similar and worse abuses were rampant in the Atalaya region, where the patrons were expanding their timber extraction activities and were in urgent need of indigenous labour (cf. García 1998, Hvalkof 1998). Several complaints were filed, but the local and regional authorities ignored them completely. This denial of human rights abuses was understandable in the light of the history of colonist-indigenous relations, and the fact was that the authorities were no different than the colonists themselves, having unrestricted political power throughout the entire Ucayali Region. The colonists and patrons saw this as an expression of their pioneering effort to civilize the savages and develop the country. The conflicts grew rapid-

ly and several violent clashes between Ashéninka peons and colono patrons occurred. The situation was tense and threatened to develop into a wider inter-ethnic conflict.

THE INDIGENOUS MOVEMENT
Organising and land titling

The general political scenario both in Peru and internationally was changing in the 1980s. Regional indigenous organisations were beginning to form and a new indigenous movement was developing. The first indigenous organisations had been founded in the Peruvian Amazon in the 1970s. A national indigenous umbrella organisation, with the somewhat unusual name of the "Interethnic Association for the Development of the Peruvian Rainforest", AIDESEP[12], saw the light of day in 1979. It had only three regional member organisations in the beginning, one representing the Aguaruna peoples in northern Peru, another representing the Shipibo-Conibo of Pucallpa, and a third representing the Yánesha of the Selva Central. More local organisations were formed and began joining AIDESEP through the 1980s, including the first Asháninka organisations in the central forest. Gran Pajonal and Atalaya were still on the margins of this emerging movement, but the Ashéninka and Yine did not tacitly accept the growing oppression from the colonists and began organising.

The indigenous populations were increasing rapidly, primarily as a result of efficient vaccinations campaigns launched by the Protestant US missionaries. Missionaries from the American evangelist Summer Institute of Linguistics (SIL) had, since the 1960s, been working on translating the Bible into the different indigenous languages. As part of their proselytising strategy, they had built a bilingual school system with small local schools scattered throughout the indigenous communities both in Gran Pajonal and around Atalaya. Indigenous evangelist schoolteachers were trained to teach in their own native language. The entire programme was accompanied by logistic support, with light aircraft able to land and take off on very short airstrips in the communities. Besides the crucial vaccination campaigns, they also provided basic health services and other support to the local population. The SIL was soon joined by other evangelist missions such as the Swiss Indian Mission and the conservative South American Mission from California. The new indigenous schools established in the communities were quite popular and the Ashéninka, in particular, who lived dispersed in Gran Pajonal and the interfluvial areas of the Ucayali, began moving closer to the schools. The schools soon came to play an organising role for the local groups and settlements, where

---

Ashéninka woman in her garden, Gran Pajonal.   *Photo: Søren Hvalkof, 1995*

opposition to the encroaching colonists could foment. The evangelist Protestants also symbolised opposition to the Catholic Church and missions who, for centuries, had been equated with the power elite and local colonists. The SIL was widely criticised during the 1980s for destroying the indigenous culture, propagating US middle class values, being a covert agent for US imperialist interests etc. (Hvalkof and Aaby 1981, Stoll 1982). However, in retrospect, it must be stressed that had it not been for the work of the SIL missionaries, their bilingual schools and their vaccination campaigns, notwithstanding their dogmatic agenda, there would have been no indigenous organisations, neither in Gran Pajonal nor in the Ucayali. Furthermore it is unlikely that small languages like Piro (the Yine language) would have survived. (cf., Hanne Veber 1991 for a study of the SIL school system in Gran Pajonal.)

In Gran Pajonal, it was SIL-trained school teachers who initially took the initiative to call in local headmen and their kin and followers, in an attempt to create an organisation that would counter the colonist expansion and put an end to land invasions and abuses. New legislation in Peru following the agrarian reform in the Andean highland had opened up the possibility of creating indigenous communities in the Amazon region. The new indigenous organisation in Gran Pajonal, OAGP, began promoting the establishment of "Native Communities", *Comunidades Nativas,* in the 1980s. A Native Community is a legal administrative unit recognized in the Peruvian constitution and other laws, which grants the indigenous inhabitants exclusive rights to demarcated and titled communal territory, exclusive rights to renewable resources inside the community, a certain degree of self-government, and special indigenous rights to education in their own languages etc. What the Ashéninka leaders of OAGP wanted was titles to their land, in order to stop the colonists' destructive cattle expansion. The new indigenous leadership asked the SIL missionaries, the anthropologists working in the area and others resource persons for logistic and technical help to get a land titling process on track. The first five communities were demarcated and titled in 1984 and, by contacting the World Bank, the OAGP leaders succeeded in convincing the otherwise disastrous Special Projects to fund and implement the demarcation and titling of the rest. By 1988, some 24 communities in Gran Pajonal had their own titles. Although the colonists protested and hindered the process as best they could, the political weight of the internationally-funded development programme overruled the local colonist administration and power hierarchy. More Ashéninka communities were established, demarcated and titled in the following years. The indigenous people were gradually regaining the territory and the control they had lost fifty years earlier and were succeeding in stopping the colonist expansion, halting the emerging conflict at the point where it was about to burst.

In the Atalaya area, local patrons along the Upper Ucayali and Lower Urubamba were equally eager to consolidate their expansion and control with the aid of indigenous labour. Although several Native Communities had been established and titled with help from the Adventists back in the 1970s, most of the indigenous population was still unorganized, and many were living in pure serfdom with the local patrons, descendants from the rubber barons who settled in the area after the bonanza. When the abuses increased in the mid 1980s, some indigenous leaders from Atalaya contacted AIDESEP in Lima asking for intervention and help. They succeeded in instigating an independent investigation. A so-called multi-sectorial commission under the auspices of the Ministry of Justice and the Ministry of Interior visited the zone and investigated the allegations. The commission issued an official report in 1988, presenting appalling evidence of innumerable abuses, including rape, multiple murders, abduction of women and children, chattel slavery and debt bondage, slave trade, theft and a series of other crimes (García et. al. 1998). However, although the report was little more than another piece of paper and did not change anything in itself, it did create good leverage for the indigenous cause. With this document in its hand, AIDESEP contacted the Danish-based NGO, the International Work Group for Indigenous Affairs - IWGIA, asking it for financial support to carry out a land titling project throughout the whole of the Ucayali Region. It seemed obvious to apply the methodology and positive lessons learned from Gran Pajonal in order to put a stop to the intolerable and dangerous social situation around Atalaya. IWGIA applied to the Danish International Development Agency, DANIDA, for funding of the project and the response was positive. A demarcation and land titling project was designed for the indigenous communities in the Ucayali region and the project began work in Atalaya in 1989, supervised by AIDESEP and IWGIA, through a cooperation contract with the Peruvian authorities.

Conflict and democracy

At that time, Peruvian society in general was sinking into a deep social and economic crisis, with rocketing inflation of several thousand percent annually, no production and general political decay. This fostered the two notorious guerrilla movements, the Maoist Shining Path and the socialist MRTA. An MRTA commando made the big mistake of killing one of the Asháninka leaders in Rio Pichis in the winter of 1989-90 in revenge for the capture and execution of a MIR guerrilla leader back in 1966, allegedly informed against by the Asháninka man. This caused an immediately uprising in the Pichis Valley north-east of Gran Pajonal, where the Asháninka very quickly organized a standing militia and, armed with shotguns and bows and arrows, they cleaned the area of guerrillas and sympathizers. Shining Path was also on the war path, killing indigenous leaders and community members who, for one reason or another, did not support or obey them. Chased by the Peruvian military and anti-guerrilla troops, Shining Path took refuge in Asháninka territory south and west of Gran Pajonal and in the Tambo river area, where for years the guerrillas sustained a regime of terror against the Asháninka communities. The leaders in Gran Pajonal were threatened after several disturbing incidents. The OAGP in Gran Pajonal interpreted the situation as highly dangerous for the stability of their newly-gained territory and their freedom, and decided to take over the colono settlement of Oventeni and grant all guerrilla infiltrators safe conduct to leave within 48 hours. Finally, OAGP organized a militia, named the Ashéninka Army, to patrol the Gran Pajonal borders in an attempt to avoid both military intervention and a takeover by the Shining Path guerrillas. This all happened in 1990.

The city of Pucallpa had been placed under martial law by the Peruvian military and a curfew was imposed, due to the high guerrilla activity in the area, with constant armed incidents. This was the situation and complicated working conditions under which the demarcation and land titling project in Ucayali began operating. In the Atalaya region, the indigenous organisation, OIRA, had been founded and, together with AIDESEP, were responsible for implementing the difficult demarcation and community titling project. Offices were set up in Pucallpa and Atalaya where the indigenous staff and topographers worked twelve hours a day. Despite all odds and fierce resistance from the colonist society in Atalaya, along with innumerable other problems of a logistic, technical, legal and political nature, besides high-level attempts to stop the project, by July 1992 OIRA and AIDESEP had succeeded in demarcating and securing titles for 114 communities. A second project phase was applied for and supported by DANIDA in 1993 and, by 1998, 209 Native Communities had received collective titles to their communal lands, and were now the legal owners of some two and a half million hectares (cf., Gray 1998).

The collective land titling of Gran Pajonal and a large part of the Atalaya Province and the rest of the Ucayali region meant that the indigenous population now had a legal position as land owners in modern Peru. The process had changed the position of indigenous peoples within local society radically. Owning land means controlling resources and political influence. During the process, the indigenous population underwent a metamorphosis from exploited peons and serfs to Peruvian citizens with civil rights and voter registration. They had consolidated their representative organizations, resisted the guerrillas' attempts to take over, and shown the astonished colonists and other non-indigenous Peruvians that they were very well capable of organising themselves. For the first time in modern history, they were able to participate in civil society and take part in the decision-making processes. They also attempted to run for political office in the local election on their own electoral list outside the conventional political parties. Both in Gran Pajonal, Atalaya and Tahuanía they succeeded in gaining the posts of mayor and a majority of seats on the municipal councils in 1995. This was an incredible turnaround in a place where the indigenous population, only a few years previously, had had no rights, no registered citizenship and did not even appear in the census or other national statistics. Peruvian society gradually overcame its crisis. The guerrilla movements eventually withered away and the conflicts with the colonists decreased drastically. The indigenous peoples of the Atalaya Province were now an important part of civil society and the process of democratization in the region. It is paradoxical that it was the indigenous population that gave the western concept of democracy meaning for the first time in Atalaya's history, and not the colonist and mestizo population, who all along had legitimized their presence by claiming their "civilizing" function.

But the new indigenous communities still needed social services in order to be able to cope with modern society in the long run. They lacked education, health care and infrastructure, not to mention the most important: a new sustainable economy. The people now understood that they had rights and obligations, and they wanted the rest as well. OIRA and AIDESEP agreed that the next complex issue to be addressed after territorial rights had been secured was the health situation in the indigenous communities. It was seen as crucial that the child mortality rate should be brought down and that the general increase in indigenous population was maintained. The last aspect may surprise outsiders, who often believe that birth control would be a necessity to bring down the average family size. But this is not a problem in an indigenous society that is mainly based on a subsistence economy and where land is not scarce. One of the reasons why the Ashéninka lost their territories to colonists in the first place was an abrupt decline in population due to epidemics and, had it not been for a fast growing indigenous population in the 1970s and 1980s, it would have been impossible to fill the space and establish the communities, which was the only possible way of regaining their right to land and territories. Thus a numerous indigenous population is on the political agenda of the indigenous organisations; it is seen as a necessity in order to consolidate and gain the needed political influence and control, so that they can develop their society in the way they want to. This is what they understand as self-determination.

Indigenous Health - the latest step

The Indigenous Health Programme - the PSI - is precisely such an attempt to take the next step and secure the indigenous population a better rate of survival and integration into modern Peru as indigenous citizens, with their own world views and beliefs respected, and with their own development agenda in force and controlled by themselves. Viewed in such a context the PSI is not only about health, it is equally a very important initiative to consolidate the organisational process and the territorial gains in a place where no one else cares, and where the odds are still against indigenous success. The Indigenous Health Programme of AIDESEP in Ucayali - named DESSAI - played a very important part in following up the land titling process. It did so by recurrently visiting all the communities, working with local midwives, healers and shamans, and establishing general health services and systems. The results of this included that the communities themselves became more viable, that people felt that their fight for land and efforts to organize were honoured, and that they were respected and part of a larger society. The mobilising and motivating effect on the new communities of the Indigenous Health Programme, besides the immediate benefits of a better health situation, should not be underestimated. The PSI represents the latest episode in the ongoing indigenous saga of the Upper Ucayali, Urubamba and Gran Pajonal - a chapter dealing with implementation of democracy and dignity.

Notes

1. Søren Hvalkof is an anthropologist who works both as researcher and consultant. He is a member of the boards of NORDECO, the Solstice Foundation, and the International Work Group for Indigenous Affairs, IWGIA. He has broad experience in working with indigenous peoples and organisations in Latin America, particularly in land titling projects. His academic approach is oriented around Political Ecology. He was one of the initiators of the PSI and participated in the development of the project's first phase. He is the compiler and editor of the present volume; he currently holds a research position at the Danish Institute for International Studies in Copenhagen.

2. In fact, there are other areas in South America that may have as high a biological diversity index, namely the tropical forests of the Pacific coast of Colombia and Darien of Panama. However, the Montaña covers by far the largest continuous area with an extraordinarily high index, covering several ecological zones. The Pacific coastal forests are more uniform.

3. Mauritia flexuosa L. F.

4. Gran Pajonal has not yet achieved the status of District but is still an annex to the District of Atalaya, although the "upgrade" is currently being processed by the Peruvian political system. Nevertheless, it functions as if it were a District, with its own mayor and administration.

5. Quechua is the dominant indigenous language of the Andes and considered the official language of the Inca culture. It spread with the expansion of the Inca empire and developed into a lingua franca of the Andes and the Montaña of Peru and Ecuador. Likewise, it was used by the early Jesuit, Franciscan and Dominican missionaries in their mission settlements, the so called Reducciones, where several different indigenous groups were relocated.

6. Cushma is a Spanish word of Quechua origin. The Ashéninka name for the tunic is Kitharentze.

7. The dry season with clear and sunny weather is called "summer" in the Peruvian Amazon although it really is the southern winter, and the rainy season is called "winter" locally, although correctly it is the southern summer.

8. The Ashéninka use the term "simirintsi" when referring to the Yine, meaning something like "those who speak differently", however, it also has a slightly deprecating significance.

9. The term Piro is still used among linguists when referring to the Yine language, which is of Arawakan stock but most closely related to the Apuriña spoken in the Purus area in the far east of Brazil.

10. I usually prefer the terms high-jungle and low-jungle as the best translation of the Spanish words, but several people have commented that it is politically incorrect to use the term jungle at all as a designation for rainforest, hence the choice of terms here.

11. One of the well-known rubber barons and slave traders operating at the time in the upper Ucayali and Urubamba was Carlos Fermín Fitzcarrald, romanticized and immortalized by the German filmmaker Werner Herzog in his movie "Fitzcarraldo", which was produced on location in 1980-81 with Asháninka from Atalaya and Ashéninka from Gran Pajonal and Ucayali as extras. The part as Fitzcarrald was played by the late Klaus Kinsky.

12. Asociación Interétnica del Desarrollo de la Selva Peruana - AIDESEP.

References

Bodley, John H.
1972 *Tribal Survival in the Amazon: The Campa Case.* IWGIA Document
      No. 5. IWGIA, Copenhagen.

Brown, Michael F. and Eduardo Fernández
1991 *War of Shadows. The Struggle for Utopia in the Peruvian Amazon.*
      University of California Press, Berkeley, California.

Cárdenas Timoteo, Clara
1989 *Los Unaya y Su Mundo. Aproximación al Sistema Médico de los Shipibo-
      Conibo del Rio Ucayali.* Instituto Indigenista Peruano. CAAP, Lima.

Erikson, Philippe; Bruno Illius, Kenneth M. Kensinger and María Sueli de
Aguilar
1994 *Kirinkobaon kirika (Gringos books). An annotated Panoa bibliography;*
      Amerindia, Supplement 19(1). Association d'Ethnolinguistique
      Amérindienne, Paris.

García Hierro, Pedro
1998 "Atalaya: Caught in a Time Warp." In: *Liberation through Land
      Rights in the Peruvian Amazon*, pp. 13-79. Parellada, Alejandro and
      Søren Hvalkof (eds.) IWGIA Document No. 80. IWGIA, Copen-
      hagen.

García Hierro, Pedro, Søren Hvalkof and Andrew Gray
1998 *Liberation through Land Rights in the Peruvian Amazon.* Parellada,
      Alejandro and Søren Hvalkof (eds.) IWGIA Document No. 80.
      IWGIA, Copenhagen.

Gow, Peter
1991 *Of mixed blood. Kinship and History in Peruvian Amazonia.* Clarendon
      Press, Oxford.

Gray, Andrew
1998 "Demarcating Development: titling indigenous communities in
      Peru." In *Liberation through Land Rights in the Peruvian Amazon*,
      pp.163-216, Alejandro Parellada and Søren Hvalkof (eds.) IWGIA
      Document No. 80. IWGIA, Copenhagen.

Hvalkof, Søren
1989 "The Nature of Development: Native and Settlers' Views in Gran
      Pajonal, Peruvian Amazon." In: *Folk Vol. 31.* Danish Ethnographic
      Society, Copenhagen.

1994 "The Asháninka Disaster and Struggle - The forgotten war in the Peruvian Amazon." *In Indigenous Affairs No. 2/94.* IWGIA, Copenhagen.

1998 "From Slavery to Democracy: The Indigenous Process of Upper Ucayali and Gran Pajonal," pp. 83-162. In A. Parellada and S. Hvalkof (eds.) *Liberation through Land Rights in the Peruvian Amazon.* IWGIA Document No. 80. IWGIA, Copenhagen.

2002a "Beyond Indigenous Land Titling: Democratizing Civil Society in the Peruvian Amazon." In *Space, Place and Nation: The Geographies of Neoliberalism in Latin America.* Editor Jacquelyn Chase. Kumarian Press, 2002.

2002b "Peoples, Pastures and Progress: A political ecology from the Peruvian Amazon." In *Imagining Political Ecology.* Aletta Biersack and James B. Greenberg, eds. Ecologies for the Twenty-First Century Series. Duke University Press, Chapel Hill. Forthcoming.

Hvalkof, Søren and Peter Aaby
1981 *Is God an American. An anthropological perspective on the missionary work of the Summer Institute of Linguistics.* IWGIA Document No. 43. IWGIA/Survival International, Copenhagen/London.

Lathrap, Donald W.
1970 *The Upper Amazon.* Ancient Peoples and Places Series vol. 70. Thames and Hudson & The Camelot Press Ltd, Southampton.

Metraux, Alfred
1942 "A Quechua Messiah in Eastern Peru." In *American Anthropologist, n.s., Vol. XLIV,* pp. 721-725.

Morin, Françoise
1998 "Los Shipibo-Conibo." In *Guía Etnográfica de la Alta Amazonía, Vol. II,* pp. 275-439. Fernando Santos & Frederica Barclay, eds. Smithsonian Tropical Research Institute. Editorial Abaya-Yala, Quito.

Myers, Thomas P.
1988 "El efecto de las pestes sobre las poblaciones de la Amazonía alta." In *Amazonia Peruana, No. VIII (15),* pp. 61-81. CAAP, Lima.

n.d. Conservatism in Conibo Dress and Ornamentation. Manuscript. University of Nebraska State Museum.

Peñaherrera del Aguíla, Carlos
1986   *Gran Geografía del Peru. Naturaleza y Hombre.* Chapter III. pp. 67-
        186. Manfer-Juan Mejía Baca, Lima.

Sabaté, Luis
1925   "Viaje de los padres misioneros del Convento del Cuzco a las
        tribus salvajes de los Campas, Piros, Cunibos y Shipibos en el año
        1874." In *Historia de las Misiones Franciscanas y .... Padre Fray
        Bernardino Izaguirre, vol. X*, pp. 19-197. Talleres Tipográficos de la
        Penitenciaria, Lima.

Santos-Granero, Fernando
1987   Epidemias y sublevaciones en el desarrollo demográfico de las
        misiones Amuesha del Cerro de la Sal, siglo XVIII, *Historica, Vol.
        XI* (1), Pondificia Universidad Católica del Perú, Lima.

1992   *Etnohistoria de la Alta Amazonía.* Del siglo XV al XVIII, Editorial
        Abya-Yala, Quito.

Santos, Fernando and Frederica Barclay (eds.)
1998   *Guía Etnográfica de la Alta Amazonía, Vol. III*, pp. 275-439. Smith-
        sonian Tropical Research Institute. Editorial Abya-Yala, Quito.

Santos-Granero, Fernando and Frederica Barclay
1998   *Selva Central: History, Economy and Land Use in Peruvian Amazonia.*
        Smithsonian Institute Press, Washington D.C./London.

2000   *Tamed Frontiers. Economy, Society, and Civil Rights in Upper
        Amazonia.* Westview Press, Boulder, Colorado.

Stoll, David
1982   *Fishers of Men or Founders of Empire. The Wycliffe Bible Translators in
        Latin America,* Zed Press and Cultural Survival, London and
        Cambridge, Mass.

Varese, Stefano
1973   *La Sal de Los Cerros. Una aproximación al mundo Campa.* Retablo de
        Papel, Lima.

Veber, Hanne
1991   "Schools for the Ashéninka. Ethno-Development in the Making."
        Paper presented to the 47th International Congress of
        Americanists. New Orleans, July 7-11.

1992   "Why Indians Wear Clothes: Managing Identity Across an Ethnic
        Boundary." In *Ethnos 57 (1-2)*, pp. 51-60.

1996   "External Inducement and Non-westernization in the Uses of the Ashéninka Cushma." In *Journal of Material Culture Vol 1, No. 2*, pp, 155-182. July. Sage, London.

1998   The Salt of the Montaña. Interpreting Indigenous Activism in the Rain Forest. *Cultural Anthropology No. 13 (3)*. August.

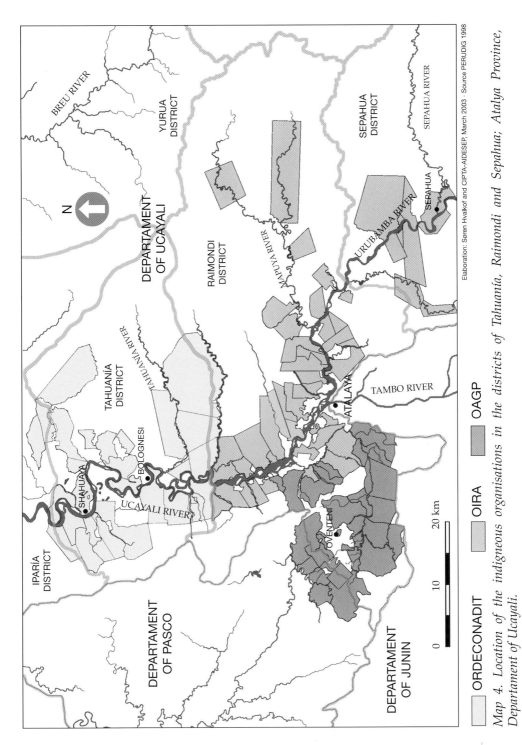

Elaboration: Søren Hvalkof and CIPTA-AIDESEP, March 2003 · Source PERUDIG 1998

Map 4. Location of the indigneous organisations in the districts of Tahuanía, Raimondi and Sepahua; Atalya Province, Departament of Ucayali.

Photo: Søren Hvalkof, 2000   *Warming up in the cool of the morning, Gran Pajonal.*

Asháninka house, Ucayali.   *Photo: Søren Hvalkof, 2000*

Ribereña indigenous family, Ucayali.   *Photo: Jim Thuesen, 1994*

Town of Lagunas, Lower Huallaga River.   *Photo: Thomas Skielboe, 1993*

Preparing fish, Shahuaya community, Ucayali.   *Photo: Cæcilie Mikkelsen, 2002*

Conibo house, Ucayali.   *Photo: Dorte M. Jensen, 1998*

Chayahuita community, Cahuapanas Rivers.   *Photo: Jim Thuesen, 1993*

Ashéninka house, Unini. *Photo: Jim Thuesen, 1994*

Health post, Unini. *Photo: Rune Hvalkof, 2000*

Town of Yurimaguas.   *Photo: Thomas Skielboe, 1993*

Hostal Denis, Atalaya.   *Photo: Jim Thuesen, 1994*

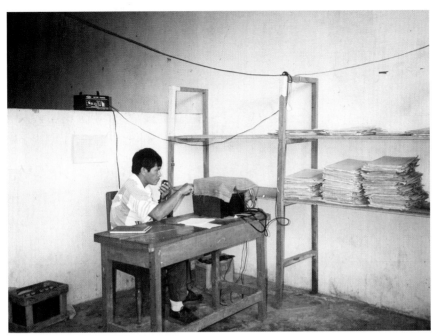

Operating the radio, OIRA, Atalaya. *Photo: Jim Thuesen, 1994*

Land titling unit, AIDESEP, Pucallpa. *Photo: Jim Thuesen, 1994*

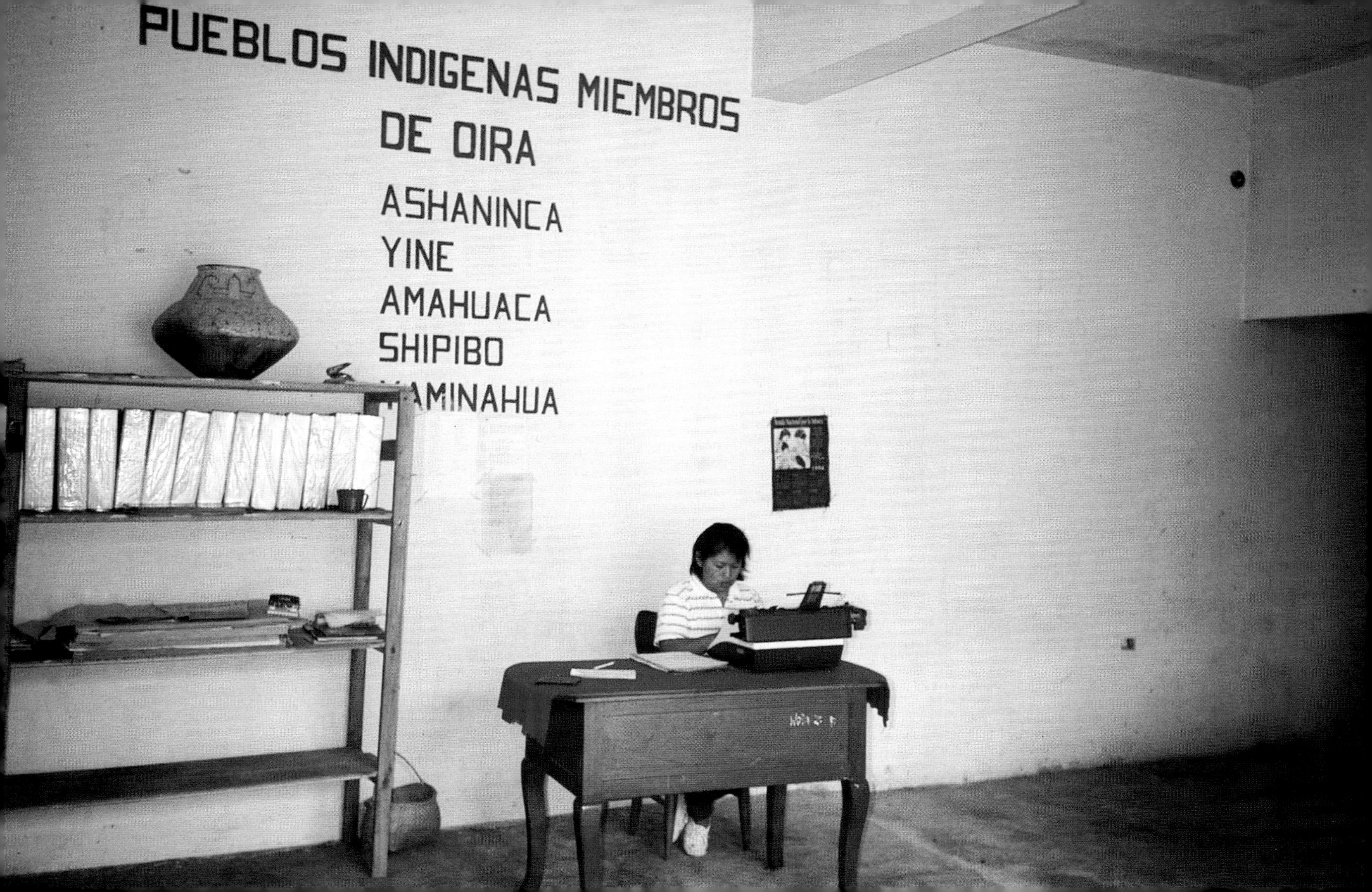

PUEBLOS INDIGENAS MIEMBROS
DE OIRA
ASHANINCA
YINE
AMAHUACA
SHIPIBO
YAMINAHUA

The OIRA office, Atalaya. *Photo: Jim Thuesen, 1994*

3. The Project History

The Origins of the Indigenous Health Programme

An Interview with the Programme Director

Juan Reátegui Silva, born in 1962, belongs to the Aguaruna people. He grew up in Borja, in the province of Alto Amazonas. He is the director of AIDESEP's Indigenous Health Programme and has been the driving force behind it.

An idea is born

First I would like to tell you about my childhood, and about when I was young. It was difficult because there were deaths in my family, my brothers, my two first brothers died from common illnesses, one caused by the "perro del monte", the bush dog [*Speothos venaticus*] and the other by more diarrhoea. So I grew up with this rather particular background. I finished my primary education and went on to secondary school. After that I wanted to study medicine. I was in Trujillo for a while, but I couldn't study there and I so came to Lima. I didn't achieve the necessary grades to study medicine, instead I began to study in the faculty of nursing. Out of that grew a need to learn all about nursing. I gained a certificate for best conduct of all the students and, for this reason, the school where I had taken my secondary education wanted me to return to work with them as a teacher, teaching mathematics, physics and chemistry, because these were my areas of strength. They wanted to give me a place teaching from first to fifth grades. If I had stayed there, that would have been it, for my dad had no money. I could not continue my studies, even though I wanted to study medicine, because my parents were simple people. But thanks to the encouragement and support of the Aguaruna-Huambisa Council, AIDESEP gave me a grant to study nursing.

I finished the courses in 1989 and, in 1990, I obtained my degree. In 1991, I received my professional title and, in 1992, I undertook a basic post-graduate course in Public Health and Health Service Management at the National School of Public Health. I began to work for AIDESEP in 1989 until the end of that year, and throughout 1990 I worked on the Titling Project. When I started, I visited the whole of Río Urubamba which, at that time, had 29 communities. It was my job to make an assessment on the basis of which a project would be formulated for a way in which to build up the health of the communities. But all the work I did centred around what I had learnt at university, and I was surprised to find that many services did not reach the communities in any effective way, and that in fact they had no access to them. There were many problems but, at the same time, I found out something very peculiar, and very important, from which an initiative was born: This was that all the communities, the mothers, the traditional healers and vapour healers who had been identified, all used medicinal plants, and I thought it would be the best idea to take this as a starting point. My Shuar and Aguaruna family also uses medicinal plants. My father is a *huaymaco*, and my mother is a woman who has visions and takes plant medicine. My grandparents were great *iwishin* and great *huaymacos* [shamans and spiritual healers], this is part of my tradition. And for this reason, I very rapidly developed a great desire to move in this direction, in our direction: My desire was to begin to build on our own knowledge. Perhaps my university studies helped me to understand this much more quickly, and gave me a better understanding of the fact that this is a part of my own culture.

The beginning

From then on, I began to develop this activity, which is known as traditional medicine. In early 1991, initially with the support of FONCODES[1], I began to work in Atalaya Province, particularly with OIRA, in order to be able to recover the "shamanic resource" of the *sheripiaris* [tobacco shamans]. OIRA's president at that time, Bernardo Silva, gave me a great deal of support. He had a very clear vision of things, and wanted the work to be developed alongside that of the territorial titling with the Asháninka, Ashéninka and other communities.

We began to work, visiting the communities. We were able to motivate people, to give them incentive and to create in them a desire to develop this aspect of our culture. During these first stages, a very strong split was evident between these shamanic resources and the leaders and organisations. Invariably, this valuable community resource was not even recognised; it was unknown. Then, during this stage of the project there was a certain rapprochement and so, in 1992, a project was proposed that could now be called the second phase, and which was a second and much more integrated experience. But, in this case, we already had experience of having worked there, we had a ready-made project. It was at this point that you[2] became involved in the process to obtain funding and support. The lawyer, Pedro García, also helped to formulate the San Lorenzo Project and we completed the project from here in order to submit it to FENA-MAD[3]. We began work in 1993 and it has continued to this very day.

The first participatory experiences

This project has had three phases: In the first phase, we believed that, using a shamanic resource, such as the sheripiaris, the most expert, we could begin to work in the communities. This was the first methodology, in order to teach and meet people, but it did not work. It started well but we found that there were apparently no such resources in the communities and some people began to question what I was doing there, asking: "Why are you coming to my community, wanting to teach me?" This meant we had to reconsider our proposal almost immediately. We proposed, instead, that it would be better to have a team made up of OIRA leaders, and an indigenous expert and a nurse, in order to make a trip to provide greater motivation to those resources the communities had, and in order to be able to draw up some statistics to find out which shamanic resources there were in each community. We followed this methodology and, by the time the second phase ended, we had found the resources. Then we moved on to the third phase, aimed at communities that had no such resources, and at communities that did not use medicinal plants. The third phase was intended to support those communities that did not have the resources and, at the same time, provide incentives to the mothers and others to use and recover their medicinal plants and to promote and pass on this knowledge to their children. This is how we have worked to this day.

Actually, in this process we also made it clear that there were illnesses that could not be cured with plant medicine. These include tuberculosis, pneumonia and some tropical diseases. Although the illness known as *Leishmaniasis* can be cured with medicinal plants, no one has yet managed this because the knowledge for doing so was lost and is still in the process of being recovered now. This meant that we needed a professional nurse with a nursing degree. The nurse participates in the team and trains the promoters chosen by their communities, along with people such as the sheripiari, the vapour healer and the traditional midwife, specialists who are already recognised within their community.

The organisation and the public sector

As a result of the above, internal organisation is being consolidated within each of the communities and this is, of course, in turn strengthening their own representative organisations, OIRA, OAGP and ORDECONA-DIT. We have moved on in this process. Now the itinerant team work undertaken in the field is also of a political nature, because we are helping and motivating the communities to understand that indigenous health also depends on their territory, particularly its assets, its natural resources, its forests, which are the greatest heritage of the peoples. The forest contains all the knowledge of the indigenous people and, if we destroy the forests, if we indiscriminately fell the trees, we are impoverishing indigenous knowledge because the medicinal plants will also disappear. Therefore, we want to incorporate all of these factors into the Indigenous Health Project. We have considered this whole aspect together with the organisation. So far, we have seen that our approach has worked well, it is a methodology that no other NGO is using, and no State body is working in such an itinerant way. In fact, our example has led the Ministry of Health to begin to implement its work at this level, too, imitating what we are doing. It is like a form of rivalry, we are forcing them to do the same thing but to do it better.

This approach to the health situation has demonstrated that the problems existing in the communities are greater than those revealed by the Ministry of Health, much greater, and now the Ministry of Health is recognising our work and using the information we are working with. They just sit in their Health Centres, waiting for patients to come, this is the way they work, this is the Ministry's system. But our system works from the bottom up, we visit community by community, family by family, on a trip lasting three months. After three months, the team evaluates the work and pinpoints strengths and weaknesses. We then try to correct the defects, to implement corrections, and the team continues on its travels once more. The information gained in this way is effective, truthful, and must attract the attention of the general public and, above all, the attention of the official system, for they are not fulfilling their designated role. This is important for the future, for we are now coming to an end, we are going to undertake a final evaluation. In this final evaluation, we will propose another initiative with which to continue the running of the system, that's to say through the training of an Intercultural Health Technician.

Why have we used this name, Intercultural? Because the most important thing for indigenous people is first of all to get to know their own culture, their reality, their knowledge and, on the basis of their technology, to incorporate elements of western technology. This combination of knowledge enables them to become stronger and, at the same time, they are far better able to tackle and resolve the community's problems in an appropriate manner. This issue will therefore be developed in a new phase. Let's hope the Karen Elise Jensen Foundation will continue to support us, and that they are able to continue their collaboration in this regard, in this integrated manner. This is how we see the continuity of the system we have been developing within the framework of the Indigenous Health Programme. We will continue working along this path and I hope that, very soon, we will be commencing a new phase of the Project.

AIDESEP

Initially, AIDESEP's leaders were rather sceptical about the Indigenous Health Programme but, with time, and as we have made progress in the work, the many doubts they - and people within the communities - had at first, have faded. In the beginning, they said we were encouraging witchcraft, that we were promoting something that was not our own but, deep down, it is recognised by all of society, even western, that indigenous culture and indigenous knowledge about medicinal plants and other things, can actually be an innovation for western society itself. With regard to the environment, following the approval of the Convention on Biological Diversity, signed by more than 140 countries throughout the world, article 8(j) recognises knowledge of indigenous practices and innovations as an element with which to promote improvements in health for all. Now this knowledge is being incorporated into the health planners' ways of working and it is for this reason that the indigenous leaders have to sort out their proposals, that is, they have to gain a clearer vision and increasingly introduce their own cultural roots. We believe that this is what comes first; I am convinced that this is where we must start. It is a much longer term development and, in addition, we can support western society with all the resources we have, within the context of the autonomy and self-determination of our peoples. It is within this context that we have to work with western society. For this reason, we believe that we have to work in this direction, and the leaders are now also clear about this. As I have already said, previously they were looking through the door, looking at the situation, now they have become a part of the situation, they are there at this very moment, particularly the leaders. I have no reason to doubt this. I have received a great deal of support from the current leaders, and this is why we have made progress, we have made so much progress. I also have a lot of friends, particularly among our brothers and sisters the sheripiaris, the traditional midwives and the vapour healers. I have been with them, I have shared with them. I am very interested in delving deeper into this area of work, so that the western world can finally see that it is a flexible and syncretic vision. This sums up all our knowledge.

International Indigenous Health

I was also one of AIDESEP's national leaders, elected in 1991. I held two posts within the areas of Integrated Health, and Development and Policy. I gained a great deal of experience as a result of this and one of the consequences was that I began to travel to many countries, attending many congresses, many indigenous seminars, learning from the experiences of others. This has also enabled me to develop my area of specialisation, to improve the work I do. Now, as director of the Indigenous Health Programme, I am learning many things and also helping other organisations, giving advice to indigenous organisations concerning their work and organisation. There is one detail I would like to mention with regard to the Indigenous Health experience. When I was a leader, in 1993, I was invited to participate in the UN Human Rights Group. The subject was Indigenous Health and I took this opportunity to put forward a proposal. I spoke to the assembly to propose the establishment of an indigenous peoples' commission within the United Nations to undertake an evaluation of all indigenous organisations throughout the world, in order to submit proposals for Indigenous Health for the World's Indigenous Peoples. The aim of this proposal was to find solutions to the development of programmes and projects directly related to indigenous peoples, involving the State, the Ministry of Health and PAHO[4] in the Region. This proposal seemed extremely simple to me but it had a great impact. The following year, the Indigenous Peoples' Commission was established, chaired by a Mapuche doctor, Oara Alderete. She did an enormous work in this regard. On the basis of the Indigenous Health Programme, I also

The director and dr. Torres.   *Photo: Thomas Skielboe, 1994*

contributed my experience in a document that is going to be submitted to PAHO. Our experience has been a new contribution, and it has been very well received, for which reason, like AIDESEP, we feel rather proud. We have made progress in this regard, we have said to the world "the indigenous organisations have proposals too". I have continued working with the Indigenous Health Project, with the Karen Elise Jensen Foundation and with NORDECO. If this international support had not existed, I would be working as just another State bureaucrat. But my commitment, as I said earlier, is to the indigenous peoples and I will continue this to the very last. If there is no support from the indigenous organisations, I can propose initiatives to continue developing the experiences we have gained so far. Well, in 1998, I was working a great deal on the cultural side of things but I also wanted to understand the methodological side, the technical side, and so this encouraged me to suggest that I should study for a Master's Degree at the San Marcos National University. I proposed Amazonian Anthropology and I have been studying ever since. I want to continue studying, to learn more about what goes on within Amazonian circles but also, at the same time, I want to continue in development. When all's said and done, from this perspective, I can defend indigenous rights from any angle, and I can help to develop things within the context of self-determination, the autonomy of indigenous peoples and their cultures. This is what I am preparing myself for, because I want to support my people 100%.

Notes

1. FONCODES is the acronym for Fondo Nacional de Compensación y Desarrollo Social, the National Foundation for Compensation and Social Development.
2. This refers to the interviewer.
3. FENAMAD is the Federación Nativa del Río Madre de Dios y Afluentes, the Native Federation of the Madre de Dios River and Tributaries.
4. Pan-American Health Organisation.

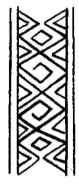

Ashéninka design

3. The Project History

The Development of the PSI-AIDESEP Project

By Thomas Skielboe, Co-director of NORDECO

Introduction

The PSI project has been carried out over three phases. The first was designed as a pilot phase with the aim of testing out different strategic possibilities for integrating the indigenous health systems with the Peruvian public health system. This turned out to be a triple challenge: In many places, indigenous health knowledge was not in use any more (or so it seemed) and had to be revitalised. The public system faced a series of difficulties in working in the remote and difficult areas of the rain forest: insufficient resources, major cultural barriers to be overcome by staff that were not at all trained for such a challenge and, lastly, the challenge of integrating two very different systems into one indigenous system that was more or less self-sustaining. The main approach for the work in the field has been the use of mobile integrated teams of nurses, indigenous health experts and political representatives from the local organisations, which have worked in different ways with capacity building at all levels in the areas. The pilot phase was undertaken in three different project areas with very different socio-cultural characteristics. The project was later concentrated in one area.

Choice of areas, organisations and peoples

In 1991, AIDESEP decided to strengthen its involvement in indigenous health work and established a Health Secretariat within the organisation. The Secretariat was to co-ordinate the health work and develop specific health policies and strategies for AIDESEP. The three project areas for the pilot project were identified in 1992 by the AIDESEP Health Secretariat and were initially based on a few preliminary experiences. The project areas were in the province of Alto Amazonas in northern Peru, Atalaya province in central Peru, and Madre de Dios in southern Peru. (See map 2, p. 26.) In the region of Alto Amazonas, AIDESEP had since 1991 been involved in a project financed by the European Union. This project was not specifically designed to incorporate indigenous health approaches but was rather aimed at strengthening the public health system in the area, focusing on the involvement and participation of the local population. Additionally, it supported the implementation of national campaigns for vaccination, hygiene, child care etc. This project was scheduled to run for a period of six years but problems with the financing of the programme meant that it came to a halt after only one year. The strategy of the PSI project in Alto Amazonas was therefore to bridge the activities until further financing could be found, with greater focus, however, on an integrated indigenous health system. In Madre de Dios, the regional indigenous federation, FENAMAD, had just completed an ethno-botanical project on traditional medicine, AMETRA 2001 *(Aplicación de la Medicina Tradicional)*, focusing on the use and cultivation of medicinal plants. This project had been implemented since 1986. The project had, however, not shown the expected results within the local communities.

The Atalaya province was primarily selected because of the organisational work carried out in the region by AIDESEP, rather than for its previous experience with the health work. The situation of the indigenous population in the Atalaya province had, over a relatively short period of less than fifteen years, changed dramatically. Former indigenous slaves and indentured labourers on local farms were now about to lawfully receive deeds to their community lands, and had established their own organisation working for their legal rights in their local area. One single programme covering these three areas was developed, focusing on building the capacity of the communities to deal with their own health situation and problems. This was to be done both in relation to indigenous medicine, to be focused upon as an important part of indigenous life, and in relation to the public health system through the appointed health personnel in the communities, the *técnicos sanitarios*, as well as through the establishment of community pharmacies, promoter training and the involvement of the indigenous population. The programme did, however, take the former projects as its starting point, thus developing an indigenous angle on the project in Alto Amazonas, and amplifying the indigenous focus in Madre de Dios with a focus on the work in the communities. In Atalaya, the aim was to develop a full-scale indigenous health programme, and work both with indigenous health experts in the communities, western medicine and the public health system through a team of travelling nurses. The Project in Atalaya was by far the largest project of the three and likewise demonstrated the most complete idea of an indigenous approach to a health system in the Amazon.

The pilot project was developed and implemented, together with AIDESEP, through the regional federations in the three areas, all of which are members of AIDESEP. In Atalaya, the project was carried out in cooperation with the regional federation, the *Organización Indígena de la Región de Atalaya*, OIRA. Fifty communities under OIRA, covering six indigenous groups, Asháninka, Ashéninka, Yine, Yaminahua, Shipibo-Conibo and Amahuaca, formed part of the project. In Alto Amazonas, the project collaborated with AIDESEP's regional office in San Lorenzo, which was established in 1987. Through the office, the project chose three federations, CHAPI SHIWAG, ONAPAA and FECONADIC, and worked with two indigenous groups, the Aguaruna and the Chayahuita, covering some 42 communities in their totality. In Madre de Dios the project collaborated with FENAMAD, which is the regional organisation for a federation of some 11 indigenous groups[1]. The project covered all 11 groups in just 26 communities. As mentioned, FENAMAD had worked for many years (until 1991) on the AMETRA 2001 project, trying to build a basis for the traditional indigenous medical system, and the PSI was an opportunity to consolidate this work and develop it further into an actual indigenous health system.

The initial pilot phase generated important experiences from all three regions, particularly in relation to coordination between the indigenous and the public health systems. Based on the lessons learned, the idea of a second phase took shape. It was decided to focus the work in one area and to concentrate efforts, with the aim of developing a system that could be duplicated in all indigenous areas of lowland Amazon, in Peru.

Expectations were great regarding the potential of developing an indigenous health system in the Madre de Dios area, as they already had years of experience in working with indigenous health in FENAMAD. The Alto Amazonas area also needed support, but already had several NGOs and church institutions involved in health programmes. In the final evaluation of the pilot phase there was, however, no doubt that the Atalaya region had the best results by far and was showing the greatest potential for further development. The Atalaya project was the largest of the three and had been able to create an important base for further development. It was thus decided to focus the work in the Atalaya region, and possibilities for expanding the project were investigated.

As a result, it was decided to work in three areas in the Atalaya province. The project would continue to work in the 50 communities involved during the pilot phase, and which formed part of OIRA, and only expand into four new communities, bringing the total to 54. However, two other areas were incorporated into the project: one further down the Ucayali river bordering onto the OIRA area. Here 27 communities from the district of Tahuania, forming part of the Organisation of Indigenous Communities of the Tahuania District, ORDECONADIT, were incorporated. The third area chosen was the higher lying zone of Gran Pajonal, and the Organisation of Gran Pajonal, OAGP, with its 27 communities was thus the second new area of the project (the OAGP today has 38 member communities). (See maps 4-7, pp. 87,118,170 and 189) The development of the second phase drew heavily on the experiences gained during the pilot phase. In the following section I have summarized main changes made as a consequence of these experiences:

- The indigenous health experts, shamans, *vaporadoras* (vapour healers) and *sabios* (persons of expert knowledge) in general, and the significance of these people, was still very much a part of indigenous society and everyday life. This came as a surprise in some areas, as the work of the *sabios'* was seen as the work of the devil and had been strictly forbidden by the Christian missions for decades (and in some cases for centuries).

- More emphasis should be put on working strategies and adjustments to make the indigenous health experts suited to the specific indigenous groups and their specific health understandings. This was a very clear outcome of the work in the pilot phase. The very different meanings, connotations and understandings of, for instance, witchcraft had proved how important it was to use micro-local indigenous health experts. Specifically, the work with the Harakmbut of Madre de Dios had shown this. The importance and danger of witchcraft and its association with the shamans in these societies had shown that the system of travelling shamans, meaning that unknown shamans could enter a village, was potentially dangerous. This strategy had to be changed, leading to a much more flexible approach to each indigenous people participating in the project and their various understanding of health.
- Constant focus on sustainability and long-term supervision systems and a closer involvement of public health. Two crucial aspects in relation to the sustainability of the indigenous health system seemed to be how to ensure the sufficient and long-term supervision of the work carried out in the villages and, secondly, how to ensure the long-term involvement of the public administration in the support of the work.
- More organised training, combined with the development of ongoing evaluation mechanisms supporting the trial and error approach.
- Strong focus on capacity building in the organisations. The local regional organisation has a crucial role to play in ensuring management, supervision and maintenance of the system.
- Decentralisation. It was obvious that, in order to secure local ownership and involve as many people as possible in the use and maintenance of the system, project management and project funds needed to be decentralised. All three new organisations were to manage their own budget and have responsibility for their own project staff.

Project strategies, methodology and priorities

The main objective of the programme is to ensure the health and improve the living conditions of the indigenous peoples of the Peruvian Amazon. This is achieved through the provision of an integrated health programme co-ordinating the curing practices of each indigenous people with non-indigenous medical support. The aim is to strengthen both systems within one framework while targeting the needs of the different communities.

The overall strategy of the PSI has been to try out different implementation strategies during the pilot phase and use the lessons learned to develop a "prototype" of an integrated indigenous health system. This "prototype" is then tested in the ensuing implementation phase, during which actions for long-term sustainability should be identified. The overall strategy for the implementation phase has focused on the following four main input areas:

a) Identification and capacity building of the available health resources in the communities, including both the indigenous health workers and the public health system.

b) Development of and support to collaboration between the different persons involved in health work in the community and in the area as a whole (including both the indigenous health workers and the public health system), and establishment of a health committee in each community.

c) Capacity building of the regional indigenous organisations and development of a system of support and supervision of the health work, between the community, the regional organisation, and the national health office in the nationwide indigenous organisation, AIDESEP.

d) Developing well-functioning cooperation between the integrated indigenous health system and the Peruvian public health system.

Key players in this strategy have been the travelling health teams composed of three persons: a nurse, a female expert in indigenous medicine (specifically targeting the women) and a male co-ordinator from the regional organisation, to be responsible for the indigenous medicine input and for linking with the organisation which, in the future, will be responsible for maintaining the health system through support and supervision of the health work in the communities. The three project areas have been divided into six sections and, for the last two years of the project, six health teams have each been allocated one area. The nurses have, with a few exceptions, not been indigenous but have been thoroughly trained before entering the work, through courses set up by the indigenous programme.

The main work of the health teams has consisted of:
- collecting data in all the villages
- conducting village meetings, thoroughly discussing the programme and the whole idea of integrating their own medicine with public western medicine
- visiting all households and discussing health problems
- establishing community pharmacies
- training a minimum of two health promoters per village to be responsible for the pharmacies
- collaborating with the indigenous medicine experts

Moreover, the teams have encouraged gatherings of indigenous medicine experts and workshops with health promoters, and supervised a new system of training for both shamans, vaporadoras and indigenous midwives. The teams have reported back to the local indigenous organisations and have, together with the organisation, been supervised and trained by the director and the field staff representing the AIDESEP health programme, the PSI.

Cooperation with the public health system has developed remarkably well during the implementation of the project. One central aspect to be dealt with in relation to the public system was to inform the health administrations about the whole idea of working with an integrated approach to indigenous and western medicine, and to overcome the ignorance surrounding work with indigenous peoples and their specific situations, which is still very much alive at most levels. The PSI has negotiated an agreement with the regional authorities, outlining the cooperation during the project period. The content of the agreement has primarily involved highlighting actions that are already compulsory services and which should have been carried out, but which, for many reasons (logistics and economics being the main ones), have not. The programme has used the logistical means established by the integrated health system, which has made it possible to carry out the different national health programmes for tuberculosis, malaria and *Leishmaniasis*, provide free treatment at certain hospitals, and complete two so-called surgical campaigns, consisting of operating mainly on hernias. Both the regional and the national authorities have shown a growing interest in the work carried out by the programme and, in the last phase, both parties have participated in the development of a long-term solution to maintaining the programme.

It has been important in the strategy to ensure that each organisation is responsible for implementation of the project in their area. The health work has likewise been presented and performed as part of the political agenda of the local organisation, and it has been important to strengthen the ties between the people in the communities and the organisation. During implementation, it has proved crucial that the project is implemented by the organisation, including taking responsibility for the budget. This organisational structure has markedly strengthened the sense of ownership of the project all the way down to the villagers. It is undoubtedly more difficult to decentralize budgetary tasks and, in some instances, this has caused problems and double work, but it does create a feeling of ownership which has been very important in implementation, and which is considered essential for future sustainability. An important aspect to note, however, is that thorough supervision and monitoring is crucial for this strategy to work.

Implementation, supervision and dynamics

Each health team has visited all villages in their area approximately three times a year, each time for a period of 3-4 days. During a visit, the teams collected data about every household in the village, which was then recorded and is used and kept by each local organisation. All members of the health teams have been appointed by the local indigenous organisations, OIRA, ORDECONDIT and OAGP. Only the licensed nurses received a salary; the other team members received only a small remuneration to compensate for the 3-4 month absence from their families and villages while in the field. None of the project participants from the villages has received a salary. The people involved directly in the villages include the following:

- Promoters
- Shamans
- Vaporadoras
- Midwives
- Apprentices to indigenous experts

These groups have, as part of the system, received a small package, containing items needed for their work, as an incentive. This would normally include a machete, a mosquito net, a flash light, batteries, soap, matches and the like.

When the teams arrive in the villages, a meeting with the village chief is always held. A village meeting is announced, in which the work for the coming days is explained in detail by each of the team members. During the stay in the village, the nurse visits all households, accompanied by the promoter (or promoters), specifically focusing on training through learning by doing. The nurses, together with the promoters, attend to patients in the villages and carry out the specific programmes on tuberculosis, malaria and leishmaniasis. The indigenous experts visit shamans and vaporadoras to discuss how the trainee programme works, specifically focussing on coordination between the indigenous health knowledge and work, and the work carried out by the promoters.

Four longer training sessions of 10 to12 days are then held, gathering promoters from 8-12 villages in one place, giving training in management and maintenance of the pharmacy, simple medical attendance, and planning and coordination of the health work in the village. Get-togethers for shamans, vaporadoras and traditional midwives are also arranged twice a year.

During the first two visits to the communities, a pharmacy is established in each of the project communities. These pharmacies are very simple and contain only the most needed medicine. They are managed by the promoters of the project. The communities are required to build or donate small premises to house the pharmacy. Each community is responsible for the sustainability of the pharmacy and for developing a strategy to replace the medicines. The method for raising funds for restocking varies greatly from community to community. Some charge patients for the medicine while others have communal cash crop fields, or raise and sell products like chickens to finance the revolving fund. At the end of the project, an inventory of the medicine stocks showed that close to 75 % of the communities had good functioning strategies for restocking.

Table 1. Numbers of indigenous experts involved in different areas of the project.

	Native	Shamans	Vapour Communities	Midwives	Promoters healers	Medicine Chests
OIRA						
Sector Ucayali	29	23	45	20	72	29
Sector Urubamba	26	10	20	23	55	26
ORDECONADIT						
Sector Shipibo – Conibo	13	23	15	18	28	13
Sector Ashéninka	20	16	51	21	41	20
OAGP						
Sector I	13	59	71	24	13	
Sector II	17			36	17	

Before and after every trip, the field teams in each organisation held meetings with the local organisation, the field coordinator and the director. During these meetings, a thorough evaluation of the work was carried out both in relation to the project monitoring system and in relation to the implementation strategy. For monitoring, performance indicators from the logical framework matrix were applied as part of the project steering tool, highlighting possible adjustments in the working strategy. These meetings have been very important to ensure flexible implementation, and have involved both the political part of the organisation and the project staff. The project has played a key role in the work and development of the organisation itself, and the capacity building within the health system has also been addressing the organisational capacity to develop, organise and coordinate the work with the communities. The meetings would be concluded by planning the work of the next trip.

Collaboration with the public health system, specifically with the regional health administration – the DRSU (*Dirección Regional de Salud Ucayali*), is an important part of the indigenous health programme. The enhanced capacity of the organisations to deal with the health problems in their area should, at the same time, leave the organisation in a position to negotiate health agreements with the DRSU, specifically agreements for free treatment at the hospitals, the implementation of national health campaigns and the organisation of "surgical campaigns".

Results and problems - current status
It has proved to be of great importance to keep the project very flexible, not least the implementation strategy. Working with indigenous peoples

in the Amazon area means working with different ethnic groups that have very different understandings of the world around them, totally different languages and, importantly for this project, different understandings of health and curative methods. Implementation strategies for the health work that have shown themselves to work very well among the Asháninka of central Peru may face serious problems, for example, among the Harakmbuts in the south or the Chayawitas in the north. Specifically, the close connection between the work of the shamans and the ever-present potential threat of witchcraft calls for flexible and sensitive implementation strategies.

Implementing through the indigenous organisations, both national and regional, has proved to be important, particularly in relation to the strengthening of the ownership of the health system developed. Using the local organisations also prevents the development of new structures, specifically developed for the project, a strategy that usually does not work very well. Apart from strengthening the ownership of the project, this strategy also has the potential for strengthening the organisational structure and the organisations' political work.

The constant focusing on the sustainability of outputs is an important issue in the implementation of all projects. PSI's programme in Atalaya, DESSEI *(Desarrollo de la Sistema de Salud Indígena),* has focused on the sustainability of the system in many ways. By focusing on the capacity building of the local organisations, it has sought to develop a system that ensures communication with the villages through contact and supervision from the health workers (promoters and indigenous experts). At the same time, the organisation, supported by the national organisation (AIDESEP), should be able to negotiate health agreements with the regional health official from the Ministry of Health. The second major aspect of sustainability is the more permanent link to the public health system. This has been achieved through the certification of health promoters, who have all received a certificate and ID card from the regional health authorities, the DRSU, stating that they have been trained as promoters. An important aspect of this is that it has been achieved by developing a proposal for a 3-year training course for indigenous health technicians. (This new project will be dealt with below.)

The local organisations are thus, as explained above, seen as a crucial link in the chain. They are, however, also the weak link in the chain. If the organisation cannot bear this burden, it will be difficult to sustain the project in the long run. This, on the other hand, puts important responsibility on the shoulders of PSI in AIDESEP. PSI is the central unit responsible for health within the indigenous organisational system, and must therefore monitor and supervise the development of the work and the health system very closely. This is a most important challenge for the organisations to deal with in the near future. Now that the project has come to an end, the situation is that the Integrated Indigenous Health System (PSI) has been implemented in the three areas in the Ucayali region, covering three

Nurse Lidia explaining reality.   Photo: Jim Thuesen, 1998

local organisations, and 119 communities. All communities have between one and three health promoters, and the focus on the indigenous health experts and on co-operation between the two health systems has been significantly strengthened. There is a good relationship with DRSU and good potential for further cooperation with the public health system. As already mentioned, one important output of the project has been the development of a proposal for a training course for indigenous health technicians. This idea grew out of the project and its focus on the long-term sustainability of the integrated health system. It was further motivated by a comparison with AIDESEP's education strategy and a closer study of their institute in Iquitos, FORMABIAB.

There was a need to link into the public health system, and there was a need to ensure the supervision of the promoters working in the villages over and above what the local indigenous organisation could provide. The public health system is, apart from one hospital and a few clinics in the small towns in each region, represented by small health posts, approximately one for every 10 communities. A *técnico sanitario* (health technician) is stationed at each health post, employed by the Ministry of Health. These technicians, however, very seldom speak the local indigenous language and have no significant knowledge of the indigenous understanding of health. This has very often created problems both for the technician work-

Down the Ucayali River.   *Photo: Thomas Skielboe, 1998*

ing in the area and for the indigenous people living in the communities. The technicians have a 3-year education in basic western health. The idea would be to create a new training course, producing qualified inter-cultural health technicians who receive training designed specifically for working in indigenous areas. They should be educated both in western medicine and in indigenous understandings of health in order to support the integration of the two different systems. The new training course should enable the indigenous health technicians to supervise the promoters working in each community, and to support the local organisations in their health work. The idea of the course was presented to the Ministry of Health, which has showed a genuine interest in developing an institute for this kind of study.

During the last year of the project, a proposal for this new educational programme was accordingly developed in close collaboration with the Ministry of Health, the DRSU and the National School for Public Health, ENSAP. A proposal for the establishment of a National Institute of Intercultural Amazonian Health, INSIA, has been finalised and approved by the Ministry of Health, and a four-year pilot project proposal has been formulated. Karen Elise Jensen Foundation has agreed to finance the first year of INSIA's start-up phase. The establishment of the Institute and the new programme will be an important step towards consolidating the

Integrated Indigenous Health System, developing a better approach through which to cope with the health problems in the indigenous areas. Achieving this will be an important political step for AIDESEP and for the indigenous peoples of the Peruvian Amazon.

Note

1. Amakaeri, Ese-Eja, Amahuaca, Hachipaeri, Yine, Pukiri, Machigenga, Yaminahua, Shipibo-Conibo, Kichwa Runa and Arazaeri.

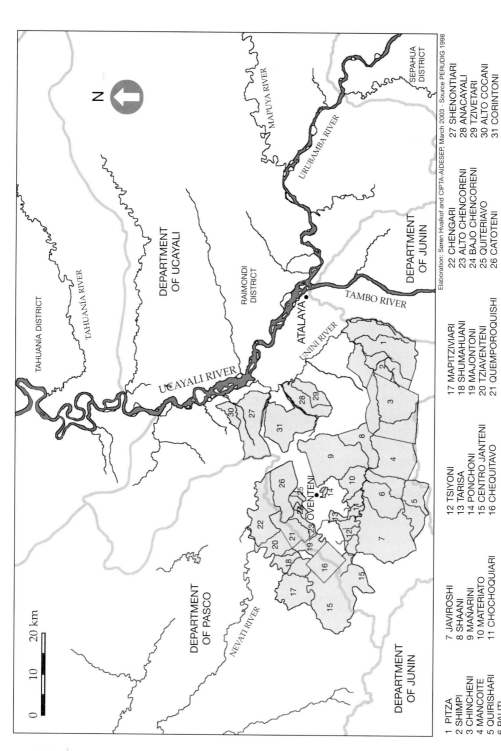

Map 5. The Ashéninka Organisations of Gran Pajonal, OAGP - affiliated communities.

Ashéninka design

A Funding Soul – Notes from the Field

By Dorte Mette Jensen,
member of the Board of the Karen Elise Jensen Foundation

The K.E.J. Foundation and the PSI

The Danish foundation supporting the Indigenous Health Programme (PSI) was established in 1986 by Mrs. Karen Elise Jensen as an endowment, dedicating her inheritance to the patronage of medical science. Her motivation for establishing this foundation was gratitude to the medical profession for its efforts in attempting to cure her daughter, Suzanne, who died of leukaemia at only 29 years of age. The Foundation was established in memory of Suzanne.

The Board of Directors, chosen by Mrs. Karen Elise Jensen, consists of three members with a background in medical science, one lawyer and myself – also a daughter and a former schoolteacher, now an organic agriculturalist. The projects supported cover medical science ranging from basic research to special topical studies, including international cooperation between research teams. The decision to support the indigenous Amazon organisation, AIDESEP, was indeed very different from the usual high-tech medical research projects hitherto funded. The project presented by the indigenous organisation was a low-tech preventive health pilot project, which was, nevertheless, acceptable to the Foundation given that preventive medicine falls within its mandate.

The application was forwarded by the Nordic Agency for Development and Ecology (NORDECO), a non-profit consultancy firm acting as the link between the Karen Elise Jensen Foundation and the indigenous organisation in charge of the project, AIDESEP. It was proposed that NORDECO should assume responsibility for supervising the project. The foundation's Board discussed this atypical project proposal extensively and, after due consideration, we unanimously agreed to support the Indigenous Health Programme, provided that certain conditions were fulfilled. Apart from administrative and audit requirements, the Foundation insisted on being an integral part of the project supervision in order to gain a first-hand knowledge of the project. This implied that at least one member of the Board would participate in the semi-annual review missions to Peru.

Learning from the field

Two Board members, the physician Dr. Jim Thuesen Pedersen and I, were appointed as the K.E.J. Foundation's representatives in order to participate in the review missions and in reporting from the field. I was very enthusiastic about participating but wondered how it would work out. Would we be mere spectators on the sideline or could we actually contribute to the impact of the project? These initial concerns were soon overcome as we became well integrated into the review team. My combined background as a schoolteacher and a farmer were useful tools in the team work, and the meeting with a very different indigenous culture in the setting of the Peruvian Amazon turned into an important learning process. Apart from the cultural dimensions of the work, both Dr. Jim Thuesen Pedersen and I had to learn Spanish. Initially, we worked through interpreters but eventually reached a level of understanding where we could get by on our own. The participatory observation and approach in the field, working with the AIDESEP project teams, contributed immensely to our learning of Spanish. A contributing factor to the improvement of our language skills was the reading of project reports and the participation in numerous meetings and discussions at all levels.

Obviously, the enormous amount of new information we accumulated was overwhelming and difficult to handle and transmit back to the Board. Names of persons, ethnic groups, institutions and organisations, titles and posts in different hierarchies, functions and tasks, and innumerable acronyms and abbreviations had to be conveyed. One eventually gets familiar with such networks, once the inclusive and complicated structures permeating the entire system are recognised. However, this raised another question. Was it really necessary that an indigenous organisation like AIDESEP should maintain such a wide network and hierarchically organised system reaching from the level of the smallest indigenous community way out in the forest to the national office in Lima and even up to representation on a pan-American level? I was amazed and puzzled by this organisational structure. But recurrent field trips visiting indigenous communities where the health programme operated convinced me of the relevance and necessity of such a wide and organised network. Indeed, in my opinion, this is the most crucial aspect. The success of the project depends on a well-functioning network of independent indigenous organisations. Although the project paper described this structure in detail, this alone would not have assured me of the need for such a large "bottom up" system and administration had I not personally experienced it in the field. The fact that ordinary people in far-off communities are part of a larger system in which they have both influence and even a named position, is of great pride to the communities. People involved in the projects appreciate their titles and responsibilities - it is prestigious and creates self-confidence to be actively engaged, and the process makes them aware of their network and organisational strength. The projects have created a new sit-

Mrs. Dorte and Dr. Jim.   *Photo: Thomas Skielboe, 1998*

uation for communities which hitherto have been completely margin-alised in the national society.

Dynamics of supervision

The project would never survive without being closely linked to the indigenous organisations, and the organisations would not have gained the momentum they have achieved without such a focussed project - a mutual effect of promoting a self-confident and sustainable network.

In this context traditional knowledge of illness and cure merged with western knowledge of health into a holistic view, and the fact that the indigenous people themselves were responsible for the implementation and daily work, considerably strengthened the project's capacity. Problems and solutions were discussed and dealt with at community meetings, and changes and adaptations to local cultural conditions were proposed and discussed with the supervising team, making it possible to adjust the project along the way. Such adjustments to the project ranged from structural changes affecting the entire set up to deciding on very concrete problems. One major change was the decision to let the shamans stay in their home communities, as opposed to the initial decision that they should form part of the itinerant health teams visiting the communities. The education and training of shaman students has all along been part of the immediate objectives of the Programme. So the students would now travel to the shamans to undergo their training rather than vice versa. This required changes in both budgeting and planning which, however, could be agreed upon on the spot. More specific adjustments were the decisions to purchase large aluminium pots for steam healing rituals performed by traditional midwives; besides extra pairs of rubber boots in the rainy season for the nurses, and bars of dried tobacco for the shamans to use in smoke-healing. These are all but a few examples of adjustments that were made in line with local needs and traditions, making it possible to improve implementation and even sharpen the objectives. This trial-and-error methodology, in combination with direct interaction between the supervising team, the project staff and the people in the communities, has been very encouraging and efficient. Donors and recipients now have "faces". They become interacting people with mutual responsibilities. Donors are not just an anonymous administration far away but well-known persons showing an interest and a visible engagement in local matters.

Another effect of the permanent supervision by project teams and the semi-annual review involving the donors has been the widespread awareness of the Indigenous Health Programme in the entire project area of the Upper Ucayali. One consequence of the permanent follow-up by the travelling field teams has been a considerably improved communication between involved communities and people up and down the river system. This has made it possible for the indigenous organisations involved to organise the registration of the indigenous inhabitants as Peruvian citizens, thus enabling them to participate in elections both as voters and as political candidates, creating a new democratic reality in the Ucayali region.

The communities visited were very proud to show us their project, to teach us about their culture and traditions and their gardens with medicinal plants, presented as their "pharmacies". We always received a very hospitable reception with "samples" of local culture and often with an impressive banquet of local delicacies such as crayfish, herbs, cooked and roasted manioc, green plantains, bananas, cooked caimans, smoked monkey meat and roasted caterpillars. During such a meal the whole community would be the audience and witness to our strange eating habits, openly pointed out and laughed at. The indigenous people of the Ucayali are extremely patient. They can wait for hours just observing with no problem at all. Being seated at meetings in the community school, I was more than once amazed at such group discipline. Almost all the inhabitants would be present watching the visitors, squatting on the undersized children's seats beneath the blackboard. Women and children of all ages, men with bows and arrows lined up all over the class room, sitting on the floor, on school benches, standing along the walls - everybody aware and airing their opinions to the assembled party. Half the people present at such meeting would be small children and babies in their mother's baby slings, but one would hardly hear an infant cry. They felt safe despite the strange looking guests and unusual circumstances so different from everyday life. The balanced human and communal coherence strikes a busy European used to a stressful life in a fractured reality, emphasising the importance of supporting the continuation of indigenous culture.

Excerpts from a diary

A meal:

"I am eating the soup and the noise from the tin plate signals the end of the meal. I am in eye contact with a beautiful young mother of about 18 or 19 years old, sitting with her two children - a little baby boy at her breast and a girl of three at her feet. She smiles and at the same time has an expression of kindness and dignified distance framed by calmness and harmony. After the meal, the local manioc beer "masato" will be served. The luxury meal is followed by music welcoming the guests and inviting them to join the locals in a dance."

A typical community meeting:

"The meeting will start and all the participants will introduce themselves and make statements to be discussed. The local coordinator will then refer to the project, asking for supplementary details and making conclusions

Visit from the K.E.J. Foundation.   *Photo: Thomas Skielboe, 1994*

regarding the current situation. The course of recent events will be presented by the project team and commented on by the audience, who will then evaluate their specific health project. The different points of view will be clearly specified and possible irregularities and problems discussed in an adequate way. The conclusions from the visit will be drawn and, usually, presented as an example of their successful implementation of the project as witnessed by both the visitors and the community members."

The nurses of the PSI:

"The core of the success of the travelling project teams are the nurses and the local coordinators. In each community, they train community members to maintain indigenous health care - presenting, organising, recording, preventing and curing. The communities love their nurse because of her capacity to cure and counsel, and her teaching of important rules of prevention of sickness - a learning process increasing their influence over their own quality of life. The implementation of traditional indigenous medicine has become ever more visible. The indigenous leaders are expressing growing confidence in their own systems. In the communities, the number of "sheripiaris" - Ashéninka tobacco shamans - women vapour healers, traditional midwives and experts in herbal medicine is increasing, and there is a growing knowledge and production of traditional crafts, conceived as part of the same spiritual powers."

Glimpses from a visit to Gran Pajonal:

"On arrival at the Ashéninka community of Chequitavo in the mission's small plane we could see the whole community - more then a hundred people - lined up along the airstrip in rows two by two. Men, women and children as young as two years of age were there. They had been standing in rows for hours, patiently awaiting our arrival. We were given a warm welcome and shook hands with almost everyone. A traditional meal was served in the schoolroom with all the locals curiously watching us as we ate. Then the meeting started - introducing, referring, discussing and evaluating. The strength of the project lies in its decentralised structure. Each local indigenous organisation is responsible for the activities in their member communities. The local coordinator has his local network and feels responsible for both the organisation and the project.

"We were accommodated, together with the project nurse Isolina, in the small house of the Protestant missionaries, who were absent at the time. Isolina is a nurse working in more than 30 communities in Gran Pajonal. Her eleven-year-old son would accompany her over the next couple of months during his summer holidays. Isolina is a single mother. Her son normally lives with her sister and goes to school in Lima. Isolina sees her son during the summer holidays and every third month, when she has some time off. By candlelight, we talked with Isolina until 8:00 p.m. Then it was time to set up the mosquito net and make up the beds inside.

"I woke up very early at dawn - 5:00 a.m. The Ashéninka women all wake at this hour, to make their fires and begin cooking. They brought fire to our hearth and food - plantains, manioc, pineapple and chicken soup. It had rained all night. It was doubtful whether the plane would arrive at noon as planned. We were soon invited to a vapour healer's session. The *"vaporadoras"* - the vapour therapy women - take a big pot of water mixed with different herbs and place it on the fire. When the water boils, stones are heated in the fire and placed in the water to increase the vapour. The patient is placed in a sort of "tent" - using their *"cushma"*, a cotton tunic - over the boiling pot. When the treatment is over, the leaves and herbal residue in the pot are carefully examined. Small objects such as bones may be found, exorcised from the body as evil waste. The bad things causing the sickness have been removed.

"It rained all day, and it was a little cold even in this tropical setting - maybe not surprising as this place is situated at an altitude of more than 1,200 m. From this high altitude community, we can watch the grazing cattle on the slopes across the ravine. They come from a cattle programme supported by the Peruvian government. The original purpose was to improve the nutrition of the indigenous peoples of the Upper Amazon, who were supposed to eat the meat and drink the milk. The government took it for granted that the indigenous population drink milk and herd cattle for domestic consumption. They do not - at all. So now the cows are left to their own devices, growing old, on the green slopes.

"The plane was supposed to fetch us at noon but the rain continued, making us realise that we would have to stay one more night. Up with the mosquito net - an act becoming almost ritual. I went to sleep after our own evening meal, hard-boiled eggs, biscuits, bananas and left over Nescafé. No rain during the night. A beautiful morning, the mist disappearing and the quiet smoke from the cooking fires rising among the houses. The women bring soup. The sun rises. This will be another beautiful day. Early in the afternoon, the plane arrives and we leave Chequitavo. Isolina, her son and the coordinator will pack their horse to make the long walk along the difficult trail to yet another community."

Concluding remarks

From the point of view of a Board member of a funding foundation, I can wholeheartedly recommend direct involvement in a professional review team and participation in follow-up field work. The direct linkage between the people in the communities and the Board members taking decisions with important implications for the indigenous population has been crucial. The first-hand experience from the field has made it possible for us to explain the context to the rest of the Board, and to discuss proposals and decisions on an informed basis. We have seen, heard, touched and smelled the problems and experienced solutions within our reach. However, to make such a "home grown" indigenous health project sustainable requires the long term involvement of the Peruvian public health service, linking it to the indigenous health programme. This becomes

A shy little girl, Gran Pajonal.   Photo: Søren Hvalkof, 1995

Now, less shy, Gran Pajonal.   Photo: Søren Hvalkof, 1995

more urgent as the PSI is increasingly influencing rural health policies in the Amazon. In this context, it seems imperative to design and implement a public indigenous education programme for community health workers, integrating indigenous and western medicine. The establishment of an officially recognised health education for highly motivated and skilled students from the indigenous communities would be a commendable outcome of the indigenous efforts supported by the K.E.J. Foundation.

Photo: Søren Hvalkof, 1994   *Backlight, Unini Mission community.*

Shumahuani grasslands, Gran Pajonal. *Photo: Søren Hvalkof, 1996*

Upstream the Unini River in the summer. *Photo: Rune Hvalkof, 2000*

Summer shallow water, Ucayali River.　　　　　　　　　　*Photo: Jim Thuesen, 1994*

Paddling the rising river.　　　　　　　　　　*Photo: Jim Thuesen, 1998*

The team on the beach, Urubamba River.   *Photo: Thomas Skielboe, 1994*

Waiting on the Urubamba River.   *Photo: Jim Thuesen, 1994*

"M/S Freedom", Marañon River.   *Photo: Jim Thuesen, 1994*

Down the Ucayali River.   *Photo: Jim Thuesen, 1994*

Loaded barges, Ucayali River. Photo: *Thomas Skielboe, 1998*

Asháninka children fishing. Photo: *Søren Hvalkof, 2000*

A community on the river bank, Ucayali River.   *Photo: Søren Hvalkof, 2000*

Cattle and timber, Pucallpa.   *Photo: Jim Thuesen, 1994*

A trail in the forrest. *Photo: Thomas Skielboe, 1994*

Otilia

Otilia Tuesta Cerrón is 35 years old and comes from Condorcanqui in Amazonas region. The daughter of a Loretano father and an Aguaruna mother, she is the only indigenous nurse to have worked in the Programme. She studied nursing at the San Martín de Porres de Lima University, graduating in 1997. She became involved in organisational work in 1992-93, joining the staff of the Health Programme of the Regional Coordinating Body of Indigenous Peoples of San Lorenzo (CORPI), Alto Amazonas. In 1995, she joined the field staff of the Indigenous Health Programme (AIDESEP-PSI) with her organisation, the Indigenous Regional Organisation of Atalaya (OIRA), and worked there until 1998.

The Antichrist in San Lorenzo

I started as a nurse in AIDESEP's Indigenous Health Project, initially visiting the 25 Chayahuita and Aguaruna communities to inform them of the type of work that was going to be carried out, and explaining to them what was meant by indigenous health. During my second visit, it was above all the women who welcomed us by demonstrating their greater openness. But there were some misunderstandings on the part of several community members. They began to say that "the Antichrists are coming", and so we were welcomed in the first community but when we arrived in the second, we found no-one. The men and women had disappeared into the countryside, there was no-one about, which surprised us very much. The information had already been passed on and there was only one family left. They told us that everyone had fled into the countryside because the Antichrist was coming. So they did not agree with the sort of work we were going to do because, according to them, plants could not heal, plants could not make you better. The idea of the "Antichrist" arose from a church that had been working there for many years. They were evangelists, and this was their idea. They feared they would be "marked with the 66" or I don't know what; they had this biblical idea. Everyone would be branded on the forehead and, out of fear of this, they all fled into the countryside.

Well, we went back and had to tell the leaders about this in a meeting. We did manage to undertake the planned work with the women we met; this was in the Aguaruna group. The Chayahuita also had some fears, but they did not leave their communities. And so we carried out the work with them, particularly the work consisting of collating the types of medicinal plants used in the communities.

The women in Urubamba

This initial phase took place during 1992 and 1993; a number of difficulties then arose in the Programme. It had to be closed and I was invited to join the Project that was going to be implemented in Urubamba-Ucayali. So, there we devoted ourselves to the work. We were welcomed very differently: their ideas were different, they wanted to work, and there were no nurses there, only leaders and community members. They were very happy with the idea of the Indigenous Health Programme. They asked for our help, particularly the women, who wanted us to visit them all the time, for they said the Ministry did not reach them. The women were happy because, generally, when there were visits, the men would go to the meeting and the women would say: we cannot take part because of our indigenous customs. They cannot tell a male health worker that they have, for example, a vaginal discharge, or that they are pregnant, or have such-and-such a problem. So this trust was very different.

Then, with regard the uses of their plants, they also had to trust someone to be able to tell them: this plant can be used for this, this one for that, this is good for such-and-such an illness. And so they began to express themselves. They could not just tell anyone, because there had to be trust. We were received very differently. I was very happy to work there, from 1995 to 1998. The people were also very happy with the kind of work we were doing, there were no problems with the Church, nor with the "Antichrist".

Ethnic differentiation

The work was primarily statistical, on the basis of common illnesses, for example, leishmaniasis and diarrhoea, then on the basis of transmissible tropical diseases, such as malaria, dengue and others. Medicinal plants were also collected, both among the Yine and the Asháninka, and also the Yaminahua. The way in which plants were used was very different among the three indigenous groups or peoples. For example, the three peoples have very different uses for *toe* [*Datura sp.*] and *ayahuasca* [*Banisteriopsis sp.*]. The three peoples have different beliefs, to them health is linked to nature. For example, if there is a scare, or a child suddenly becomes frightened, it is because the Mother of the Water or the Mother of the Countryside has hurt it. The concept of health is very different, they link it to the environment in which they live. To cure an illness, the Yine use *toé* and the Aasháninka use *ayahuasca*. I also observed that the Yaminahua take *ayahuasca* to find out what illnesses they have, and the Asháninka use tobacco quite a lot. Each people has its own beliefs and culture. We had to respect this and, in line with this, apply their own particular kind of health system. We could not impose on them or tell one people that they should use what another is using. To cure a particular illness, they had their own plants.

In the beginning, they said that they did not want a Shipibo traditional healer, who might be in the area of the Asháninka and Yíne, to visit them because they had their own traditional healers, their own vapour healers. In other words, every people had its own doctor. So this is how the method of work was improved for it to function better, this is when it was decided that the people themselves should choose their own vapour healers and their own *sheripiaris* [tobacco shamans], their own health systems. This was being developed in each community, to a very advanced stage, so that the people themselves could continue to implement it. Work was also undertaken to provide vegetable plots that were not communal but family-run. Only in this way could the health system be improved, because the people felt that the community vegetable garden system did not work very well. When it is communal, everyone begins to say: you go and work, I don't feel like it, but when it is family-run then the family, and each of its members, begins to look after the plants.

Food and civilisation

It was clear that, with regard to nutrition, there were differences in the way the fields were sown. Indigenous communities that are nearer to a village, for instance, a mestizo village, have few sown fields, there is little food, for example, there is a shortage of meat and of fish. But the distant communities, a day or more away from a mestizo village, do have fields and gardens, they have fish and better food than those communities that are closer to mestizo villages. The closer ones do not have adequate food and those that are more isolated do.

I think this is because there is a form of dependence. For example, if there is a family in an indigenous village that prefers to exchange a chicken for a tin of tuna or a couple of kilos of beans, what is it they are doing? It is a bad trade-off. They have been told they mustn't do it, but they say they prefer to eat things from outside rather than their own produce – as they put it, "we want tuna". In this aspect, the programme has also had to talk to the mothers about what good nutrition is or, more particularly, about a balanced diet. They should not lose sight of the fact that, with all food, it is not quantity but quality that counts, but there is no satisfactory agreement. In the meetings they say yes, that's OK. The nutritional content of every product is individually explained to them and then they, well some of them at least, grow more aware.

Nurse Otilia drinking masato. Photo: Thomas Skielboe, 1994

Chatting in the health post. Photo: Thomas Skielboe, 1994

Gloria

Gloria O. Bullón López is 26 years old and comes from Tarma. She has been working in the Indigenous Health Programme since 1998. She worked in Sector I of the Gran Pajonal with OAGP, together with Rómulo Leiva Rossi and Esther Chiri Santiago, the two Ashéninka coordinators. They work with 13 Native Communities: Materiato, Ponchoni, Chochoquiari, Pauti, Javiroshi, Anexo Javiroshi, Quirishiari, Anexo Pauti, Anexo Pitza, Bajo Shimpe, Chinchini, Mancoite and Shani.

The jungle? Not me!

We began the field work in November 1998, following our training in Lima. I had undergone my nursing practice in the school in Tarma and was on the point of taking up a post in the neoplastic hospital. Dr. Torres was there looking for nurses, as other nurses from Tarma had already gone to work in the Programme. The director spoke to me; she asked if I was interested in working in the forest, around Pucallpa. I had sworn that I would never work in the jungle because I don't like the heat or the mosquitoes. For me, it was a completely unknown world. I had always wanted to work in the mountains, or by the coast ... but never in the forest! But I began to think seriously about this, particularly as I was single. I didn't know what experiences I would have to tell my children about in the future, so I told myself that at least this would be something different, something new. Besides, it was a great opportunity because things were economically very difficult at that time.

Well, I made up my mind and I told my family I was going, although at first they didn't believe me because I had said I would never go to the jungle.

On arrival, I handed over my documents and was explained a little about what the work consisted of with the promoters and the communities. Then I had an interview with Mr. Juan Reátegui, the Programme Director. He began by asking me if I knew much about the forest. I told him that it was very hot and that there were mosquitoes. I told him what I knew. I told him quite sincerely that I knew very little about indigenous peoples but I knew that their culture was different to that of the mountain peoples. They ate some kinds of animals that I would never have thought could have been eaten, such as caterpillars and ants.

The thing was, I was interested in getting to know new places, different people and, as I had only recently qualified, I wanted to prove to myself that I could do something professional. This was the challenge for me. So I said, "I have to prove what I can do" and it took even more courage when they said that there was no water in this place, no electricity, no television, no civilisation, that you had to walk miles. But I believe that people can adapt to many things and learn from them.

First impressions

I began working with Isolina Valdez, trying to find out through her what the area was like, what sort of people lived there and, above all, getting to know who the leaders we would be working with were. She told me that Mr. Pascual Camaiteri, Mr. Ydelfonso Campos and Mr. Miguel Camaiteri were there and she told me about the coordinators and the type of work they had been doing over the last two years. She told me the work was quite hard because you only occasionally got to travel by horse.

I had never seen anything like Oventeni, only on television, in films of long-forgotten places. She told me there was one community here, another there. We managed to reach the community of Ponchoni by plane, where I was introduced to the wife of the community President as her husband was not there. That first night they put us up and we got to know the residents and, with time, it all seemed much easier.

At first it was a bit of a shock to leave my family, to have to share a room with a person I had never met before. Isolina helped me a great deal; she is a very special person, very noble. We were there about a week, sorting out our details for visiting the first communities: a nearby one called Quirahuanero, and Catoteni.

Field induction

We began in Quirahuanero, it was the first contact I had had with a native community. They already knew we were coming and they welcomed us warmly. They already knew Isolina and there were great expectations at meeting the new nurse. So, at the first meeting, I introduced myself and told them of the issues I would be tackling with them. We spent around three days there, visiting three communities. It was right in the middle of the rainy season, winter, so the road was quite muddy. I asked Isolina if all the roads were like this, if it was always so difficult to get anywhere, and she said that this was not bad, that they were worse in other communities. My boots were full of mud, my trousers filthy, and I had never sweated so much in my life. Slowly, she made me understand that this was how it had to be, that everything could be overcome. I talked to her a lot, not only about work but about personal things too.

If the Ministry of Health...

If the Ministry of Health were to go to the communities, it would achieve a great deal. I saw that there was a great need to treat patients, many required care within these communities. I could see that professionals were rather strange to these people. In the community, professionals were viewed with mistrust; this is how they were perceived. The people wait to see what they will do, what they will say. And the Ministry staff only stay a few hours, a day at the outside, and do not make contact with the people they are supposed to be working with, despite the fact that this is their job. If they were to work as we do, their work would be greatly improved. The first thing you have to do when you arrive in a community is try to find out who the leaders are, or who is in the community, to introduce yourself and tell them why you are there, take their opinion into account, what they say, what they think about what is going to be done, how they would like to be involved and to draw up a small work plan with them for the days you are going to be there.

Social solidarity

We began to visit more distant communities, where nobody had ever been. Nobody there had ever encountered God, or experienced another kind of culture, other ways of life. It's very different there; they are less complicated than we people from outside. If they are hungry, it's not important that it's not time for breakfast or lunch, they just eat whenever they are hungry, whether it's ten o'clock or five in the morning.

Something else that caught my attention was the fact that they know how to share. When they boil their cassava, or they eat their fish or they catch a bird or something, they roast it or make it into a soup, and everyone eats from the same plate or the same bowl. Sometimes they eat on the floor with their candles, their leaves, their mats, whatever, they eat right there. From a health point of view, some things are not right, for example, eating with dirty hands, or eating on the floor. I told them about these things. Go and eat but wash your hands, eat on the floor if you like but your plate must be clean. We tried to teach them simple things, without changing what they do, because this idea of sharing begins with the family, it is unique; these things should never change.

Little changes in their daily lives can greatly help to prevent illness, primarily nutritional deficiencies and parasitosis. They fall ill quite a lot with diarrhoea and are very afraid of influenza, for it is a killer. Last year there was a huge epidemic around May/June, and many people died.

Sadness and suicide

Something else I noted during the flu epidemic was in the community of Chochoquiari, where a *sheripiari* [tobacco shaman] died. He had a pupil who, on seeing his teacher die, committed suicide. He hung himself from a liana because he could not bear the pain of the thought that his teacher had died. On seeing him dead, the sheripiari's wife and children also went into the countryside and hung themselves. A whole family, even their parrot which, it was said, bore the spirit of the sheripiari. The community was left with no sheripiari, no pupil, not even anyone interested. This was very sad to see. These were great emotions that could not conceive of life without the being that had departed. They preferred to be together, as the people put it, wherever that may be. They know it as neither heaven nor hell.

Education and health

Some parents have questioned the value of school, they say that the children come home lazy when they go to school, that they play and don't do what they have to around the house: collecting wood or going to the fields. We tell them that they are using their brains and that this work will help them a great deal. And that they can do the chores in the afternoon. But there is a great deal of concern about this in Gran Pajonal and some distant communities.

Other parents are disappointed with their children's teachers, despite the fact that they have tried to ensure, together with the organisation, that most of them are bilingual. Cases can be seen of teachers going to the community merely because they have to, or to make money. But they have no real feeling for their work. Sometimes, they send a class of children out into the world who cannot read well, they get their letters mixed up and have no facility for expressing their ideas. So the work of the teachers has not always been completely effective.

But this varies from one place to another. The work of the teachers can be very helpful, not only in teaching literacy but in terms of the development of their people. It can be assumed that the teachers have a little more education than the community members and so they can contribute their ideas, help to organise the people, given that they spend more time with them. But the teachers, like the promoters, have to learn as they go along and so the fruits of this work will only slowly be seen. In contrast, we health workers have already prioritised the issues: diarrhoea, all respiratory infections, particularly tuberculosis, and malaria. And we already have trained promoters who can deal with these illnesses.

The public health system is not very effective, due to a lack of continuity. People from the communities do not go to the medical post in Oventeni. A new doctor in his internship cycle, or a new nurse, is always arriving, staying just one year and then moving on. There is no continuity. The most distant native communities do not even know them, they think nurses are just there to give injections, vaccinations, they do not know the truth of the work, which is why I say that if the Ministry worked like the Programme does, visiting the communities for at least a few days, it could do a lot of good for the people.

The Indigenous Health Programme and development

The communities have received this programme extremely well and now they do not want it to finish. They are sad because the nurse and the coordinators will be leaving and, once they are gone, there will be no-one to see if the promoters are doing their job, or if things are going wrong. We tell them that we have been working there for four years now and that this work should be bearing fruit; that, of course, in the beginning it will be a bit shaky, there will be difficulties, but that they must continue to strengthen their organisation, the OAGP. The work with the organisation must continue, supporting them, coordinating with them, providing help and doing whatever possible in negotiations with the public authorities, the Ministry of Agriculture, and Ministry of Health. They have a lay magistrate, they have Authorities, they have representatives there with whom they can negotiate. They can improve their nutrition, become multicroppers, not grow just yucca and coffee. They are also beginning to plant orange trees, bananas and pineapples. To ensure a variety of foods in some communities, they are growing garden produce, some green vegetables, but they don't have the necessary knowledge, they don't know when it is good to sow, how many seeds or what type of soil to use.

As I said, the people who go there as representatives of the Ministry of Agriculture don't have a particularly good relationship with the communities. I believe this is due to difficulties in accessing distant communities and the lack of government budget. This cannot be resolved so easily. We try to give the communities, the leaders, the organisation, ideas as to how things could be improved. The point is to see how they can adapt our ideas to their ideas and do something. But the truth is there is quite a lack of coordination with the authorities.

There was a time when there was no coordination at all between the OAGP and the Ministry of Agriculture and other authorities but, luckily, Don Pascual managed to get the message across as to what point of view the organisation represented. Now, if an organisation goes to work with the indigenous communities, it has to coordinate with the OAGP. They have achieved quite a lot in this way. The Ministry plans its trips in accordance with the censuses undertaken by the Programme. We have, for example, assessed the proportion of children who have not been vaccinated. They are now working on the basis of this, and they are also educating patients with regard to respiratory problems or malaria.

The organisation and the future

Everything is now coordinated with the organisation and we are supporting this in all ways, saying that this work must continue, that the nurses are not indispensable. And that, just like us, somebody else could arrive at any moment, and they need to be prepared. They must also bear in mind that, now that the new road to Pauti is crossing their land, cars will be entering, and so they must remember that people, both good and bad, will also be entering, that they must be prepared for this. In fact, the first car arrived in May to buy coffee. Other cars had arrived in relation to the roadwork itself, but that day a small car arrived to buy coffee and they welcomed it with some happiness, because they sold their coffee at a better price than when it is taken out of Gran Pajonal by plane. Now they had gained a little more profit and they were excited. I told them to store their products, for purchasers would come not only for coffee but also to buy bananas, cassava, but I stressed that they did not have to sell. They should make sure they kept some for themselves. Then they knew that we were not deceiving them, we were not exaggerating. They themselves then understood that strangers would come to buy their bananas, their cassava. They saw I was right and asked me to tell them who was good and who was bad.

This is going to be a big problem. We have already spoken to Don Pascual to see how a good organisational structure can be maintained in this community – because there are people here who have completed secondary education but who are not working for their community. Quite the opposite, they have gone to Santa Cruz, they have left for Satipo and sometimes they come back with bad ideas for their community. These produce envy, meanness and jealousy. The Pauti community was the oldest, the best organised and now, with the change in leadership, it has many ideas for community development but it lacks strategies, ways to do these things, how to implement ideas and motivate the people. Whatever you say, they now have ideas from the outside world.

It has been a great experience for me to have spent almost two years there. A huge change has taken place in my life for, with some trepidation, I have realised that this work is very important and that they need to realise this and I think they are aware of the changes that have taken place in the communities because of the Programme. Now they have *sheripiaris*; they have motivated vapour healers and vegetable gardens to produce cash crops, and each of the specialists have their students. Now they realise they are not alone, that together they can find answers to the community's problems and that being organised is by far the best solution.

Voices I: The Nurses

Maria Isolina

Maria Isolina Valdéz Felipe is a graduate nurse who qualified in 1988. She is 34 years of age and originally comes from Chanchamayo in the Selva Central. In 1990, she began working in the Perené Hospital in Chanchamayo, where she visited some of the Satipo communities, working in the area of immunisations for the Ministry of Health. Since 1993, she has worked as a nurse in various of AIDESEP's indigenous member organisations: with CECONSEC in the Selva Central, with FENAMAD in Madre de Dios and with OIRA in Atalaya. She began working with OAGP on the Health Programme in Gran Pajonal in 1996, where she remained to the end of the project.

Working with the organisations

AIDESEP needed six nurses to work in an anti-cholera campaign. This was how I became involved, in September 1993, with CECONSEC's work, and this included my visiting 83 communities. I worked alone there, with just the organisation's health representative. I received some training in Lima, to know how to make best use of the communities' human resource potential. I needed to know how the indigenous people care for their patients, how they cure them. There were vapour healers and herbalists where I came from, but I did not know anything about them.

I contacted the headman of one of the communities in Chanchamayo, as this community was badly affected by cholera and we had to carry out an anti-cholera campaign there. I set off to visit all the communities and, because I was working alone, I had scarcely finished a trip, then I had to set off again two days later. This was really difficult. It was the first time that I had worked and talked with indigenous people, getting them to defend their culture. They did not want their children to learn their language. They would say to me, "If they do, how will they go to Perené, how will they go to college?"

I was not particularly well prepared, and we were very much seen as outsiders. Yet, gradually, we were able to teach them something. In the campaign, we managed to prevent cholera. Some traditional healers gave out herbs to be taken, using one plant that smelt of cinnamon to save their patients. The traditional midwives were also organised; they came to the talks in Perené or Chanchamayo, and were given work gear and medical supplies. In this respect, the Ministry of Health was reaching the midwives, but not the *sheripiaris* or vapour healers in any effective way. But now we had planted a seed.

Terrorism, time and resources

When I arrived in Chanchamayo, the area was suffering greatly from terrorism. I could not stay long in the communities because of the danger. Sometimes I had to take medicines from CECONSEC in my rucksack and, with the person in charge of Human Rights Defence, I managed to get a pass to be able to cross some of the military bases en route to the communities. They asked me loads of questions. The communities' chiefs were in charge of looking after me. They were responsible for bringing me and waiting for me and, if there were any signs of danger, getting me out - even in the middle of the night - and taking me as near to Chanchamayo as possible. There was a real problem with terrorism.

Another problem for the communities, apart from cholera, was malaria. CECONSEC is an organisation with few resources and so we had to negotiate and ask for help from the Perené municipal authorities. We had to coordinate with the hospital in La Merced to ensure it provided support to the indigenous communities. They gave us medicines for the campaign because what we brought from the Programme was insufficient. The municipality helped us and this was how we worked for seven months.

The first results

At that time we used to say that "they should have a promoter". But that was as far as it went, we had no training sessions planned, we could not leave someone in charge of dealing with the health care. Well, this was how it was when I started. I had arrived to work in the indigenous communities without much thought, and it was a good experience, something different. You had to be creative, to find ways of getting things done.

We held an evaluation in Iquitos and, on our return, we met up with six nurses who had been working in different areas, and we realised that we needed far more training. There was one of us who had worked with indigenous communities before, but neither I nor the others had much experience and we needed to know more, to know a little about the history of the communities.

In a meeting in San Lorenzo, policy guidelines for indigenous health were drawn up, and there we began to understand a little more of what was required of us. The main thing was to integrate western medicine within the indigenous communities. To see which health system was more advanced and to make the two traditions complementary on the basis of the indigenous health system. It was not a question of saying "you have to wash your hands" or "you must drink boiled water" but of understanding how they have been living, and for how long, with their own system.

And so we began to understand a little more about what working with the indigenous communities meant. My feeling was that I should carry on educating myself so that I would be able to continue with other work at a later date.

Putting the Indigenous Health Programme into practice

They again asked me to work in OIRA, to begin a trial of the Health Programme. Four nurses started working, and they told us we had to meet with the communities' human resources and form an Indigenous Health Council. We worked with a coordinator who was also a boat driver and who helped us with the work in the communities. As the boat driver spoke the local language, we were able to communicate well with the communities. The Health Council functioned well, and we were spending more time in the communities. We covered 50 communities in all and each nurse worked with 12 or 13 communities. I worked in the Unini area. We were finding out what resources were available, the vapour healers, the midwife, the promoter. They were being trained, from our point of view, in the academic side of things. Also, in the evaluations, we wanted something specific to the communities and to the Indigenous Health Council and we also wanted to organise them around the use of western medicine. Finally, we held an evaluation meeting with Otilia Tuesta, who was already better integrated into the communities, for she had worked in San Lorenzo a long time. An earlier project, ADAR, had already formed a Health Committee, that is, there were already nurses. Latrines had been built and they had been constructed very well, but the community members did not want to use them, they said that they were full of flies and mosquitoes and that they smelt bad. We tried to tell the community members to use them and that they should wash their hands afterwards.

After these first trials, we could see in the evaluation that we were already better organised. In Atalaya we had already begun the first data collection with the sheripiaris. In the initial stages, OIRA itself had undertaken the data collection but we felt the organisation lacked something, it was still rather weak, and yet we – as a part of the western side of medicine – could not do that work, it had to be done by the indigenous side through their own system.

At that time, FENAMAD launched its work in Madre de Dios within the Indigenous Health Programme.

The Madre de Dios experience

Two of us went to Madre de Dios, and we found a very different situation there. It was an organisation, which, according to its members, had a great deal of experience, and that had been working for many years. We went with a coordinator to the communities and we found a very different reality. There was a huge mix, a lot of mestizos who spoke very good Spanish. Where I was working in Madre de Dios there were Shipibo, Harakmbut, Arawak speakers and Quichua. I was faced with a really difficult situation. The AMETRA 2000 project had been in operation there, there was the Botanical Hospital and they talked quite a lot about a French consultant. When we arrived in the communities to seek out the human resources, they rejected us at first, rejected the Health Programme.

Paralized after an accident. Maria Isolina's patient.   Photo: Søren Hvalkof, 1994

There had been problems with the Frenchman, who had told the Harakmbut traditional healers to take *ayahuasca*. They were not accustomed to taking either *ayahuasca* or *toé*. They said that *ayahuasca* made them ill and so they wanted to know nothing about the Health Programme. We told them that we did not want to change their customs. The Harakmbut only used tobacco whilst the Shipibo use *ayahuasca* in their health system and there are other ethnic groups who only sing, who cure their sick by singing.

It was only during my second and third visits to Madre de Dios that they began to accept me but, after nine months, the work ground to a halt due to bad financial management. So then we travelled to Lima to undertake an evaluation and we had to face up to everything on our own. We had proved to the Madre de Dios Hospital that there was no tuberculosis in the communities. The Hospital said that all the communities had tuberculosis and that the costs in Madre de Dios were very high, that in 1994 they were the ones with the highest TB frequency. We carried out some intensive research and only found one case of ganglionar tuberculosis. It was a community member who was working with the gold diggers and who had arrived in the community ill. Each group of miners, who came from Cuzco and Ayacucho, had seven, eight or ten people with tuberculosis. So the hospital staff began to realise that it was not the indigenous that had tuberculosis but people from outside, who came to work in the gold mining industry, they were the ones with tuberculosis. The staff were very appreciative of the support we had given in this regard. For each community health post, we had trained health promoters and technicians. We had left medicine packages, because these were necessary in the area. The work we did there was not at all bad, but after nine months it came to a halt and we had to return to Lima.

Hepatitis and malaria

When we returned to Lima, AIDESEP was in the process of preparing research into prevention of hepatitis B and Delta in the Amazon, for the National Health Institute. To be able to assist in this task, I was sent for training at the National Health Institute, to gain experience in taking blood tests and undertaking sampling throughout the basins of the Río Marañón, Putumayo, Tigre, Napo before returning to Atalaya, in Ucayali. I carried out the first sampling with Dr. Torres and then they sent me to all the basins to take blood samples and send them back, in order to be able to see what types of parasites there were in each area. We also treated the cases of malaria that were appearing throughout the area of Marañón. For the research work there, we worked in coordination with the Ministry of Health.

We had a few problems with the Aguaruna–Huambisa Council, as we had to ask the Council's permission, but the people wanted us to help them. We also had the full support of the Ministry of Health, of the Municipality, in reaching these people and, thanks to them, we are now vaccinating against hepatitis B, at least the children under one year old. The aim was to cover all children under 5, because of their increased tendency to catch hepatitis. Now the Health Programme is proposing to continue the work where Dr. Torres and Otilia are working. At first we thought it would only be done with OIRA, but part of the Gran Pajonal can also be covered.

The OAGP's strength

The third phase of the project, which had already been prepared with OIRA, was delayed a little. I was chosen to work in Gran Pajonal and so I arrived at the Ashéninka Organisation of Gran Pajonal – the OAGP. Given my experience of other organisations, I found that OAGP was very good, with strong foundations.

I had scarcely arrived when they said to me, "Nurse, we have no boat or car, you have to walk 3 or 4 days to reach a community." This rather shocked me as a first impression. They asked me where I had worked previously and I told them mostly along the river, walking very little in Chanchamayo. Then Don Pascual Camaiteri told me, "Well, nurse, here you walk. The first community is four days away." I told myself not to be frightened and they saw that I would be OK. I thought, well, work is work, wherever you are. We began the journey and our objectives were the same, to recover and strengthen indigenous medicine, complementing and integrating it with western medicine. In the team we had a male coordinator and a very expert female coordinator. There was also a women's organisation with which we worked. We made a very long trip, getting to know the whole area. The indigenous people were rather scared and did not want to say what they did or did not have.

The Swiss Indian Mission was also working in the area and we began to identify promoters that were being trained by the Mission. We were warmly welcomed because they knew that we were going to start a new Programme. During a training session for all the promoters, I got to know Sister Liselotte from the Mission. We talked, we coordinated and no-one was opposed to the work, because OAGP needed to strengthen its indigenous health system. The sister understood that we had to treat the people within their own health system.

The community members told us that the *chori* [Andean settlers] brought them illness, brought them joncawontse [gonorrhoea], that these were new illnesses. Then we looked at whether it would be possible to work with the two medicines, in coordination. The sheripiaris or traditional healers said that they could only cure up to a certain point, and from then on, they could not. So this was for the promoter. Thus we were able to work out in what direction the Health Programme should go.

Ways of working

Our team comprises one coordinator responsible for each organisation and who, in our case, is Ashéninka, a female coordinator, also Ashéninka, and the nurse. We also have a female expert, a vapour healer, but she is not used in the communities where there are already vapour healers. There were also two schools involved in the first phase, one in the community of Chequitavo and the other in the community of Tarisa, where the sheripiari teacher lives. This is where the students go to train. We also have an administrative assistant.

A trek visiting communities would take us months. After two years of work, we had promoters working and new promoters had been identified for training. It was the same with the sheripiaris.

We also worked with the settlers. When we carried out the census, we visited everyone, indigenous and non-indigenous. We also focused the work on communities that had families from outside. In Oventeni, there are people who have only recently arrived, they live outside the communities themselves, they are not in any community. We also included them within the census. They live on the farms, with their patrons, and it was they themselves who approached us. They have accepted the Programme very well. They told us that they have their Ashéninka vapour healer and that they go to him to be cured. He is a very good vapour healer from Oventeni, and we have invited him to our meetings on several occasions. There is also a bonesetter and a traditional midwife, who have been identified and introduced to the village.

Evaluating the work

We undertook an evaluation, in which I said that there had been inadequate training, that we were working with promoters in a community, that we then left them for five months without seeing them or providing any continuity of training. We raised the need to expand the work, insisting that we needed another team in order to be able to reach the communities easily. This was how the programme was extended and we now have two teams.

We worked out an agreement between the Municipality and the OAGP to include the Oventeni settlement within the Programme. We contacted people who have supported us for years in Oventeni. The organisation considered the inclusion of Oventeni as being strategic, in order to reduce the political problems with the settlers.

In the course of our work, we have recovered many indigenous specialists and doctors, and we have 60 promoters, of which 33 are now at a good level. They have participated in all the training sessions, have had good practical experience. In addition, medicines have been replaced, fields are being worked to pay for the medicine stock in the communities and products are sold to purchase medicines. The difficulty is in the western part, because there is no system for purchasing medicines. This still remains an issue on which a strategy needs to be found, an alternative in order to be able to ensure that our promoters continue to make progress. It is important that we are able to work with the Ministry in order to be able to supply the Oventeni health post and that the promoters there can buy medicines.

For me, it was a very good experience working with OAGP, there were no problems and the administration was always on a par with the work. This was always our request, that the administrative side should be closely linked to the technical side of the work. And this was how it was in Gran Pajonal. We are very happy with OAGP's recognition, with the work done with the organisation's leaders and I would like to thank them warmly for having allowed me to work in this area.

Nurse Lidia.   *Photo: Jim Thuesen, 1998*

Voices I: The Nurses

Lidia

Lidia Orihuela Zapata is a graduate nurse from Tarma in the Andean department of Junín. She is the team nurse with the most experience in the Amazonian forest. She began working with AIDESEP in 1991, taking part in the "Anti-Cholera Campaign" in Atalaya. Since then she has worked with the Health Programme in various regional projects, including in the Bajo Huallaga and Achual Tipishca with FEDECOCA (1993) and, later, in the Pacaya-Samiria National Reserve with the Cocamilla and riverine mestizos. Her extensive field experience benefited this programme, in which she worked with OIRA and ORDECONADIT until the end of the project in 2000.

The cholera epidemic

I was initially appointed to work in CECONCEC, which is in the Satipo area of the Selva Central. There was a lot of terrorism in this area at the time, so they sent me to Atalaya. I worked in Atalaya, in the "Anti-Cholera Campaign". At that time, AIDESEP's health department was headed by Mr. Juan Reátegui Silva. We began working in 1991, training the promoters in how to treat cholera because, at that time, cholera was devastating the population. In Ucayali, we found that 144 people had died from it. The promoters did not know how to give intravenous rehydration treatment, despite the fact that the Atalaya Health Centre had provided them with intravenous serum. They did not know how to administer locally-produced rehydration solutions, and so many people died in 1991. That year, I began to train the promoters in water purification, raising the people's awareness about cleanliness and the importance of hygiene. Then, with this as a basis, the promoters began to bring cholera under control and the death rate from this illness fell. At that time, the people were called to attend mass meetings and I was surprised to see that not only the promoters but the *sheripiaris* came too, along with the community leaders, bilingual teachers, authorities, traditional midwives and vapour healers. All received training in cholera treatment and they were very satisfied because they wanted to overcome this illness, they wanted to eradicate it. The whole population felt very concerned. Later, when we were monitoring, we were surprised to see that the vast majority of the population, some 70% or 75%, had built their own latrines and had improved their cleanliness, in other words, they had understood the importance of hygiene and cleanliness in the fight against diarrhoea and cholera.

Health and indigenous specialists

In 1993, I went to Bajo Huallaga, where FEDECOCA works, and I also worked with AIDESEP in the Pacaya-Samiria National Reserve, in Samiria. There we began to set up Indigenous Health Councils, comprising spiritual chanters, traditional midwives, and herbal healers, along with the promoters and those responsible for training. We did work with them on western medicines, pharmaceuticals, but also on indigenous medicine. We found that indigenous medicine predominated there, it was used quite a lot, particularly by the women. The women were the ones who used medicinal plants, those that the Ashéninka here in Atalaya call *piripiri* and *pinitsi*. We also worked on issues of cleanliness and with the spiritual chanters, the icaradores. There are very good *icaradores* among the Cocama-Cocamilla people. In 1995, I went back to Atalaya to again work with the Indigenous Health Programme in OIRA's communities. We continued working, now increasingly strengthening indigenous medicine and its associated human resources. There it was different, the sheripiaris, traditional midwives, and vapour healers were not recognised because, among the Ashéninka people there had previously been no traditional midwives. In a community there were three, four or maybe five midwives but they worked within their own family. A midwife would deliver the babies of her daughters-in-law, daughters, granddaughters, great-granddaughters and so on. Another family would have their own midwife and if, for example, a family's midwife died, this would sometimes be made known. That was how you would find out who the midwives were, because they were never actually recognised in an assembly as midwives. The vapour healers were, however, recognised. There would be one or two vapour healers in each community.

Religious resistance

Some communities had no vapour healers because, with the arrival of the evangelists, even the sheripiaris and vapour healers disappeared. People said they were anti-Christian, that they were the devil's work, and so we had to fight this, because the people were turning against what was their own, their own culture, their own medicine. These things had survived the ups and downs of so many centuries and, well, now they were beginning to demonise them.

We continued this work, with ORDECONADIT again, from 1996 on. There were still many communities here, many more Adventist communities, in which the sheripiaris were demonised in the full sense of the word: They were demons, witches, it was against the law of God, there were even strong and well organised communities without sheripiaris because of this. There were vapour healers, because, as they say, their work with plants is all right, but no sheripiaris because they are demons. This is what the people belonging to these Adventist communities thought.

Recognition and success

We continued the work, and we are very satisfied, at the end of the project, for we now have a number of sheripiaris who enjoy good recognition in their communities. The same goes for the traditional midwives and vapour healers in each community. We also have promoters who are working in the communities. The vast majority of families have their own vegetable plots, and they recognise the value of medicinal plants. A respect for sheripiaris, for vapour healers, has once more been restored. The sheripiaris no longer have to work in secret, in hiding. There is now even an Integrated Health Project for the native communities, being implemented by the Ucayali Regional Department, in which the sheripiaris, the traditional midwives, the vapour healers, all the human resources of the indigenous health system, are taken into account. This is defined by the Community Health Agents in the head office. So what is happening now, in our communities, is that our sheripiaris feel stronger, as do our traditional midwives, our vapour healers, our promoters, because they now see that even the Ministry is recognising them and valuing them. The western system has understood the importance of indigenous medicine as being the main form of medicine in the area, and is beginning to understand that western medicine is now a complement, albeit a necessary one. The staff from the Ministry no longer work in isolation, they now coordinate, they work with the traditional midwives, the vapour healers, and now they even want to work directly with the sheripiaris. However, it is a bit difficult for them because, even now, the sheripiaris still feel suspicious of them, there is still some distrust.

Supervision and follow-up

The promoters are also very satisfied. They are now coordinating with the health posts and centres. What they are asking for - and what they need - is greater strengthening in terms of their knowledge of how to handle medicines. This is what they need. So now, on this latest trip we are making, I am placing more emphasis on supervision. I can see that some of the promoters are still weak, and we have also had promoters being replaced in some communities. One promoter, for example, has gone into the logging industry and spends long periods away. He has bosses to report to now, and can't just return to the community. So another promoter has been chosen and is being trained. Now, on this trip, we have travelled with a group of promoters and, in travelling from community to community, they have learned a great deal because they learn more from seeing than from sitting in a classroom. This is a very positive experience for them. To learn through demonstration and through practise is far preferable, and we hope that their knowledge is already bearing fruit. We now have our strengthened, our valued, indigenous medicine, and the health resources of each community now come forward far more willingly. For example, they will approach the Health Ministry's team saying, "I am the midwife" or "I am the vapour healer". The sheripiaris are still a little hesitant, but the traditional midwives and vapour healers do approach the teams, they make themselves known and talk to them. And closer links between the Health Ministry and the communities can be observed.

Asháninka specialists and technicians, ORDECONADIT.   Photo: Jim Thuesen, 1998

Beatriz

Beatriz Cuellar Contreras was born in Pucallpa and is 32 years of age. She is a nurse with more than nine years' experience of working in Public Health in Lima. She has worked with the Programme for two years, with OIRA in Atalaya. She works with the Yiné, Asháninka, Yaminahua and Amahuaca peoples in the Río Urubamba sector.

The beginning

I am from Pucallpa and was born exactly two hours from San Alejandro and there, too, there are rivers, similar to those of Atalaya, and the local people are Cacataibo. I never thought I would work directly with indigenous peoples, despite the fact that I was born in the forests, and the truth is, I really like it, it's great. People recognise us, they thank us, and we are always welcomed warmly. I'm used to the work now. We know how to work in the rainy season or the dry season, when we have to walk a long way to see a patient. When we are in the communities we work seven days a week.

Atalaya is different and particularly the Urubamba sector, because people are always moving around. Sometimes, we choose a promoter and then they tell us that she or he has gone to study in Pucallpa. So there are opportunities for support, perhaps it is due to the parents, who want their children to succeed. Nor are there such serious illnesses as in other communities, because there are health posts. I think maybe the food is better and that's another reason why there are fewer illnesses. Clothing is better too. People in the Urubamba sector now only wear their *cushma* [long cotton tunic] when it's cold, then they use it like a coat. They are always commenting that those upriver in the Urubamba sector have more money. The difference is that upstream they work in the logging industry, there's a lot of that sort of work there.

In the community of Onconashari, you can see the benefits they have. There, for example, most people have small radios. It's never silent in that community, the radio is always on in one house or another.

We found women with venereal diseases in these communities. There are a lot of logging companies there. The first time we went, there was a party going on with more than 30 loggers and, you know, with a lot of boozing and drunkenness, they must have passed it on, maybe the women went with one of them. Wherever there are loggers we have seen venereal diseases but we can treat them. We always talk to the vapour healer, and the young people are told to continue the treatment using the herbs that are prescribed.

In the Bufeo Pozo zone, in Puija, there are communities with more medicines than others. These are people who know how to handle their medicines better. In the case of Bufeo Pozo, the promoter is an excellent administrator. They also have the PISAQ organisation, which is continually training them and giving out medicines. They have double or even triple the training of those downriver. Apart from PISAQ, they also have OIRA and the Health Centre.

Indigenous and western medicine

We have had the opportunity to travel out with Señor Angel, who is an expert in indigenous medicine. The course has been very interesting because, in addition to the promoters, the traditional midwives, vapour healers and traditional healers have also been trained. We always say at each meeting that it is easy to gather medicinal plants, that pills cost money, and there are some communities that put this into practice, but others do not. Others say that it is easier to take a pill for a headache and this is what they are used to. But the promoter always works with the traditional midwives, and so the promoter can see whether something can be cured with western or with indigenous medicine.

There was one woman whose son had pneumonia and so the birth attendant blew on him, that is, he blew tobacco smoke into his lungs. She thought it was caused by fright and that was why she had gone to the traditional healer. But the boy also had pneumonia, so she came here and the child was at death's door. He arrived at the health centre in a bad state. They should not have been giving the poor child tobacco, as he was already in a bad condition with pneumonia. So we had to tell them that there are only some things that traditional medicine can cure. But they believe in curses.

Two of the best *sheripiaris* are in Urubamba. Two of them are masters; one is in Pucani and another in Capirona. People did not believe much in the one in Capirona because they said he used curses, but the real problem was that this man had got involved with two sisters, and so the community did not want him. They virtually threw him out, although for him it was normal to have children with the two women. Other people had accused him of putting a curse on their grandchildren. Sometimes, although they are experts, they don't only do good things, they do bad things as well. This is what people are always saying. We also have 10 trainee *sheripiaris*, as the Asháninka call them, or *kajonchi* as the Yine call them, or yowu as the Yaminahua or Amahuaca call them. They practise in different ways. The Yaminahua do not use ayahuasca [hallucinogenic concoction] but tobacco. They cure with tobacco. There was another healer in Bufeo Pozo who cured everything through his Bible and he was designated the community's *kajonchi*. Not all take ayahuasca, or purge themselves as they call it, in order to see into the future.

The Indigenous Health Programme

I think the programme has a potential, it is the help they really need. Also because of the trips they take to bring the manioc and bananas to Pucallpa. Since a motorboat can get down to Pucallpa in four days, the Programme can help in all sorts of ways, not only in health.

I have worked in this area for four years and I think that the promoters are well trained. If, suddenly, the Programme were to go, the health centre would still remain and they would train new promoters in how to administer the medicines. Now they are sad because they know the Programme is coming to an end, so they say that we must always visit them, always help them.

We explain that the Programme was extended for two years, that the financial support was for two more years, and they ask us if there is going to be another project. We tell them that the promoters from here will perhaps have work to do, and that the best thing is that the indigenous people themselves treat their fellow people, because they understand them better, they speak the same language. A mestizo will never treat an indigenous woman for fear that the men will see him, they all care a lot about this, about intimacy, shall we say.

Health specialist Luzmila grilling fish.   *Photo: Cæcilie Mikkelsen, 2000*

Sofía

Sofía Vivanco Hilaro, 37 years of age, is a graduate nurse. She joined the Indigenous Health Programme in September 1998 and works in the Ucayali sector with 29 communities belonging to OIRA Atalaya.

Incorporating different systems

I think our experience of work in this Programme has been a good one because of the diversity of systems with which we have been working and our reasons for doing this work. The communities continue to maintain their traditional health systems, which they use to prevent and treat common illnesses. Another important aspect is the mortality rate among children caused by diarrhoea, parasitosis and malnutrition.

The 19 months I have been working here have been a good experience. I have worked with the vapour healers, sheripiaris, traditional midwives and bonesetters, and training the health promoters by means of a system that takes the use of their traditional medicines into account. It is an innovative experience and cannot be compared to simple training. Western medicine is very systematised, but we cannot act the same way in every community because they practise different types of medicine. These traditional systems have been maintained for generations, and they do not change. Nor does the preparation of medicinal plants and this knowledge is passed on orally.

We have tried to adapt our language, our way of life, and our customs to the indigenous reality, and we have seen the importance of the health promoter in the communities. We have been training promoters in each community and this is important because, if a promoter has to leave because of other work, another must take their place. Similarly, we have emphasised the need to replace medicines, and this also takes place under systems created by the communities themselves. Communal plots have been encouraged, there is poultry rearing, and products such as rice are sold. But in Atalaya, rice only sells for 25 to 30 *centavos* a kilo and so the profits are not enough. This is a problem in that it restricts medicine replacement significantly, and hampers the efforts made by each health promoter and community chief to maintain and sustain this type of work. But, in spite of these limitations, the communities' promoters are sufficiently motivated to continue maintaining the community medicine chest for emergency cases. We have drawn up a list of 12 emergency medicines: analgesics, antipyretics, antispasmodics, antiparasitics and antibiotics.

These are medicines that can be used in an emergency or for complicated treatments. We also have an agreement with the Atalaya Health Centre that ensures their collaboration in diagnosing illnesses, because there are cases that the health promoter cannot resolve in the community.

Last February, we held a meeting with the Atalaya Health Centre, with the health technicians who work in the outlying posts. These are people who work only from a western health perspective and, in the meeting, they understood the need to modernise their way of working, so we invited them to travel with us, from community to community, giving them enough time for the community members to get to know them, respect them and include them in their way of life. Because if an unknown person arrives in the community, they are not easily accepted. It took a good four to five months for people to accept us, confide in us and make a place for us in their society. This is a new way of working, and it was accepted by some of the health post technicians. Visiting a community for two or three hours is not the same as staying there one or two days. As for us, we have chosen to live side by side with the people, and the results have been very good.

During our fifth trip, we worked with a man who is an expert in the use of plants, he has studied and trained with the master Shipibo, Mr. Angel Ruíz, from the organisation ORDECONADIT. With his help, we brought vapour healers, sheripiaris, midwives and health promoters together so that they could all learn to use and prepare medicines for the treatment of common illnesses. To treat diarrhoea, respiratory infections, influenza, shock caused by "bad air", frights, sickness or parasitosis, *ojé* tree sap is prepared. We have had good results with this concoction.

We have always been concerned to ensure the participation of health promoters. We have managed to bring together a group of 35 very motivated people that are willing to be involved. In each place where an evaluation has been undertaken, the results have been extremely satisfactory. Their involvement, and their learning from each other, has been very important. The vapour healers share their experiences with the newer ones. It was the first time that such meetings had been held. They learnt to share their knowledge and also to recognise plants and possibly change some methods of preparation. Similarly, the sheripiaris cure their patients with tobacco and *ayahuasca*, but they have also participated in the treatment of illnesses other than the usual ones. It has been a good experience for us to work, for example, with the Ramón Castilla community. We nurses, along with the health promoters, treat patients from a western medical perspective, whilst the vapour healers give their opinion from a traditional perspective. The same goes for the sheripiaris and the midwives. Take, for example, a case of diarrhoea treatment. The patient was questioned and explained his or hers symptoms and, after this consultation, the promoter gave us his opinion from a western perspective and the vapour healer his opinion from a traditional perspective. This has been an extremely dynamic way of treating patients, and has been really good because we agree on a lot of things. In this case, we chose the treatment according to the traditional system. The vapour healer decided to use boiled mango tree bark, with a flower whose name I don't remember. If there was no improvement in the patient within two days, it was agreed that we would start western treatment with antibiotics. This way of working has generated quite a lot of interest and many think this is how we should work in all the communities.

The promoters, vapour healers, sheripiaris and midwives can use this system. It is good because there have often been cases of patients going to a sheripiari for 40 days without receiving a second opinion. We had one case of a gluteal abscess in the community of San Francisco. The patient received tobacco treatment from the sheripiari. He was blown on [with tobacco smoke] and vapour healed but there was no improvement. The abscess was growing to such an extent that the right gluteus was four times larger than the left. Then, after 40 days, the sheripiari said that it was an illness for the doctors. The patient was in a very bad way, severely anaemic and malnourished. He could no longer walk and, given these circumstances, we began treatment with antibiotics. The patient was scared, the head of the community even intervened and we left him in the hands of his family. After six days, I returned to the community and the patient was already a lot better, he thanked us for our intervention and agreed to continue the treatment, which we extended for another 15 days to avoid complications. After six months he was a great deal better, and this showed people that sometimes the sheripiaris can make matters worse. We have used these examples to explain to the sheripiaris that they should not be so set in their ways, that sometimes the patient needs more, and that the promoter, midwife, sheripiari and bonesetter are part of a team. They need to keep in close communication with each other. The training sessions we have held on all our trips have been aimed at this, so that they get to know each other, so that there is less rivalry between them, so that they become more open, more communicative, and learn to respect other opinions.

We have also had situations in which it was very difficult to be allowed into the house of a family to attend a birth, when the midwife and the husband were present. Sometimes they prevent us from being involved, through embarrassment on the part of the woman, or fear or jealousy on the part of the husband. In this respect, our work has sometimes been severely limited. We had one case, in the community of El Pozo, of a six-hour labour in which the baby was not descending. The midwife called me and when I arrived at the house there were four birth attendants, the nurse, the mother of the 15-year-old girl giving birth, and the husband. Then, when I began to put her into the right position the mother was shocked and said that was not how it was done and the other midwife said the same, that she had to be sitting, she had to be lying down, she had to be standing. So I told them that they were also going to learn what I knew, so I moved the patient and the baby was born. But the problem continued when it was time to cut the umbilical cord. There was no way they wanted this done until the placenta had been delivered. Everyone said she would die. We waited a whole hour with the baby attached to the mother by the cord. When the labour was over, the women said that it was also a good birth the way we did it. The cord was cut at 15 cms with a special knot and the placenta was dealt with by the husband. He crushed it so that he would have no more children. He didn't want any more after seeing his wife suffer so much. And so I too learnt something that day.

In the community of Pensilvania, about two weeks after I had started my work, I came across a little boy of eight years old with arthritis. It really saddened me to see the little boy laid up in bed, with a temperature of 40 degrees, on the point of going into a convulsion and the family unable to do anything because they had no money. They had no fuel to take him from Pensilvania to Atalaya, a six-hour boat ride. They couldn't even buy a tablet for his fever. So we began to treat him and, after eight days, he was quite a lot better. Dr. Torres also helped us in the diagnosis and treatment. In these cases, a lack of money is quite common.

Lastly, I would like to thank the donor and AIDESEP for the way of working that has been chosen in the native communities. This doesn't exist in any book, it is something new and the creativity of this work has been growing daily, as problems, needs and opportunities have arisen in each community. The training methods have been modified because there are many issues that we wanted to raise from a western point of view. We have had to change our way of working to bring it in line with the reality around us, and this has been very hard. It took us months of learning, time and patience. For their part, the promoters do not have the level of education we would wish them to have. Sometimes they haven't completed primary school, or only the second or fourth year of primary school, and it is very difficult to teach things that are in writing. We have had to use practical sessions to help them learn. We want our contributions to be valid for native communities in any country.

Rosario

Rosario Vega Camarena is a 30-year-old nurse. She only began working in the forest with AIDESEP and its Indigenous Health Programme in 1999. She works in the Ucayali sector with the regional organisation, ORDECONADIT.

Introduction to indigenous culture

I first heard of the existence of AIDESEP in 1991, through Lidia Orihuela Zapata, who - like me - comes from Tarma. She told me about the project, she showed me photos and then my interest began to grow. They offered me a job in 1994 but at that time I had problems with my health and couldn't go. Later, I came into contact with AIDESEP again, through Mr. Juan Reategui, and this is how I came to be here. For me it was something new. Although I had visited the forest around La Merced in Chanchamayo, this was very different. I had always worked on the coast or in the mountains. When I arrived in Ucayali, I began to work with Shipibo-Conibo communities. Nine were Shipibo communities and four were mixed.

I could see that the Shipibo culture was more closely linked to fishing than the Asháninka. These people are hunters and harder working. The Shipibo are also rather more dependent on western culture, relying on outside help. My work was to try to revive an appreciation of their culture in them, to prevent it from being lost, westernised, because this would mean losing everything. They have managed to preserve their culture for thousands of years, and what we are trying to do is get them to maintain their ways of working, their traditional midwives, vapour healers and shamans.

The 13 communities I work with have an indigenous health system. In the case of Shahuaya, they already have a trainee and in Tumbuya there is also a bonesetter, although there is no traditional healer there. But people are treated between the neighbouring communities. They come from Shahuaya, from the community of 9 de Octubre, from Tumbuya or Nueva Fenicio, or they come down from Santa Ana. There was rather a barrier between them and the promoters but now we are trying to make contact between them, so that they coordinate, work in collaboration, are alert to any illness that may occur. For example, the promoters cannot treat a shock of "bad air" and so know they must take the person to the traditional healer and, when there are things the traditional healer cannot cure, they have to go to the promoter. This is how we have worked and it continues to function well.

Medicine stocks and loggers

Now we are on our last trip, and replacement of medicines for the community medical stocks are more or less 80% on medicines for short term treatment and 20% for long-term and emergency medicines, for example for epidemic situations. There is one community that has not replaced the medicines and whose money is in the hands of a logger, who is dragging his feet. He always tells them they should come back tomorrow because he doesn't have it, or not all of it. So the organisation intervened and so did we, as nurses, and the logger, the man, told us that he would let us know when the money would be returned to the organisation, so that we could tell the community and they could replace their medicines.

The Shipibo rarely work in the logging industry and so have little dependency on the loggers. Last year, for example, everyone was fully involved in fishing in their communities but this year the loggers have entered, and sometimes they do not keep their promises to the community. They always talk to them about a percentage, that the percentage is already set, but they don't keep to it and the indigenous wait and wait and, in this case, the organisation had to intervene.

The loggers are a problem for the communities. They take people from their communities to the forests, and they are not looked after properly. They are provided with no benefits, little food and, if a snake should bite them, they are not taken to the health post.

Health and indigenous rights

We have had meetings with community members, together with the *onanya*, the vapour healer, the *sheripiari*, the traditional midwife, the promoter and some of the leaders. Seminars have been given telling them about ILO Convention 169, the Peruvian Political Constitution, and so on. They are becoming more aware and they now know what resources they have and how to use them. We have also held one or two meetings with the Asháninka to resolve similar problems.

We don't only focus on health but we also provide advice to the organisation, to our team, so that they can reach the community and fulfil their objectives. Sometimes, we stay one night more in a community to sort out little problems, but always in coordination with the team. We also teach prevention, for example, giving them an understanding of the symptoms of respiratory problems, of leishmaniasis or malaria. In my area, there is no malaria, well, only among those who come on visits from the Upper Ucayali, for example. There are a few cases of leprosy among the Asháninka. In cases of leishmaniasis, cancer or tuberculosis, the promoters provide treatment, under our supervision. We provide the follow-up so that the treatment is completed and the chain of transmission stopped.

The work of the Programme is very extensive and complex, from all points of view, but very satisfactory. For example, with the Ministry of Health, when one nurse's shift finishes, each patient is passed on to another and it's her responsibility. Here, we take the patients the whole way through their treatment. You see them improving little by little and it is very satisfying to see both start and finish of the treatment.

I came here with a great desire to work with indigenous people, persons with great needs. And for me the work has been very important, I feel I have made a contribution. You can't do everything all at once but I feel good, I have adapted to them and, what is most important, I have learnt to think like them and to interpret what they are trying to say.

I am a highlander from the Andean mountains and, both in the forest and the mountains, there are traditional healers who, through different procedures, manage to cure their patients. So it was not so unknown to me because sometimes I used traditional medicines in my village and also used indigenous medicine. I have been vapour healed twice, once in Paraíso, because I felt a little unwell, and the other in Santa Ana. So, in a way I have also been a patient and it worked.

If I get the chance, I would love to carry on with this work. It is a great experience, and one that I will never forget.

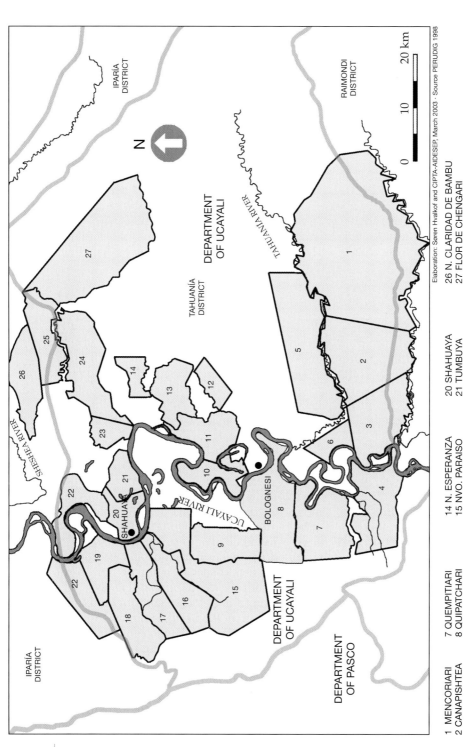

Elaboration: Søren Hvalkof and CIPTA-AIDESEP, March 2003 · Source PERUDIG 1998

1 MENCORIARI	7 QUEMPITIARI	14 N. ESPERANZA	20 SHAHUAYA	26 N. CLARIDAD DE BAMBU
2 CANAPISHTEA	8 QUIPATCHARI	15 NVO. PARAISO	21 TUMBUYA	27 FLOR DE CHENGARI
3 TONIROMASHE	9 SHIMA	16 FERNANDO STAHL	22 SEMPAYA	
4 DIOBAMBA	10 BETIJAY	17 BAJO ARUYA	23 SAN FERNANDO	
5 PTO. ALEGRE	11 STA. CLARA	18 ALTO ARUYA	24 SANTA ANA	
6 JATITZA	12 N. ROCA FUERTE	19 N. DE OCTUBRE	25 MAPALJA	
	13 TUPAC AMARU			

Map 6. Organisation of Native Communities of the Tahuania District, ORDECONADIT - affiliated communities

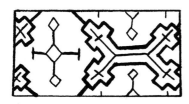

Shipibo-Conibo design

4. Emergencies

The Cayman Attack

Andrés' version

Andrés Ruíz Ferrari is a Conibo and inhabitant of the community of Tumbuya. In 1997, he was attacked by a Cayman while out collecting wood from a lake to build a new office for his organisation, ORDECONADIT. Andrés lost his arm in the incident. Miraculously, he managed to make his way back to the community where the nurse from the Indigenous Health Programme, Lidia Orihuela, decided to take him overnight by boat to the Regional Hospital in Pucallpa. Andres' life was saved but now, with only one arm, he has difficulty working and surviving in the forest. His hope is to find an administrative post in a project or within his organisation, given that he has a secondary school education. Andrés is married with two children.

I live in Tumbuya and the organisation had given me the task of finding wood for the new office in Shahuaya. Sunday, I went to find wood, and it was on Monday the accident happend. The alligator was under the water and I frightened it because, in April, it has already laid its eggs. So it overturned my canoe and threw me in the water. As I came up, I saw the caiman in front of me and, before it could bite my whole body, I offered it my arm. It bit it off just below the shoulder. The sun was almost up and I began to scream and shout. The caiman wasn't following me any more and I wanted to get out of the water, grabbing a branch, but I couldn't. The caiman was there, with my arm .... then I passed out like I was dead. For more than three hours. Blood was pouring out as if from a bucket.

I somehow succeeded in getting up. I fainted for a moment and then made it for my house. I started off at 6 in the morning and arrived at 4 in the afternoon, walking, rowing. I arrived almost naked, wearing just a pair of shorts. Luckily, I met the teacher, Silo Santos, who had a *peke* [canoe or boat with a low horsepower four-stroke outboard motor] and he took me to the health post in Nueva Italia. As soon as I arrived, my brother-in-law got in touch with Miss Lidia Orihuela to come and see me. She cried when she saw me and immediately gave me an injection and took me to Shahuaya.

Photo: Søren Hvalkof, 2000   *Andrés, his wife and daughter.*

By ten my shoulder was very swollen and I couldn't move or eat, and I couldn't stand the pain. Then Miss Lidia took me to Pucallpa. There is a medical post in Nueva Italia, but they couldn't do anything, so they took me to the hospital in Pucallpa where they operated on me.

Lidia took me in the project's boat. If there had been no boat I would have died. I am very grateful to Miss Lidia for helping me, it is thanks to her I am alive.

I returned home in May, recovered. But now I cannot work. I have a little girl of four years old and my wife is pregnant. Things are very bad. Sometimes I only eat a few days a week. I have my brother, my brother-in-law, but they never give me anything, not even a fish, nothing. I have been suffering for six years and I can do nothing. It's tiring having to row with only one arm. Sometimes it swells up because my blood doesn't circulate well and it hurts. This is how I live.

Lidia's version

Nurse Lidia Orihuela saved Andrés Ruíz by taking him by boat to the hospital in Pucallpa. They navigated the waters of the river Ucayali the whole night. Lidia tells us her version of events and reflects on other emergencies and initial problems with the hospital.

Mr. Andrés went to gather wood from the lakes because, at an extraordinary congress of the organisation, it had been decided to build an office to operate from. Various communities agreed to provide the materials and Mr. Andrés went out to cut wooden house posts. He was rowing in a lake and he felt as if the canoe was being prevented from moving by a floating branch. He stopped himself with his oar, so that he could push the canoe away, but he did not notice that it was actually a crocodile or caiman, measuring approximately 8 metres in length. He hit it with the oar and, with one slap of its tail, the alligator threw him into the water. It went right at him with its mouth open and he offered it his arm. The young man struggled with the crocodile in the water and then managed to get away. He grabbed a tree to pull himself out of the water but, when he stretched out his arms, only one responded and, when he looked down he realised his right arm was gone. He hadn't felt anything, no pain. On seeing his arm was not there, he swam to the canoe because he was bleeding and he was afraid of attracting the piranhas [carnivorous fish]. He then rowed with just one arm and made it to the path. This happened at around 10 in the morning and he got back to Tumbuya at 4 in the afternoon. It is a very long way from the community to the lakes. He arrived at his community almost unconscious and all the people were shocked by what had happened and took him to Nueva Italia. I had never seen anything like it in all my life.

At that time, there was no doctor in Nueva Italia. There was only a technician. It was already 6 in the evening and, by some miracle, the

Shahuaya radio was still on, because their hours were from 3 to 5. I was preparing packages of medicines for delivery to the communities and the technician called me to tell me there was an emergency in Nueva Italia. I went running and they told me they didn't know what to do, that a community member from Tumbuya, 23-year-old Andrés Ruíz Ferrari, had lost an arm to a cayman. I had no experience of anything like that. I gave the technician instructions as to how to stop the bleeding and ease the pain and went straight away to Nueva Italia. I got there around 9 at night. It was an awful sight to see him lying there, his arteries and nerves all in shreds. In spite of everything, I finished giving the treatment, covered the wound and gave antibiotics, and we went immediately to Shahuaya. The boat was there and at 11 we left for Pucallpa. When there is an emergency, you don't think of the danger. We travelled in the dark, the whole night, with lanterns. The boat pilot's wife came along as he did not want to leave her alone. The patient was in a great deal of pain and I gave him painkillers every six hours and penicillin. As soon as we arrived they took him into the hospital and into the operating theatre.

When we arrived, I called upon the Agreement we have between the General Health Department and the Indigenous Health Programme-AIDESEP. The Agreement stipulates that patients do not have to pay the costs of hospitalisation, examinations, operations and special treatment. They exempted him from the operation expenses but not from the cost of the special medicines.

I felt bad for him, and my heart went out to him. When he was released from the operation, I went into his room and he welcomed me with a huge smile, cheerfully asking me, hello, Miss, how are you?

Despite the fact that I had brought medicines with us, they asked me for other special ones as the wound was a large one. And so we exchanged some of the medicines I had, coordinating with the social assistant and head of the pharmacy. In the end, I ended up owing 25 *soles*, which I paid out of my own pocket. They did not want to release the patient until it was paid. It took me two days to pay the debt and the patient was already discharged, getting bored and wanting to leave. He spent 11 days in hospital and, as soon as he left, we went back to Shahuaya and I took him to Tumbuya.

Now I know that he is alright but he has problems because of the loss of his arm. At first, he used to lose his balance and fall when he was using a machete. His physical limitations have caused problems with his wife. They wanted to separate but Andrés' family made them get back together, so that she could help him.

A congress of the organisation agreed to help him by giving him work but it has not been possible. Now the current leadership is looking for a way to help him.

This was a dreadful experience, but it has not been the only one. Our bad luck is that sometimes bad situations occur at night and we have to travel in the dark. In this phase of the project, we have had two seriously ill patients: one woman in the community of Bambú, with a torn cervix. Her baby was wrongly positioned and only one tiny foot had emerged. The midwives had manipulated the baby too much and had torn the neck of the womb. The placenta came out but not the baby, and so we had to take the woman to Pucallpa. It took 12 hours with a Yamaha 40 HP motor. It was a miracle she was saved because a torn cervix can cause death by haemorrhaging. But because the baby was outside the cavity and putting pressure on the uterus, this stopped her from bleeding too much. When the doctor from Nueva Italia, who thank God was in Shahuaya, saw her, he told me that the woman had a torn cervix and he didn't dare touch her because the slightest movement could set off the bleeding. And so I had to transfer the patient to Pucallpa. The same thing happened later when a colleague turned up with another women, who was suffering from placental retention. The obstetrician tried to remove it but couldn't, and so we also had to go to Pucallpa.

In the previous stage of the project, we had a case of intestinal infection that had to be treated immediately. We couldn't wait for them to operate. We have had a six-year-old girl die in hospital through intestinal infection. On another occasion they operated on a woman and it turned out that she had a cyst. So there are good experiences and bad ones.

Shipibo-conibo design

5. Concepts and Projects

The Indigenous Health Programme – PSI-AIDESEP

By Juan Reátegui Silva, Director, PSI-AIDESEP

Origin

In 1991, AIDESEP decided to create an internal structure to be responsible for the institution's health policies, in much the same way as it had done with education issues previously. This organic authority within AIDESEP was to be responsible for designing strategies, and for formulating, implementing and evaluating the corresponding projects and programmes. From 1991 to 1994, it was called the Health Secretariat but, from 1994 onwards, it became known as the Indigenous Health Programme – PSI and this is how it has been known ever since. From the very start, it has been headed by an indigenous health professional.

Why create an Indigenous Health Programme - PSI?
- Because of indigenous peoples' negative experience of the health care provided by the Ministry of Health (in terms of management).
- Because of the series of health projects being undertaken with indigenous peoples by various NGOs, with very limited participation in decision-making on the part of the indigenous peoples, and with unsatisfactory results and frustrated expectations.
- Because of the increasing frequency of epidemics, caused by illnesses introduced from the West. It was the 1990 cholera epidemic that finally precipitated the decision.
- Because of the increasing trend in indigenous policies in the Amazon basin towards a cultural reappraisal which is closely linked to the public health culture in key areas.
- Because of the western demand for Amazonian health knowledge.

Indigenous Health

In 1992, the then Head of the Health Secretariat submitted to AIDESEP's various levels of organisation an Indigenous Health proposal, comprising its philosophy, policies and strategies. From 1995 onwards, the Indigenous Health Programme (PSI) was to develop the central ideas of indigenous health, which incorporate a political and strategic proposal of the organisation of indigenous peoples of the Peruvian Amazon, aimed at preserving and improving the health of its peoples.

The concept of indigenous health has two components: first and foremost, that of re-appraising and developing indigenous health systems as a central part of the structure of indigenous society; and, secondly, within the context of interculturality, that of seeking complementary spaces in all fields with western or modern health systems, guaranteeing a better level of health care for indigenous peoples and the Peruvian population as a whole by making a combination of different world views possible, each one contributing from its own reality.

It was from this perspective that this proposal arose, aimed at activating indigenous peoples' capacity to recover and modernise their rich cultural heritage in the area of health, while at the same time coordinating it with new knowledge coming from other cultural universes. The way in which the health-illness-treatment-death processes are tackled, as phenomena that affect every living being, is directly linked to the culture of each human group, and these different cultural responses inform the medical systems or health systems of such human groups.

In our legal code, the Peruvian population is recognised as being multicultural, that is, made up of various cultures, and this implies the co-existence of various health systems among the Peruvian people. However, Peruvian society works on the basis of monocultural paradigms across all sectors. These paradigms emanate from western culture, the effectiveness of which is already being questioned, both in relation to its monetarisation and it's dependability. It has now also been shown that no single health system alone is able to solve all the population's demands and problems, not even those within its own cultural sphere.

In this respect, this indigenous health proposal, whilst prioritising and emphasising a reactivation of the health systems of the indigenous groups, does so from an intercultural perspective that does not rule out the possibility of combining two or more visions in order to resolve the health problems of the Peruvian population as a whole. Moreover, this interculturality makes possible the generation of intercultural paradigms that facilitate the complementarity of indigenous and non-indigenous knowledge, particularly in the area of health.

Objectives

- To develop the indigenous health systems of the ethnic groups represented by AIDESEP.
- To improve and increase the access of these groups to the resources of the western health system.
- To promote and develop research that contributes to fulfilling objectives 1 and 2.
- To undertake health training activities from an intercultural perspective.
- To contribute to strengthening indigenous organisations, primarily at regional, federational and local levels.

Strategies

The PSI's overall strategy is to link health actions with a strengthening of indigenous organisation and to develop the Indigenous Health System (Programme) in collaboration with grassroots organisations, as the only alternative that will guarantee its sustainability.

Specific strategies have been developed to identify, coordinate and support the human resources of each community in the area of indigenous health, promoting the re-establishment of their social prestige and personal self-esteem.

Strategies have been undertaken to link experts in plant knowledge and traditional preparations within the community with apprentices and with the western health promoters themselves.

Creative strategies have been developed to improve the access of the indigenous populations to western health services, such as maintaining medicine depots, and conducting vaccinations and surgical campaigns.

Each and every one of these individual strategies has been in line with the overall strategy of linking the health work with the organisational strengthening of the indigenous peoples.

Activities

Indigenous Health Projects:
- Design
- Negotiation
- Implementation
- Monitoring
- Evaluation
- Advice and support to AIDESEP's leadership on issues related to this area of work.
- Workshops bringing together health workers from all of AIDESEP's federations in order to redefine health policies and strategies.
- Negotiation and signing of agreements with various state and private institutions (Ministry of Health, Cayetano Heredia University, National Institute of Health).
- Establishment of a consultative council for the Indigenous Health Programme.
- Presentation of papers at national and international events on behalf of AIDESEP.

Projects

- Traditional Medicine with FONCODES: 1992.
- Anti-Cholera Campaign: 1993.
- First project with NORDECO: 1994.
- Indigenous medicine with the Cocama-Cocamilla: 1995.
- Prevalence of serological markers for Hepatitis B and Delta: 1996.
- Extension of the DESSAI project: OIRA, OAGP, ORDECONADIT in Atalaya: 1998.

Shipibo-Conibo presentation.   *Photo: Jim Thuesen, 1998*

PSI and the indigenous movement

Recovering and strengthening indigenous health systems signifies a revitalisation of the central structure of indigenous societies, with a subsequent reaffirmation of their identity and self-esteem.

- The traditional knowledge of indigenous peoples, the main repositories of which are the shamans, is the basis that guarantees their development and that of the Amazon as a whole.
- The shaman, as leader of his people, is the repository of the comprehensive knowledge of the people and fulfils the role of guiding force within his community. He is the political resource *par excellence* to lead any indigenous process. This should be taken as a potential not as a reality.

The indigenous approach to the concepts of:
health, illness and treatment

Culture can be defined as a pattern of beliefs, thoughts, values, practices, communications, behaviours and world views. Within its process of historical development, each culture has identified ways of resolving its fundamental problems. These obey not only the internal dynamic of the society but also, to a large extent, external influences.

With regard to the specific problem of illness, very individual categories, models, ideas and practices have been created that depend on the world view, social history, economy and nature of each culture. For this reason, these solutions are not necessarily identical or valid for all cultures. The concept of "health" has also developed in western culture. The World Health Organisation (WHO) defines health as the biological, psychological and social well-being of an individual.

For the indigenous peoples, "health" signifies the harmony of all elements that make up the balance, that is: having their own understanding of and control over their life, and the *harmonious co-existence of the human being with nature, with himself and with others, aimed at holistic well-being, at spiritual, individual and social fulfilment and tranquillity.* For this, the peoples, through their wise men and women, have developed a set of very complex practices and knowledge that is well structured in its content and logic. Their strength and capacity for survival is due to the effectiveness of their health systems, the conceptual focus or world view of which is based on balance, harmony and holisticity.

The indigenous world view defines the relationships of the individual with other individuals, and of these individuals with society, with nature and with the spiritual beings, in conditions of harmony, balance and holisticity. This world view as a whole – to which can be added all the norms, habits and customs passed on from generation to generation via oral tradition, besides the plant, animal and mineral resources used wisely by their shamans and other specialists – forms what we know as indigenous medicine and which is now more appropriately known as the indigenous health system, which is unique to each people, to each culture.

In the languages of most indigenous cultures, there exists no equivalent term for the English word "health". This is understandable, because indigenous thought is holistic, comprehensive. It segments neither reality nor individuals. If the latter are not ill it is because they retain a harmonious balance between their mind, their spirit and their body and, at the same time, with other individuals and with nature. And when they fall ill, it is because this balance has changed in one or several ways and, therefore, the individual is also altered in some way, both in mind or spirit and in body. Then, the individual becomes truly ill and, consequently, his/her treatment must be holistic.

There are indigenous terms to denote illness and its different forms, and almost all indigenous cultures attribute it an external origin. Illnesses *come from outside*, they are *blown from outside* and are attributed to outside malevolence or to the forest spirits. They are classified according to the incapacity to fulfil everyday tasks and according to the attributed cause. As explanatory theories of illness, in general, there are two hypotheses: firstly, the presence within the organism of a foreign body or, secondly, the exit of spirits from the body. A dispossession of the vital organs. In the first case, the shaman puts extraction techniques into practice and, in the second, techniques to reincorporate the spirits.

In the treatment of illness, the role played by plant resources is decisive. Yet this is not primarily for their therapeutic function but because they are a source of knowledge and of many powers. This is not only the case in Amazonian cultures. The world over, there are many societies that grant a privileged place to plant resources in their way of thinking. The role of the shaman in the Amazonian world must be viewed from this perspective. In the language of the shaman, the *spirit* or *mothers* of the plant

1. Comparison of Approaches to Health

Western approach	Amazonian approach
Separating man from nature	Integrating man and nature
In the human being, the spirit is separate from the body	In the human being, the spirit and body are inseparable
Illness is an individual problem of the body or the spirit	Illness is an imbalance between the person, their family, community and nature
Treatment is an increasingly specific and specialised task	Treatment is a task of wise people, men and women whose discipline and wisdom enable them to better communicate with the patient and his/her environment
Highly commercialised. Not only are there systems but also medicines for those that have and those that do not have money	Completely separated from the market and production. Wisdom and the private and economic appropriation of knowledge are incompatible
Standard medicines aimed exclusively at the body	Specific medicines, aimed at the patient, the traditional healer and the context. Aimed at the body and soul of all of them

resources are known as beings that teach and act for themselves. In the case of the *mothers* of the teaching plants, these are linked to a specific method of knowledge and learning, hence the compulsory use of these plants in any process of shamanic initiation.

The Indigenous Health System

This comprises all the elements created by the Amazonian peoples to preserve and maintain the ecological balance within which they develop. The Indigenous Health System has thus not developed a System to treat the

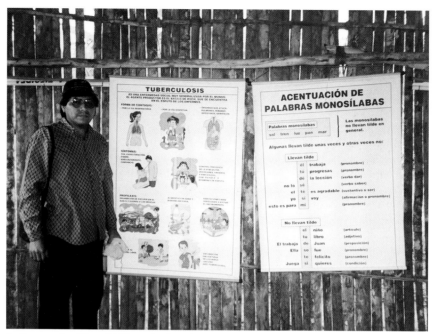

Indigenous health and bilingual education.   Photo: Thomas Skielboe, 1994

"sick" individual but a System to *re-establish* the ecological balance of which the subject forms a part. It comprises all the ideas, concepts, beliefs, myths and procedures relating to physical and mental illnesses or social imbalances of a particular people. This knowledge explains the etiology, nosology and procedures for diagnosis, prognosis, treatment, prevention and establishing the origin of illnesses. This knowledge is passed on by tradition (from generation to generation), orally and according to the restrictions established in each world view, which means that this knowledge is circumscribed, local, collective, anonymous and carries a deep universal message, in which the holistic and the systemic are concepts that have always been present within the indigenous people.

In indigenous health systems, *illness* is defined in the social sense as interference in the normal social behaviour and in the competence of the individual to work. The majority of indigenous peoples divide illnesses into two groups: backcountry illnesses caused by supernatural effects such as charms, winds, spirits that act autonomously or are called up or directed by magic; and illnesses of God, the origins of which are not found in the mythical indigenous world. In general, each traditional healer uses indigenous health technology in accordance with his training, powers and preferences but always in spiritual communication with nature. This communication can be obtained under the effect of teaching plant spirits or by interpreting dreams. Treatments include rituals, plants, minerals and animals. The individual visits the traditional healer in search of help when faced with an illness, in order to protect himself/herself from a possible illness or to reaffirm his/her health status.

The *treatment* seeks to recover the balance that has been lost, and the action of the traditional healer is effective when, once the origin of the ill has been identified, restoration of the unity and harmony of the sick person is achieved, along with the concord of the sick person with the surrounding world. The traditional healer is irreplaceable within his community because he has deep knowledge of the laws governing balance, and of the imbalances caused by health and sickness. In him, the indigenous peoples recognise the indigenous defender of their own identity and the indigenous person who, through his skills, reaffirms the knowledge and beliefs of his people.

Indigenous and Non-Indigenous Concepts and Knowledge in the Development Process

By Juan Reátegui Silva, PSI-AIDESEP Director

Concepts and knowledge

In terms of relationships with other non-indigenous cultures and societies, our history - which is not a short one - clearly shows that it is the non-indigenous who need to review and reconsider their ideas, attitudes and behaviour towards this relationship. We are aware that, on more equal terms of mutual respect, and calling upon our most far-reaching principles and values, this relationship between indigenous and non-indigenous could be of great benefit to both, and to the quality of life on our planet as a whole. And yet the term integration, proposed to designate this interrelationship, arouses in us a kind of allergy by reminding us of the many times that, in its name, the non-indigenous have wanted to absorb us, to make us disappear like little fish being eaten up by a big fish.

The tendency that still dominates non-indigenous thought and rhetoric is that of promoting the integration of indigenous peoples into the dominant society. Whether we like it or not, our daily life takes place in countries with a dominant society, on the one hand, and indigenous peoples, on the other, in an asymmetric relationship in which integration is understood as a slow form of assimilation.

Faced with this, as distinct cultural societies, we assert our principle of self-determination as a fundamental right of indigenous peoples to control our lives, our resources and our own development. And, as part of this, in our relationship with the non-indigenous, we give - and expect in return - a balanced relationship of equality, which could be called *coordination, symbiosis* or a similar term that suggests the notion of mutual respect. If we are to talk specifically about coordinating indigenous and non-indigenous knowledge and concepts in the development process, we need to specify some aspects of indigenous knowledge.

The most important, to my mind, is not to assume an automatic opposition between indigenous and non-indigenous knowledge, nor to talk of two types of opposing mentalities. Whilst the idea of "primitive mentality", which guided non-indigenous behaviour for a long time, has now been abandoned, the notion of "mythical mentality" continues to live on, exerting its power, albeit now with the recognition that we do not lack logic but merely that we follow a different logic.

For example, one of the most widespread prejudices is that shamanic thought is only expressed through concrete categories. However, this was refuted by the Colombian anthropologist, Mr. Reichel Dolmatoff, as early as the end of the 1960s. He demonstrated that, according to the level of knowledge, we can express shamanic thought metaphorically through concrete categories, at a higher level through abstract notions such as "energy" and at another level, higher still, as "very abstract thought" or "symbolic". In this way, we define the activities of the shaman as a transfer of logical patterns to symbolisms that can easily be understood and put into practice. The myths are one of these symbolic codes that the shaman uses to build culture: ideas, customs, and fantasies.

However, in practice, this coordination between indigenous and non-indigenous concepts and knowledge has been taking place for a very long time. An illustration of this is that three quarters of the pharmaceuticals today prescribed around the world are derived from plants that were discovered through indigenous knowledge. The negative side of this interaction is that, when it comes to the profits, neither the pharmaceuticals industry nor anyone can agree on the indigenous peoples' intellectual property rights. This needs to change if we truly want a positive coordination between our societies.

This coordination of knowledge is also taking place in the indigenous world: for more than 5,000 years, when our shamans wanted to enter into a "trance", they have taken a hallucinogenic mix of a liana known as ayahuasca *(Banisteriopsis caapi)* and a shrub called chacruna *(Psychotria sp.)* The number of plants that can be added to this base is limitless as ayahuasca is a means by which to explore the properties of new plants.

A few years ago, non-indigenous knowledge showed us that *chacruna* contained *dimethyltriptamine*, a hallucinogenic substance that is produced in the human brain but which is inactive when consumed orally as it is inhibited by a digestive enzyme known as *monoamine oxidase*. On the other hand, ayahuasca contains *harmine, harmaline, tetrahydroharmine*, which are inhibitors of *monoamine oxidase* and which are also hallucinogenic.

In the light of this knowledge, we now know and understand that, 5,000 years ago, our ancestors were capable of precisely identifying, out of thousands of plants, two of them, one of which had the active component they were looking for (hallucinogenic) and the other which made its oral use possible, by protecting it from the digestive enzymes that inactivate it. This shows the great quality of indigenous knowledge which, added to non-indigenous knowledge under conditions of equity and mutual consideration, has the potential to generate immense well-being for humanity.

It is said that a better mutual understanding is gained when information is shared equally, as this avoids misunderstandings. I therefore hope that this book will provide just such an opportunity.

Specialist in Shipibo herbal medicine.   *Photo: Jim Thuesen, 1994*

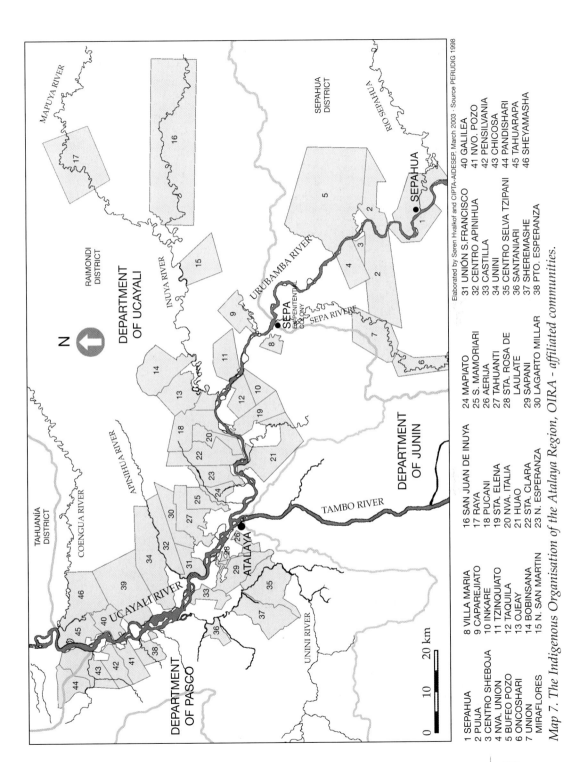

Elaborated by Søren Hvalkof and CIPTA-AIDESEP March 2003 · Source PERUDIG 1998

1 SEPAHUA
2 PUJA
3 CENTRO SHEBOJA
4 NVA. UNION
5 BUFEO POZO
6 ONCOSHARI
7 UNION
MIRAFLORES

8 VILLA MARIA
9 CAPAREJIATO
10 INKARE
11 TZINQUIATO
12 TAQUILA
13 OJEAY
14 BOBINSANA
15 N. SAN MARTIN

16 SAN JUAN DE INUYA
17 RAYA
18 PUCANI
19 STA. ELENA
20 NVA. ITALIA
21 HUAO
22 STA. CLARA
23 N. ESPERANZA

24 MAPIATO
25 S. MAMORIARI
26 AERIJA
27 TAHUANTI
28 STA. ROSA DE
   LAULATE
29 SAPANI
30 LAGARTO MILLAR

31 UNIÓN S.FRANCISCO
32 CENTRO APINIHUA
33 CASTILLA
34 UNINI
35 CENTRO SELVA TZIPANI
36 SANTANIARI
37 SHEREMASHE
38 PTO. ESPERANZA

40 GALILEA
41 NVO. POZO
42 PENSILVANIA
43 CHICOSA
44 PANDISHARI
45 TAHUARAPA
46 SHEYAMASHA

Map 7. The Indigenous Organisation of the Atalaya Region, OIRA - affiliated communities.

5: Concepts and Projects

Shamanism

By Juan Reátegui Silva, PSI-AIDESEP Director

Introduction

Shaman is a term of Siberian origin invented by the first anthropologists to describe the less comprehensible religious practices of primitive peoples. In the Tungus language of Siberia, the root *shami* indicates the idea of bodily agitation. In this language, a shaman is a person who beats a drum, enters into a trance and cures people. In reality, any concept of shamanism reflects the anthropologists' underlying point of view, whatever their perspective.

From an academic point of view, shamanism is the rational study of the irrational, until western thought reaches some kind of understanding as to what the shaman means when he states that plants themselves reveal their properties and other things to him. In the Peruvian Amazon, a man of spiritual knowledge, either acquired from his ancestors or inherited, who himself makes the choice or is chosen by the spirits and who, as he acquires powers, interrelates with his environment in harmony with nature and the teaching plants, is generically known as a shaman.

In the Amazon, each culture or people have their own name for this person. The Asháninka and Ashéninka call him a *sheripiari*; the Yíne a *cajunchi*, the Shipibo an *onanya*, the Awajun and Huambis an *iwishig*, etc.

Shamanic knowledge does not attempt to represent a "natural" order because, if it did so, culture and nature would become confused and, in the end, it would be impossible to make sense of either of them. The shamanic universe can thus be seen as an effort to impose a cultural order on nature: to look at "nature" in social terms and establish a dialogue with it. It is not the "domination" of nature that identifies shamanic knowledge but its communication with it. It is nature that makes the shaman powerful, insofar as it develops his capacity to interpret it and interrelate with it. For this, the shaman subjects himself to rigorous diets and difficult rites. Via its symbolic and ritual content, shamanism attempts to project an ethnic content onto indigenous society.

The shaman is a mediator between the social world of the people and the extra-social world of the spirits. The shaman specialises in conceiving of the inconceivable, reducing its terrible and disconcerting complexity, and daring to negotiate with it. At times of individual or collective crisis, the shaman applies his knowledge and experience to transform the powers of untameable spirits into a positive and culturally significant social force. In other words, the shaman uses the cognitive, symbolic and cosmological categories that are the essential building blocks of social order and of the definition of political power.

Shamanic knowledge is thus difficult – if not impossible – to understand for those who are unable to experience the life of the indigenous peoples of the Amazon and the personal experiences of the shaman, as a Yíne explains:

> "For the first time, just as an experiment, at 16 years of age, I took ayahuasca. Then I continued experimenting and learning the secrets of shamanism from within my family. My knowledge comes from my ancestors, from my parents in the first place. They have cultivated these disciplines and practise them to this day. My leaning towards the practice of indigenous medicine comes through inheritance. I began with two disciplines: toé and ayahuasca. They taught me to appreciate their knowledge, their technology, and the lessons taught me by the teaching plants and their spiritual world are marvellous. This discipline is very healthy: it teaches you to respect everything around you, the world and its natural resources. It is also a repository of the knowledge and cultural values of a wise harmony between man and nature, for which reason it is particularly important for children and the elderly."

Ayahuasca is associated with knowledge of the forest and the spirits of the teaching plants of the upper and lower parts of the forest. On the other hand, toé (Brugsmania sp.) is associated with the spirits of the water, from the lower, middle and upper forest areas. Tobacco is associated with the spirits of the highlands, with the animals and birds, and is particularly represented by the hummingbird.

If a man practises medicine, these teaching plants are transformed into a very beautiful woman, one who is not of this world but of the universe and invisible to those who do not practise. And if a woman practises medicine then, in a similar way, these teaching plants become a man. These accompanying spirits teach the secrets of the knowledge of medicine slowly, with great discipline and ethics, and learning is a continual process right up until death.

THE SOCIO-CULTURAL CONTEXT
The Asháninka people

According to the earliest information we have of them, the Asháninka people inhabited the lowlands, where initial forms of agriculture had been developed, resulting in significant population growth. They were living in the upper regions of the River Ucayali. Later, and as a consequence of the movement of other Amazonian peoples, the Asháninka were displaced from these areas by peoples of the Pano linguistic family, who came from the Brazilian watersheds and arrived in these areas overland. These peoples gave rise to the Pano-speaking groups called the Shetebo, Shipibo and Conibo, who settled along the Ucayali River. This is proven by the existence of close trade relations between the populations of the Central Andes and the forest area, neighbours since pre-Inca times. This trade continued even after the establishment of the Inca Empire.

Once colonisation had started, penetration took place by means of those places that had served normal communication purposes between the Incas and the Central Forest region. The Franciscans began to establish *reducciones* or settlements to facilitate the conversion of the Asháninka, whilst exploiting their labour. In 1635, the Franciscans established the Ocopa Convent and, five years later, they had seven missions, of which the most important was Cerro de la Sal. Between 1671 and 1673, the Franciscans managed to relocate more than 1,000 Asháninka to this mission. Scarcely two years later, the Franciscans had 38 missions, grouping together around 8,500 Asháninka.

Colonisation was interrupted in the mid-18th century by the rebellion of Juan Santos Atahualpa, who managed to unite the Asháninka, Yíne, Yanesha, Mochobo, Simirinche and Shipibo-Conibo peoples in a fierce struggle against the colonial power. For virtually the next 100 years, the Central Forest was to remain closed to the Spaniards.

During the second half of the 19th century, a further advance into Asháninka territory took place, with the *criollo* Republic granting 500,000 hectares of territory in the Perené river and the Ene river areas as a concession to the Peruvian Corporation, a British company formed of state creditors. Obviously, along with the half million hectares of land, the British company also gained access to the Asháninka and Yanesha peoples who had been living there since time immemorial, and they became the company's slaves. With this concession began the penetration of the Central Forest and Asháninka territory on the part of settlers from other regions and other countries, attracted by the Peruvian Corporation's "modern" exploitation techniques.

During the missionary period (17th – 18th centuries), the Asháninka suffered a serious decline in their population through epidemics caused by encounters with these very different people. "Illnesses from outside" appeared, for which indigenous medicine had no answers. According to the ethno-historian, Jay F. Lehnertz, the little reliable demographic data produced by the missionaries suggests there were a total of 10,000 Asháninka during the period of 1711 to 1723, and that the total number of Asháninka christened over the period 1709 to 1742 was between 40,000 and 50,000. This author (1974) estimates that, during the 18th century, the Asháninka population declined by a proportion of 3.5:1.

During the Republic, many external factors worked to prevent a demographic recovery: raids and violence caused by the increase in rubber prices; the capture of indigenous labourers for the *caciques* which, along with other reasons, perpetuated the demographic decline until the late 19th/early 20th centuries. In 1970, the cultural geographer, W.

Denevan, detected a rapid demographic recovery among the Asháninka people. For that year, he calculated the total Asháninka population at between 24,000 and 26,000 people. Uriarte notes a figure of 34,000 Asháninka in 1976 and, by 1989, Hvalkof considered that the Asháninka population totalled around 45,000.

The 1993 census estimated the Asháninka population at 51,063 inhabitants, distributed among 359 communities located in the areas of the tropical forest of the departments of Junín, Cerro de Pasco, Cuzco, Apurimac and Ucayali, thus forming the most numerous Amazonian indigenous people in the Peruvian Amazon. This demographic increase, along with the dynamic of latent conflict among indigenous groups of the basin of the Upper Ucayali, has meant that the Asháninka people can today be found settled along the rivers of the Upper Ucayali, Perené, Pichis, Ene, Tambo and watershed areas such as Gran Pajonal. They are also found on the floodplains of the middle Ucayali, towards which the Asháninka population of Gran Pajonal has been expanding since 1970.

The Shipibo-Conibo people

The Shipibo-Conibo people, of the Pano linguistic family, are settled along the banks of the Ucayali river and its tributaries. They were two different ethnic groups and still inhabit the banks of the Ucayali river.

In 1657, missionaries and soldiers made incursions into the territory of the Shipibo, whom they called *Calliseca*, but they were killed. In 1660, the Shipibo attacked the missions on the Huallaga river. In 1661, 2,000 to 3,000 Shetebo and Shipibo settled in two centres rose up against the missionaries and, in 1670, they attacked the Panatahua mission. From 1686 to 1698, they came under the influence of the Jesuits until, in 1698, they killed the missionaries. In 1765, various missionary posts were established and, by 1766, the Shipibo population of five settlements had been converted. Due to the Runcato uprising of 1776, these posts were lost. In 1790, there were Shipibo along the rivers Pisqui, Tamaya, Aguaytía and the Ucayali upstream of Sarayacu and in Cushabatay. The Shipibo were known, among other things, for being great travellers and salt traders. Their traditional arms were clubs, bows and arrows, and spears. The two latter are still used today for hunting and fishing. The use of shotguns and cast nets for fishing is also frequent nowadays.

In the world of the Shipibo-Conibo people there first developed a mythical culture related to lunar features, a magical-religious pan-naturalist world vision, which has influenced their methods used in the conservation of life, ecology and the environment. The Shipibo-Conibo people have created a whole way of life and culture that can, to this day, be seen in the way they fish, hunt, and produce handicrafts.

Shamans and their context

The relationship between the shaman and his environment is not a matter of competition, nor of use and exploitation, but of complementarity and respect. He takes from the environment what he needs, what he wants but, for this, he must have the "consent", the "acceptance" of nature. It is a harmonious relationship between himself and the environment. The most striking feature of shamanism among Amazonian societies is the way they think and establish relationships along reciprocal lines.

The indigenous territory, covered with dense vegetation, has managed to develop in harmony with man and nature. Its biodiversity has enabled it to take shape as the altar of indigenous medicine, and it jealously guards the knowledge acquired by each generation, the spiritual and curative power of each plant, along with its application, dosage and symbolic significance.

Knowledge of the environment is accompanied by a knowledge of soil use. The shaman protects the forests, rivers and nature because they form part of the basis for his survival. They provide food resources and preserve age-old knowledge. It is a harmonious relationship between man and nature, which is expressed in our vision of the world, our socio-political organisation, our science, our technology and our spiritual life.

Knowledge is also related to territory insofar as the different traditional systems of soil management are a part of this, ensuring that the production system is applicable and viable, in harmony with the environment. All this is only possible if there is no deforestation and the natural resources and river basins are not destroyed. The knowledge process is indissolubly linked to a cosmogony. In this respect, we can talk appropriately of an ecosystem, of connections and links that exist between each thing and its environment. It comprises a holistic vision. Many plants would not have the same function, use or importance if they were taken from their natural environment, if their original conditions were changed.

ASHÁNINKA SHAMANISM
The sheripiari

In societies such as the Asháninka, without further specialisation and no centralised authority, there are no analogous positions of authority. Social control of individual behaviour within each *nampitsi* [community or settlement] is based largely on socially-created beliefs relating to the social order and powers that threaten this. In the case of the Asháninka, hunters, fisher people and gatherers, some of these beliefs relate to man-nature relationships, referring to punishment meted out by the spirits of the animals and fishes against individuals who hunt or fish in excess, jeopardising the regeneration of resources and, hence, the existence of the group.

The other aspect of control of individual behaviour can be found in witchcraft. Through witchcraft, anyone not complying with the accepted norms of behaviour and discipline with regard to reciprocal cooperation and food distribution can be punished. In both cases, it is the sheripiari who exerts this coercive mechanism.

How the sheripiari acquires powers

To learn to be a sheripiari, a man or woman must be taught by an old and expert sheripiari. Their training can last from six months to years, and they have to keep to a strict diet, not eating certain foods such as meat, chillies, etc., not drinking alcohol, and abstaining from sexual relations. They must eat only vegetables, particularly fried maniok, and fish such as the *boquichico* [*Prochilodus nigricans*]. The master sheripiari will give the apprentice *tabaco-ampiri*, a tobacco-paste, to suck, causing hallucinations of long duration, and so the young person must be completely determined to take on this responsibility. When he sees himself flying, transformed into a tiger, united with the female spirit of tobacco in the form of a woman, he will have become a sheripiari, coupling with this spirit and having the ability to travel the forest as a tiger. This process transforms the new sheripiari, giving him a natural dimension and converting him into an intermediary between the social and cultural sphere, the group and external powers.

Access to levels and aspects of reality not perceived by ordinary people is thus conferred by means of this sheripiari–specialist ritual, via the capacity – through trance – to visit the spirits that live in the natural world, or the fathers of the animals in the caves high in the mountains, and through maintaining culturally cultivated special relationships with the female spirits of particular teaching plants.

The Asháninka, as we have seen, are very careful to conserve the animal species of the different areas of the forest, alternating their areas of hunting. Retreat of animals to other zones is caused by over-intensive hunting and is interpreted as a result of the anger of the owner of the species in question which, in the first place, sends the animals to man for food. In these cases, the sheripiari acts through a trance achieved by ingesting tobacco juice (*sheri*), identifies the hunter who has committed the offence, ritually repairs the damage, and re-establishes the balance and his behaviour in line with the social norm, taking the hunter in question to the dwelling place of the owner of the animals to ask forgiveness and obtain the sending of further animals. If the hunter violates the regulations again, he is threatened with being turned into an animal to be hunted by members of the *nampitzi*.

SHIPIBO-CONIBO SHAMANISM

The onanya

The Shipibo-Conibo, belonging to the Pano linguistic family, are settled along the banks of the Ucayali river and its tributaries. The practice of indigenous medicine, an important aspect of Shipibo-Conibo culture, is suffering the impact of western culture.

There are currently very few high category healers among the Shipibo-Conibo, such as the *meraya* or *yube*, there are only the *onanya*. It is to be hoped that, in the future, the knowledge and techniques of indigenous medicine will be given new value in order to recover the previous levels of shamanism.

The Shipibo-Conibo shaman classifies ayahuasca by colour:
a) *Panshin oni,* by its yellow colour.
b) *Josho oni,* by its white colour (this is rare).
c) *Huizo oni,* by its dark brown colour.

Each variety above represents the following spirits:
a) The boa (anaconda). In Shipibo, this plant is called *ronin oni.*
b) The cricket (grasshopper). In Shipibo, this plant is called *champo oni.*
c) The *chicua* (black bird). In Shipibo, this plant is called *chisca oni.* It is a messenger bird both for the traditional healers and for the members of the community. It presages good or ill. This bird always lives alongside ayahuasca.

These representations of ayahuasca cannot be distinguished or recognised. Only the traditional healers can do this by taking ayahuasca, and through their visions.

For ayahuasca to produce hallucinogenic effects it must be used in conjunction with the leaves of a plant known as *chacruna.* Flowers, husks, or plant roots can also be added for experimentation purposes, as they are possessed by superior spirits. The person wishing to learn must follow very strict rules, in terms of diet for example, in the same way as the master healer does. Each master healer has his own ideas depending on the way in which his teacher taught him and according to his own experience. Patients – during and after treatment – and individuals who gain access to these experiences, or to experiences with other teaching plants, must also follow very strict rules.

There are two main forms of diet for the learning and acquisition of shamanic powers:
1. Fasting: You must not less yourself be seen or spoken to. You must remain in bed for several days. Liquids may be taken.
2. Strict diet: Sexual and social abstention. You must not eat salt, herbs, spices, acids, certain fish and animals.

With regard to strict diets, the traditional healer must prepare the food for himself or for the apprentice. Another option is to give these tasks to a young girl who has not yet menstruated or a woman who is past the menopause. This latter must not be in a sexual relationship and must maintain her clothes with aromatic plants. The diets to be followed are due primarily to the fact that the spirits are jealous and weak. The spirits of the dead animals and fish make war on the spirits of the plants. If the diet is not kept, the apprentice is scolded, punished or killed by the spirits.

There are simple diets that only last two weeks and even as short as half a day after a simple treatment or after taking ayahuasca in experimental form.

How the *onanya* acquires powers

Shamanic powers can be acquired by three mechanisms:
1. Through inheritance.
2. Through the choice of the spirits.
3. Voluntarily, with or without a teacher.

In the Shipibo-Conibo shamanic world, there are three categories of apprenticeships:
1. *Onanya*. This is the healer who holds all knowledge of first aid. He uses magical powers and medicinal plants.
1. *Meraya*. A healer of this category is like a magician. He possesses the teachings of the semi-divine spirits and also their medicinal plants.
3. *Yube*. A healer of this category is specialised in extracting magic darts, for which he is protected by the father and mother spirits of the *yachay* or *chonta mariri*. He also has the same knowledge as the *meraya* and uses medicinal plants.

TECHNOLOGY AND SHAMANISM

Social interaction and the indigenous calendar are linked to the distribution of society's different productive activities throughout the yearly cycle. This adaptation to the boundaries imposed by ecology on the production of resources and social reproduction itself enables the continuity of the social system and the reproduction of its living conditions to be ensured over time.

Man's adaptation comprises a number of social activities and he is aware that, as such, they take on socially generated representations and interpretations of nature.

One aspect of these representations and interpretations enables the most appropriate moment for undertaking production activities within the annual cycle to be identified. Knowledge of when to make collective representations forms the reference point of the collective memory by means of which the members of indigenous society, masters of special agricultural technologies, adjust individual and collective behaviour towards nature to the rhythm of the biological development of the living organisms on which their material reproduction is based.

Asháninka sheripiari techniques

The distribution of time forms an annual calendar of activities whose general criteria are astronomical, climatic and hydrological. Other flora and fauna that form part of the necessary knowledge for the practice of agricultural activities of market gardening, hunting, fishing and gathering are chosen in correlation with these factors. In the Asháninka world, there are a variety of techniques. One of the most important techniques in slash-and-burn cultivation, practised by Amazonian farmers, is the choice of land. Then, the stage of slashing and burning begins with a gesture of great purifying significance. The sheripiari chews *ivenki* [*Cyperus piripiri*] and spits throughout the whole area and over his sons and sons-in-law to prevent clashes with the evil beings of the forest.

The burning stage is fundamental to the cultivation technique as the transfer of the nutrients, largely found in the plant cover, to the ecosystem of the tropical forest is sought through the transformation of the plant material into ashes. It is in the sowing and harvesting phases that the symbolic gestures accompanying the technical work show how the relationship between the farmer and the crops grown is understood. In the stage of harvest and abandon (fallow), a symbolic aspect is the women's songs at the time of transporting the harvested manioc from the fields to the house.

Of the hunting techniques, the practice of lying in wait in the feeding areas of forest animals is probably the most difficult. Arrows are primarily used in this. It is essential for hunting techniques that the purity of body and weapons is achieved in order to establish an appropriate relationship with the forest animals. Fishing is practised both by individuals and groups, generally in the summertime, in July and August. Women who are menstruating or who are pregnant are prohibited from participating in this type of fishing because "they sweeten the poison". Finally, a male and individual form of fishing is practised throughout the year using nylon and a steel hook, both obtained at market and which are modern substitutes for the cotton cord and thorn or bone hooks used by fishermen for thousands of years.

Shipibo-Conibo onanya techniques

In the case of the Shipibo-Conibo, the relation with the spiritual world is a question of aesthetics, and of therapeutic applications. Under the influence of ayahuasca, the meraya perceives information that he knows, often chaotically, comes from the spiritual world, in the form of luminous designs. He then tames this information, transforming it into various aesthetic notions: geometrical patterns, melodies, rhythms and fragrances, which play a key psychological and spiritual role, both for the patient and for society.

One of the tasks of the meraya was, in Shipibo tradition, to obtain designs from the spirits and hand them over to women in charge of their artistic elaboration. The meraya thus has a key role in art and in the dominant religious ideas that remain symbolised in individual designs and motives. In addition, meaning was transmitted through the decoration of his tools, clothes and earthenware jars etc., with the characteristic geometrical designs, in which each non-specified design symbolises Ronin, the cosmic anaconda. (Ed.note: see the Shipibo-Conibo vignettes in this book.)

Adolescent ceremonies are essential rites that served both for religious life and for the artistic activity of women. It was at such times that the best specimens of clothes, ornaments, ceramics, and weapons were gathered from all over vast areas of the Shipibo-Conibo people. Formerly inter-regional festivals were great artistic presentations and opportunities for the dissemination of the religious experience, expressed in the decoration of objects. Nowadays, wood engraving is a technology whose outlining is done by the women and the actual carving by the men. All artistic production is carried out by the women. As well as covering everything with their geometric designs, they weave or embroider textiles, gild ceramics, thread beads, create facial designs and mark people with invisible bodily designs.

Shipibo–Conibo therapy is essentially a vision of ideal designs, applied to the patient's body. The concept of the cosmic anaconda, Ronin, is central to knowledge of the symbolism of the designs. Ronin is a spirit primarily related to water, the physical basis of the universe. As the essential provider of all geometric designs, Ronin is symbolised in Shipibo-Conibo art at three levels of perception: firstly, in the production of ceramic vessels. In this technology, the rolls of clay added represent the anaconda rolled up resting. Secondly, the style of the design as a whole is related to the skin of Ronin, which shows all the existing and imaginable designs and colours. And, thirdly, Ronin and other snakes are symbolised by individual motives more or less fashioned in a snake-like form, integrated within the design.

Reference

Lehnertz, Jay F.
1972   "Juan Santos, a Primitive Rebel on the Campa Frontier", in *Actas e Memorias del XXXIX Congreso Internacional de Americanistas*, Lima, vol. 4.

Don Angel teaching traditional medicine.   *Photo: Søren Hvalkof 2000*

Meeting about the health programme.   *Photo: Thomas Skielboe, 1994*

Training course. *Photo: Jim Thuesen, 1994*

Ashéninka health technicians, Ucayali. *Photo: Rune Hvalkof, 2000*

Community medicine chest.   *Photo: Thomas Skielboe, 1994*

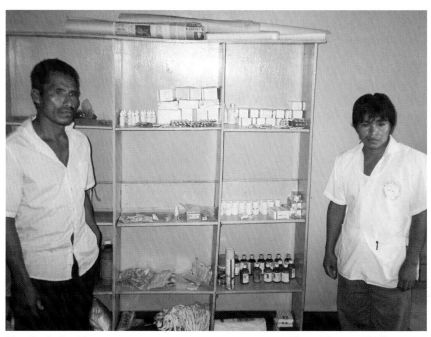

The district health post.   *Photo: Thomas Skielboe, 1994*

Vaccinating.   *Photo: Jim Thuesen, 1994*

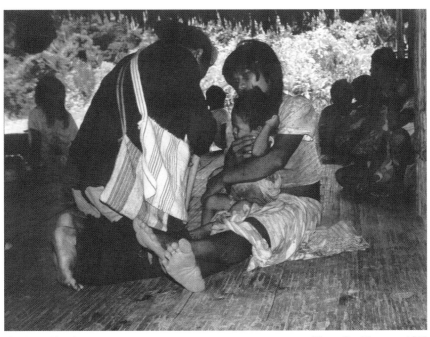

Curing with tobacco.   *Photo: Jim Thuesen, 1993*

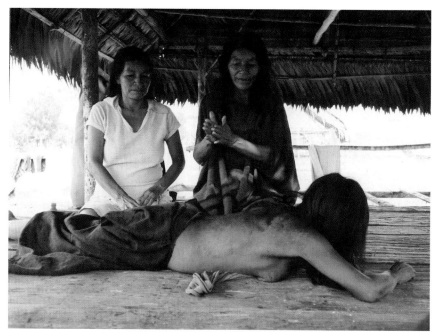

Maestra Amelia and the midwife curing.   *Photo: Thomas Skielboe, 1994*

Vapour healerAmelia in action.   *Photo: Jim Thuesen, 1994*

Vapouring.   *Photo: Jim Thuesen, 1994*

Materialising the course of illness.   *Photo: Jim Thuesen, 1994*

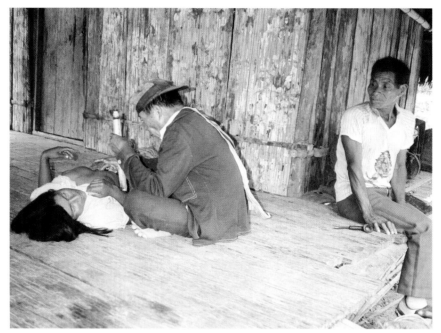

Sheripiari treating a patient.   Photo: Jim Thuesen, 1994

Sheripiari curing.   Photo: Jim Thuesen, 1993

Asháninka design

The Asháninka Healer

Dionisio Moron Rios is a very experienced shaman. He is introduced by his son-in-law, Luis Cushmariano, who is also his apprentice and a boat pilot of the Programme. They both live in the lower River Unini.

Presentation

My father-in-law is the healer in Unini and he is a doctor, a *sheripiari*. He takes the vine called *kamarampi* (ed.: *Banisteriopsis sp.*) and *jorowa* (ed.: *Psychotria sp.*), in which he has faith. When the community members fall ill, they go to him and he cures them, this is why he has faith in the two plants. My father-in-law says that if he cannot cure them with traditional medicine, he tells the patients to go to the pharmacy and buy their medicine, that it will do them good because the spirit has told him so. He does not send them just for the fun of it but because he knows what he is doing, and this is what other sheripiaris ought to do, come to an arrangement with both sides, both traditional and western medicine. But unfortunately there are sheripiaris who do not work in this way, who do not examine the people, but my father-in-law does and if he can't cure them with traditional medicine such as *kamarampi* or *jorowa*, he tells the patient to go to buy medicine from the pharmacy, that it will make them better, that he knows because the spirit told him.

The old healer's story

I learnt to be a sheripiari with masters and my father-in-law has also taught me, right here. I have taken ayahuasca with an indigenous friend, who is Cocama and with the mestizos. In all I have had three masters teaching me.

The Cocama lived in Bolognesi, and came especially as he was a small trader, and he has become my great friend. One day he asked me if there was any ayahuasca and I said yes, that I would bring it the following day. As I knew nothing of these things, he helped me to cook it all day and night. We began to take it while he advised me, he told me that this was good, that it was medicine and that I would realise this after I had taken it for two or three years, that only then would I open my eyes and realise that this cures, that it is a great medicine. And I listened to him and began to take it. Later, another man came from Gran Pajonal, which is in up there in the hills and he also invited me to take it. At that time I had already been taking it for a year and he told me that my body was well prepared, that I should keep going and not give up, that I should continue taking it and learning things about diet, that I had to diet one year. I could hardly manage to keep the diet. I left my wife because we could not sleep together. Nor could I eat pork, only roast banana with skin. I ate my rice with a little salt, no butter or fat. I could not drink *chapo* [banana and sugar drink], nor any kind of sweet things, nor fruit for a year. My master told me that it was good, that I could do it and very slowly my body got used to it. In the end I managed to learn a little, I am not saying I know a lot but enough to get by. I have now been taking it for 27 years.

Don Dionisio (centre) demonstrating a giant Ayahuasca   *Photo: Rune Hvalkof, 2000*
vine, planted 25 years ago.

Casimiro

Casimiro Izurieta Cevallos is 70 years old and lives in the community of Tzinquiato. He is a traditional healer, with many years experience as a shaman, bonesetter and herbalist. The programme appointed him master specialist in order to pass on his wisdom to the next generation.

Bones, herbs and ayahuasca

I first lived in Mapalca, where I founded our village. There was a man there, the grandfather of Javier Prishica, who brought me here and I worked with him in medicine. He taught me everything, also how to obtain *kamarampi*. At that time we were not greatly accepted by the people, they said we were deceiving them. But they would call me when there was an emergency, at any time, for example, if a young boy had an accident, because I am a bonesetter.

Now I am continuing to work with the Programme, supporting my community, and now I am more accepted. People tell me to keep on working, that I should not stop. I want to teach but some don't want me to. I learnt to be a bonesetter a long time ago, from my companion from Mapalca and I now have 25 years experience, but few young people want to learn. I tell them that tomorrow I may die and then who will look after the people here? I am the only one doing this. They come to get their bones set from Mapalca, Shiranta and Capajereato. And I don't charge a fortune, as they say, although some say I charge a lot but that's not true, they only pay what they can.

To heal bones I use a *yanchama [Paulsenia armata]* resin, there is also *renaco [Ficus sp.]* latex sap for gluing and the fat of the black boa is a great thing. I have faith in renaco resin because I too have had a fracture. When I was young, I liked to climb trees like a monkey and once I fell. I was like dead, unconscious for a while and my backbone was dislocated, and when I worked it hurt me. One day a man told me there was a thick liana that you can split in the middle and you rub it in six times when you leave and six times when you come back. Then you tie liana together again and when the renaco tree begins to heal then your wound will be healing too. Now I feel no pain.

Youngsters today don't have the same curiosity; they don't want to accompany me anywhere. Sometimes I go to train somewhere else. The other day I went to Libertad. There was a patient with a bad flu, to the point of coughing up blood. They told me it was tuberculosis and I took him to the Health Centre but an analysis of the sputum was negative. Then we cured him with plants and alligator fat.

Sometimes we prepare *ayahuasca*, but they bring it from elsewhere, because we do not grow it here. You take it and you see what illness someone has, as if in a film. You see everything, what your body is like, if you have suffered any injury, or a cold or something else. When there is no *ayahuasca* we take toé, which we do grow. You take a little to heal.

But you have to diet for three months and for this reason many do not want to do it. You cannot have relations with women for three months. For the diet, you must not eat salt or fat and "bad" fish. I dieted in order to cure my wife. Through the diet, the body takes on the gift of learning, and only then can you do what you want.

Don Dionisio (right) and his son in law preparing coconuts.   Photo: Rune Hvalkof, 2000

213

Mauricio

Mauricio Fasabi Apuela is 78 years old and a long-standing healer. He comes from Lamas in the department of San Martín in northern Peru. He first experienced the Amazon forest in the 1940s, during his military service. He married a Yine woman and settled in Ucayali, adapting to the river environment. They now live in the Yine community of Santa Clara.

The shaman from Lamas

I learnt shamanism in my homeland, in San Martín, when I was demobbed from the army. I met my wife when I was going to the Manú river and I just put her in my boat – I couldn't speak her language – and took her, we didn't come back for a year.

In my village, I learnt from a certain Ambrosio Tuanama, he taught me in the Amazon village of Jeberos. I learnt with those people and this is why I wanted to serve my country. I have been learning things but there are some healers who harm people and this is no good, because this is witchcraft. But of course the good thing is medicine. Medicine is one or two months of following a diet. After two months or so, you can return home to take ayahuasca and to learn more and you can continue to take it every month until you become a good healer and then you can cure.

The youth of today don't want to learn. I am sick but if patients come to me I cure them. This stone [he shows a stone that has been taken from his body!- ed.] is what wanted to kill me and last night we took a really strong ayahuasca. This here is my brother he will confirm that I am not lying. We took it with these men who are working here, they are from Sepahua, they want to be my disciples but it's not possible because they are not from around here, because learning doesn't happen in a couple of months, not a in week, and tomorrow they are going back to Sepahua. I have no disciples here, just me, sometimes they want to take it but in the end they prefer the girls and therefore they don't take it, they can't follow the necessary diet; when you take ayahuasca you must not sleep with women or you will fall ill.

But sometimes illness comes, because you do not purge yourself, because you do not respect the diet. My son-in-law here, Juanito, was treating a patient, Don Belisario, he was a spiritual man. He taught me and, when I knew some things, he died and I succeeded him and there is no other healer around here. I am the only one who cures all the sick people, they are always calling me from OIRA, asking questions, that was why I was recommended by OIRA.

The indigenous health project is very good because it is such an incredible thing. We are all very happy here, for example, Miss Teresa is very happy, she tells me that when someone is ill and cannot be treated with western medicine then they say to me, look old man, you'd better take your ayahuasca and treat him in your own way, and so I do. This is how we combine the two medicines.

When we came to Urubamba, at that time, my wife was still strong. She is older than I am and now when she tries to cook her bananas, all she does is burn herself. It was in 1944, I took her to the Manú river, oh how time flies.... to think I came to San Martín a young man and now look at me, my whole body aches. They operated on me in Sepahua because my testicles had dropped; it was a hernia. I came back from Sepahua very ill, then Miss Otilia arrived, she came here one day and said to me, "Hey Grandpa, what's up?" Oh, Miss, I said, I am very ill from this operation I had in Sepahua. I showed her my leg where they operated on me and she took me back to Atalaya. There people from OIRA treated me and now I am OK, even my son-in-law Juan Mozombite has had an operation. Also my grandson, Antonio, who is scarcely two months old, is calm now. I offered him his renaquilla [*Clusia rosea*], which is good for operations. Here my daughter-in-law Lili has also been following the treatment for two months, she too has completed her ojé [*Ficus insipida*], and she tells me she is better but I tell her not to eat sajino [*collared peccary*] (Tayassu tajacu), or fish with teeth, that she can eat boquichico [*Prochilodus nigricans*] because it is good, and also shrimp.

In 1944 I was planting rubber in Manú and in 45 I returned. My wife is from around here, her village is on the Tambo river. Her husband died and because of her feelings for her husband she was going to the Manú river with her uncle. Well, I met her, I took her, I put her in my canoe just like you would load an animal, I couldn't woo her because I didn't know her language. She is a Piro (Yine). Now I speak three languages, Quechua, Spanish and Piro (Yine). But not the Campa [Asháninka].

Lamas is a beautiful village, it is on a mountain and all the houses are yellow. They speak Quechua there but not in Tarapoto any more. Only a few. Now at 78 I can no longer see well.

Luzmila

Luzmila Fuchs López is Ashéninka from the community of Nuevo Paraíso, Ucayali, where the Adventist Mission has its base. Luzmila works as a traditional midwife, vapour healer and specialist in indigenous medicine with the Indigenous Health Programme, appointed by ORDECONADIT, the indigenous organisation in the Tahuanía district.

Passing on experience

I don't know how old I am but I am a traditional midwife. I am here in Boca de Tahuanía working with the organisation's nurse. I help women to give birth or when they cannot have children, and for this reason they have chosen me to teach people, showing them how to care for women who are going to have a baby. In other communities there are no birth attendants, or only those who attend their own daughters, granddaughters or daughters-in-law, no-one else. We have told them that they should deliver other babies and not only their own family and so now they are helping all women.

In some communities, there are old vapour healers and midwives, and they must teach the young women who want to learn so that when we are no longer around they can replace us and carry on teaching their children so that our culture does not die out. I had an aunt who taught me how to vapour heal before she died. She lived in Bajo Aruya and someone put a curse on her. Now her daughter has taken over from her. I go to the communities to teach interested women how to vapour heal and we tell them that plants are good. There are plants in the wild that can be used to vapour heal.

Training is undertaken with the promoters, vapour healers and midwives to see if they have learnt or not and to continue to teach those who have not learnt well. In some communities, there are vapour healers who live very far away. Now in Mencoriari they have their vapour healer, like the sheripiari, who also lives alone and only cures his family. But, through all this work, the whole community is now being cured.

The communities are now happier than before. My nephew brings them pots so that they can vapour heal. Before they used old pots and now, with the new ones, they are happier. What's more, they have been given a mosquito net so that they can cover the sick. They have all been given the tools of their trade. The midwives are also learning and teaching others to use plants. We have de-parasited 300 people with ojé [*Ficus insi-*

pida] and now we are working with both children and adults, and also with anaemic patients.

With Miss Lidia we have encountered seriously sick people, even a young man who was ill, pale and swollen. Until we offered him ojé. The patient was in the countryside and his son went to find him to carry him back to his house. He wanted to die but his son took him to Compirushari. On the second day we gave him ojé, we took his clothes off and washed him with water and he was crying out that he wanted to die. I told him that he was not going to die and the following day he was less swollen, he even got up and that was how we left him. After a few days we returned and we found him cured. He was attending meetings and the people were surprised to see him well. They thought he was going to die but, thank God, it was not to be.

Luzmila, Lidia and coordinator Manuel.   *Photo: Rune Hvalkof, 2000*

Voices II: Indigenous Specialists

Rosa

Rosa Valera Flores is 58 years old, and a traditional midwife and healer from the Shipibo-Conibo community of Shahuaya. She works in the Programme with ORDECONADIT in the Conibo sector of the Tahuanía District. (See the fotos of Mrs. Rosa on pp. 274 and 275).

The master healer

I learned from my mother, when she was young, and I continued as a midwife. Women experts should teach their daughters.

They asked me to work with 13 communities. During my travels, I taught vapour healing, treating several patients with vapour and working with people interested in learning. I also work with girls, showing them, teaching them to spin, to embroider cloth, also how to work with ceramics, making mocahuas [bowls]. I teach all this to girls and women, young and old, who are interested in learning. This work is growing in the communities, and the involved people are continuing to practise and work in their communities. I have taught them to heal with plants, for example, those with diarrhoea, vomits, they are offered plant remedies. I have also taught them how to prepare ointments and syrups. For the ointments, I taught them how to prepare chuchuhuashi [Maytenus laevis], uchpa caspi and boa sacha. I explained to people how to use these preparations to heal a wound or to use some bark for diarrhoea. I have taught all of this, showing them how to prepare the plants, what amount to use.

I also taught the preparation for vaginal discharge. We use a tree which in our language is called the isumbushite, which means maquisapa [*Spider monkey, Ateles* sp.] bushite peine. It is prepared and offered to women who have a vaginal discharge. Some women have been cured in this way, others not. There are two types of maquisapa ushumbushite: one is a slightly bitter bark and the other is a little sweet.

I also cure with ayahuasca. When the intoxication of ayahuasca overcomes me, I begin to sing to the patient that I am curing. There are people who come to my house very ill and they leave a little better. There are also deceitful healers, who do not cure the sick. There are some that think they can be healers after three months or a year. I have been working for many years and even now I may take toé or kamalampi, which is for the sick person. But if the patient resists all of this, the problem returns.

Comadre and specialist Hermila.　　　　　　　*Photo: Cæcilie Mikkelsen, 2002*

Voices II: Indigenous Specialists

Amelia

Amelia Coronado is Ashéninka, a master vapour healer in the community of Chicosa and head of Women's Affairs for the organisation OIRA, where she spent three years working in the Health Programme. She works in the communities of: Quepachari, Quempitiari, Toniromashi, Tahuanía, Canapishtea, Puerto Alegre, Mencoriari, Diobamba, Tahuarapa, Chicosa, Pensilvania, Pandishari, Nuevo Pozo, Sheripashi, Nueva Esperanza, Unini-Cascada, Shenontiari, Sataniari, Anacayali, Tzivetari, Centro Selva Tzipani, Corintoni, Boca Apinhua, Centro Apinhua, Unión San Francisco, Lagarto Millar, Aerija, Laulate, Sapani, Tahuanti, Urubamba Sepa, Capajearato, Inkare and Belén. (See map on p. 189).

Work as an expert vapour healer

My grandmother taught me how to vapour heal and also all about medicinal plants. My work now consists of teaching the women about plants, how to vapour heal, how to cure a chill, sickness and diarrhoea. They already know a little but they need to learn more. They give me a good welcome in all the communities.

Thanks to the Indigenous Health Programme we are making progress and we have pupils in my community who have been trained, and this makes me very happy. But I, and the communities, need some supplies. I ask the OIRA leaders if they are going to recognise all my work because I have three jobs, as vapour healer, midwife and bonesetter. They only recognise me as a vapour healer but this doesn't mean that I have lost my other knowledge. I am ready to help my community in any way I can. What we need is to continue training the midwives, and the vapour healers. I have seen no training of promoters or midwives this year, and there is no one supporting the nurses.

The communities keep asking me to visit them but I tell them that my work has finished, although I will always continue to support them, I will continue teaching the women. This is why I want the health project to continue.

We are all very happy with the Programme. My grandmother, Jovita, is working as a vapour healer and she also needs supplies. I stopped working two years ago and I have suffered with the 50 communities. I was first in a community for eight days and then for four days. I used to cure with piripiri, with huante, with toé. I vapour heal with toé to banish all illness far away. I also cure diarrhoea with lemon leaves. There are a number of barks that can be used as medicines and I have taught all this to my community. This is why my community is very happy now. There are three vapour healers here, Jovita, Gloria and myself. There are also three midwives but I don't know them. But they are also asking for supplies, just like the sheripiaris, who need their tobacco with which to cure. We know we need training, although when Miss Juana was here the promoters, vapour healers and midwives were always being trained.

The Programme has achieved a great deal but now it is not quite so strong. The nurses are not training the promoters any more. They are all men and we need women to be trained.

Amelia diagnosing.   *Photo: Søren Hvalkof, 1994*

Susana

Mrs. Susana Avenchani Faman is community chief and vapour healer in the community of Chinchini, situated on the banks of the fast running Unini river in Gran Pajonal. She was working with the Health Programme through OAGP, the local indigenous organisation.

Handicrafts and medicine

I weave cushmas, shoulder bags and baskets in my community. I also work with the community members in cultivating our herbal medicines and growing cotton, as well as making handicrafts.

I know how to dye yarn in colours, using the clay that you get from the lakes. I need support from the project to get me pots for boiling my yarns with the clay dyes.

With my medicine I soothe the patients; through the spirit of the leaves that are boiled for steam, the patient will be calmed.

My mother taught me this, and my mother was taught by my grandmother. Right now I am planting my medicine. I have the medicine that women use when they give birth, to remove the pain during labour. I also have herbs for not having children, and other herbs when they want to have children again. After you have your child you drink this remedy for not having more children, and when you want to have children again you drink this other one. There are lots of women who ask me for this. You can make it from a vine that grows in the forest and I also have it in my garden. One is named the "little vine" and grows on a tree and the other is a herb called pinitsi.

Teófila

Teófila Vásquez Valera is a native of the community of Shahuaya in Ucayali. She is 49 years old and was appointed by her community and her organisation, ORDECONADIT, to be a vapour healer in the Programme.

Learning vapour healing

I did not know how to vapour heal, it was only through the Programme that the people chose me as a vapour healer. Mrs. Rosa Valera taught me how to vapour heal a patient. According to the Shipibo culture, you use a mango leaf and an orange leaf for vapour healing. The leaf of the savanca, as we call it in our language, is also used from the wild. All this is cooked and you begin to vapour heal. I learnt everything from Mrs. Rosa.

I have also learnt how to prepare a remedy for diarrhoea and sickness in children and adults. The leaves of lemon grass are prepared and then given but the dose depends on the age and state of the patient. I have also cured wounds, by giving the patient crushed piripiri [*Cyperus piripiri*] but you must tell them how long they have to follow the diet for them to be cured. I have even cured a woman who was haemorrhaging, giving her the leaf of the red cotton plant mixed with yawar piripiri [*Eleutherine bulbosa*]. I also cured a child who was passing blood in its diarrhoea.

I have treated children and adults within the community for years and now I am treating patients who have swellings, using leche catahua [*Hura crepitans; Hevea spruceana*] mixed with tobacco. You put it on the swollen part and it gets better.

I am very grateful for the work I have been able to do during this time, very happy and very grateful. I have learnt and I will continue to learn many things in order to be able to treat my family, the community and people who need my services.

Medical Aspects I: Working in the Field

By Dr. Luis Torres Tuesta, Physician, PSI General Coordinator

Methodology

Field work and its methodologies constitute an enormous challenge to those working directly in this area. The key project objective that guided our overall intervention was to build a local health system in each community, comprising components from both indigenous and western medicine. The work with the organisations, the previous tentative experiences of the first phase, the methodology for planning, implementing, disseminating and evaluating the work of each trip, along with an appropriate management and readjustment of strategies, facilitated and ensured our effective development.

Forming the teams for field work

We decided to use mixed teams for field work implementation, one team for each sector made up of two representatives from indigenous culture and medicine, and one graduate nurse representing western medicine.

It was decided that the indigenous representatives should consist of one woman with experience in indigenous medical practices, and particularly in *antenatal* care and childbirth, and one representative from the organisation, preferably a leader, who would work as sector coordinator and indigenous health and culture promoter. In OAGP, the woman expert also played a role in terms of the women's organisation (OMIAGP). It was decided that the western medicine representative should also be a woman in order to facilitate the work with the indigenous women of the communities, who do not generally communicate or confide their health problems to men.

The formation of these mixed teams was in line with the expressed needs of the communities themselves. When we visited the communities at the start of the project, the inhabitants told us in no uncertain terms that they wanted both medicines, their own (indigenous medicine) and the "pharmacy medicines" (clinical or western medicine). The reasons for this was that they had illnesses that were specific to themselves, but they were also affected by illnesses brought from outside.

The teams' training and trips

Prior to each stage of the project, the team members received training on institutional issues, intercultural health, the project itself, issues specific to each person and guidance on team work.

The field work took place within the geographic range of each organisation (federation), each of which was divided into two sectors. One team worked in each sector, moving from community to community, staying on average three to four days in each. Each team made six consecutive trips in an 18-month period of field work, during the second and third phases of the project. In this way total coverage was obtained and thorough and sustained work achieved.

The team in each community

In the visits to each community, some initial formalities were essential. Firstly, an informational meeting would be held with the head of the community on the reasons for the visit and the work to be undertaken. A community assembly would then be convened in which the team would explain the work to be undertaken and the necessary agreements would be reached. Depending on their role, each member of the team had specific activities to implement, but always in mutual coordination and collaboration with the others.

The sector coordinator and the vapour healer's role was to be in specific contact with the indigenous medicine human resources (shamans, vapour healers, herbalists), promoting and supporting their work from the very first visit. As the indigenous representative, the sector coordinator was responsible for issues related to the life of the community as a whole: territory, forest conservation, culture, self-development, non-dependence and self-determination, indigenous rights, problems of community, federal, regional and national level organising and, specifically, promoting and supporting the work of the indigenous medicine human resources. The vapour healer's task was to promote and support the work of the vapour healers in each community, including the training of new vapour healers. She was also to promote and support handicraft work, food production, women's organisation and rights, and deal with pregnancies and labour.

The work of the nurse was undertaken on a house-to-house basis, her main role being the training of at least two promoters in each community and the organisation and running of a medicine chest comprising a minimum stock of medicines. She was to provide training on prevention of illness, treatment of patients, and on how to keep a record of the activities undertaken.

It should be noted that whilst each team member had their own specific role, at particular times intervention was undertaken jointly, mutual collaboration being one of the main characteristics of team work.

During the first visit, the team would assess the health situation of each community, and they would undertake a population census, identify environmental risks, for both families and individuals, for the work of training and prevention.

The work of each visit was planned, implemented, reported on and evaluated. Depending on the progress made and the difficulties encountered, strategies were changed and adapted to the results and expected objectives. The work of the teams in each sector was supervised by a representative from the indigenous organisation and culture, and by a doctor representing western clinical medicine.

Whilst the proposed results and objectives guiding each team's field work were clearly defined, the way the process unfolded involved interesting social and technical aspects. The adaptation of western professionals to a new environmental and cultural reality, the interaction of team members with each other and the people, the language difficulties, the attitude of mutual respect, the different viewpoints and conceptions of different problems, the exchange of knowledge and experiences, the commitment to work effectively to gain the community's acceptance, these were all new experiences that enriched the knowledge and strengthened the motivation of each team member and the team as a whole.

The promoter

The promoter was a volunteer appointed by and committed to the community, responsible for the western component of the local health care system. There have been promoters in indigenous communities for many years. When the project began its activities, there were already promoters in all the communities, some of them with more than eight years' experience.

Prior to the project, they received no regular training, nor any follow-up or supervision. Now, with the project working in 119 communities, their training, follow-up and supervision are systematic and constant.

Training of promoters

The main role of the nurse in the project's field work was to train the promoters in each community. In the beginning, they found that the promoters received theoretical training for three or four days from the Ministry of Health (MINSA) health centres and NGOs, but only sporadically, and in large groups in the towns or larger settlements (Atalaya, Sepahua, Bolognesi, and Oventeni).

In line with the overall project objective, "to develop a coordinated team in each community, with representatives from both indigenous and western medicine", and bearing in mind that each community had promoters interested in learning western techniques of health care but who, because of their cultural characteristics, were not predisposed to or in the habit of intellectual theoretical work, we chose a primarily practical form of training, rejecting the idea of bringing them all together in one town.

The training of the promoters was undertaken continuously over an 18-month period during the second and third phase of the project, in the following way:

- Whilst the nurse was visiting the community, from the time of her arrival until her departure, the promoters would accompany her, learning "everything" through practical work along with essential theoretical explanation.
- In small groups of four or five neighbouring communities over 6-7 day periods, combining practical work with theoretical explanations and visiting the participating communities as a group. This way of working enabled the promoters themselves to gain concrete experience (to learn by doing), with the more experienced providing support, there thus being a movement from passive reception of ideas to concrete actions under supervision.
- For periods when the nurses were not in the communities (two to three months), the promoters were left tasks to be reviewed on the return of the nurses. In the interim they could act by consulting the promoters' manual, the flipcharts, and the book "Where There Is No Doctor".
- In the last three visits, given the need to get the new promoters up to an equivalent level, it was decided to change the usual course of the visits, forming new groups with promoters from three communities and doing the work as a group, visiting each community for two days. In this way, the new promoters received training for six consecutive days, stimulated and supported by the old promoters, with their direct intervention with regard to health problems, and under the direct tutorship and supervision of the nurse. This way of working had a great impact and was widely accepted because of its essentially practical nature and its more beneficial dynamic for each participant. This was because it enabled a strengthening of weak aspects, along with a more effective use of everyone's time as the promoters were being trained at the same times as the communities' health problems were being dealt with.
- Issues were determined by the problems encountered, in terms of diagnosis, treatment and prevention of illnesses, in terms of records, management of the medicine stocks, passing on knowledge to the population in their own language and with regard to the use of medicinal plants and exchanging relevant knowledge and experience.

At the beginning of the third phase of the project, it was proposed that the training of promoters should be carried out jointly with the MINSA health centres. This never actually took place, except partially in OAGP, largely due to the rapid turnover of staff in these establishments and the lack of a team to oversee this at regional level.

One very particular feature of the social dynamic in the indigenous communities is their spontaneous participation. They are all involved in any activity undertaken by visitors that are accepted by them: leaders, teachers, students, mothers, indigenous medicine specialists (vapour healers, traditional midwifes, herbalists, shamans) and community members in general, providing information and other facilities or as observers.

Medicine chest

The community medicine chest was another important and strategic component of the work of intercultural health. It was implemented in each community as a complement to the locally available therapeutic resources of indigenous medicine, and in response to a need that was acutely felt by the people of every community. It is the first time they have had independent access to such a possibility, with little help, and with sufficient training and knowledge. They had previously received occasional donations of medicines but they did not know how to use or handle them.

A small medicine stock has been established in each of the 119 project communities, with its own premises built by the community itself, and with a list of the minimum essential medicines, in the use of which the promoter has been trained. The project initially contributed a sum to form a revolving fund. The different ways of replacing medicines – buying and selling, financial contributions generated from fishing, fundraising sports events, and the sale of wood – sometimes operate unilaterally or, in most cases, in a combined form. Work has been patiently but constantly undertaken to adapt and stabilise appropriate forms of administration.

EPIDEMIOLOGICAL REALITY
Demographic information

Editor's note: The figures for people included within the project's trial census do not, in some cases, correspond to the figures indicated from other sources of demographic information for the area, which include social science research. In general, the figures given here show a general trend towards being lower than the others.

The difference is more pronounced in Gran Pajonal, where the total population, including the mestizo and mixed population in Oventeni, was no more than 4,600 people in 1999 according to the information given here, whilst the figure given for OAGP itself is around 8,000 individuals. More conservative estimates from researchers working in the area suggest a total population of between 6,000 and 7,000 people, not including the settler population.

The difference can be explained within the normal margins of error for demographic surveys covering mountainous forest zones, in which the population live far apart and with logistical problems of access, through different methodologies and the fact that OAGP covers 6 extra communities that were not considered by the Programme as belonging to Gran Pajonal as they are located in areas closer to Ucayali.

Similar discrepancies can be found in the data from ORDECONADIT and OIRA. In general, the Programme estimates that the data is 15-20% below the current reality. Nonetheless, it is representative of the population included within the Indigenous Health Programme and valid in terms of relative statistics.

Population

The indigenous peoples have, for the first time, undertaken their own population censuses in the three project areas. A trial was undertaken in May 1995 with OIRA. In 1997, it was carried out in 113 communities of the three organisations. In 1999, the census was carried out in 118 communities of the three organisations plus one smaller settlement.

In 1993, children under 15 years of age represented 44.6% of the total national population of the poorest social stratum (5th and last stratum). Within the project area, children under 15 years of age represent 52% in OIRA, 51% in OAGP and 49% in ORDECONADIT.

Data from the last census (1999) was recorded on cards that are retained by each organisation. It has been established that the indigenous peoples themselves can carry out their censuses with little help. Throughout the project, too, the promoters have been trained in recording births and deaths. There is a book of births and a book of deaths in each community. This activity requires follow-up and supervision for it to be maintained.

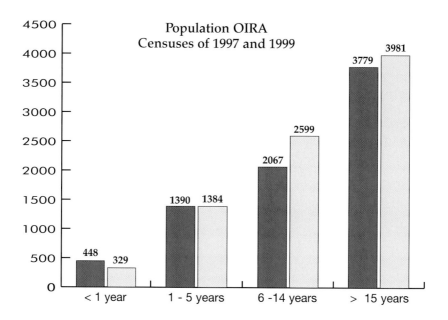

 1997
1999

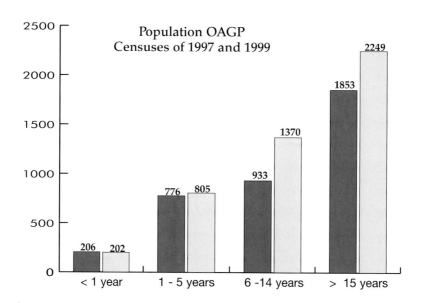

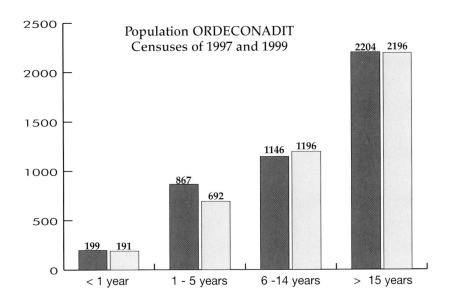

Population ORDECONADIT
Censuses of 1997 and 1999

Population by people and organisation
January-February 1999

Organisation	People	No. - Native Communities	Population	Growth Rate %
OIRA	Asháninka	44	6,152	2.0
	Yíne	8	1,967	2.8
	Amahuaca	2	100	4.3
	Yaminahua	1	74	
OAGP	Ashéninka	31(*)	4,626	4.0
ORDECONADIT	Shipibo-Conibo	10	1,856	0.8
	Ashéninka	20	2,241	
	Mixed (Sh-C. + Ash)	3	178	
3 organisations	6 Indigenous Peoples	119 Comm.	17,194 inhab.	

(*) Includes Oventeni, with 582 inhabitants, mostly mestizo.

In general, the trend is towards population growth among the indigenous peoples. In ORDECONADIT, the migratory outflow also needs to be taken into consideration.

- Births and deaths
Indicators – Three Organisations – 1999

	Births	Birth rate x 1000
OIRA	312	37.62
OAGP	259	56.00
ORDECONADIT	197	46.08

	Deaths	Overall mortality rate x 1000
OIRA	60	7.23
OAGP	89	19.20
ORDECONADIT	40	9.35

	Deaths < 1 year	Child mortality rate x 1000 live births
OIRA	20	64.10
OAGP	33	127.41
ORDECONADIT	11	55.83

	Maternal deaths
OIRA	0
OAGP	0
ORDECONADIT	1

	Deaths < 5 years	%
OIRA	38	63.33
OAGP	42	47.19
ORDECONADIT	15	37.50

Percentage of child deaths under 5 years of age.

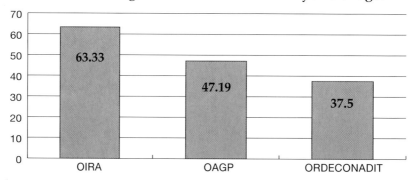

Birthrate x 1000 Inhab. – 1999

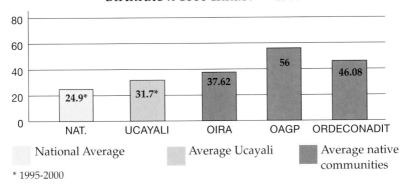

National Average   Average Ucayali   Average native communities

* 1995-2000

General mortality rate x 1000 Inhab. – 1999

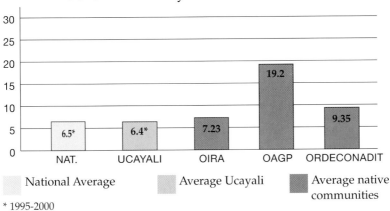

National Average   Average Ucayali   Average native communities

* 1995-2000

Child mortality rate x 1000 Livebirths 1999

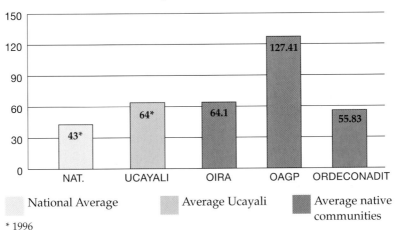

National Average   Average Ucayali   Average native communities

* 1996

Principal Causes of Death
Period: Nov. 1998–July 2000

ORDECONADIT

Pneumonia	13
Sepsis	5
Dehydration through diarrhoea	3
Anaemia	2
Other	17

OAGP

Pneumonia	39
Suicide	13
Dehydration	9
Homicide	7
Tuberculosis	3
Neonatal asphyxia	3
Sourcery	3
Neonatal tetanus	2
Snake bite	2
Other	8

OIRA

Pneumonia	19
Dehydration	10
Sourcery	7
Asphyxia	4
Drowning	4
Malnutrition	2
Anaemia	2
Sepsis	2
Other	10

In 1999, there was only one maternal death in ORDECONADIT. In the community of Shahuaya, a woman died from eclampsia. In the two remaining project areas (OIRA, OAGP), there were no deaths through complications of pregnancy, childbirth or puerperium. This fact is astonishing given that these people live in extreme poverty.

The percentages of deaths under the age of 5 are also very high in relation to the regional and national averages. The two main causes of death are pneumonia (ARIs) and diarrhoea with dehydration. In 1995, this latter was the main cause but by 1999 it seems to have been displaced by pneumonia (ARIs). It is noteworthy that in OAGP, severe depressive states, suicide and homicide occupy a significant place as causes of death.

- Morbidity

Morbidity according to the cases treated by the nurse in the three project phases. No. of cases per organisation

	OIRA	OAGP	ORDE-CONADIT
Acute diarrhoea. Dehydration.	567	206	152
Skin infections; acarosis, pyodermatosis	609	675	155
Intestinal parasitosis. Nutritional deficiencies	1,262	2,407	734
Bacterial conjunctivitis	333	120	66
STDs: urethral discharge syndrome	92	80	37
Poisons: snake bite	10	16	11
Skin mycosis	57	55	85
ARIs exc. pneumonia	1,057	279	235
Pneumonia	7	152	77
Pulmonary tuberculosis	81	6	39
Leishmaniasis	48	62	23
Malaria	97	172	6
Other (*)	494	568	179

* *Injuries, minor surgery, other problems.*

CASES TREATED BY PROMOTERS IN 55 COMMUNITIES • OIRA
Period: 1997 - 2000

COMPLAINTS		1997	1998	1999	2000	Total
Diarrhoea Diarrhoea, "cholera" Diarrhoea with mucous	ADIs	336	529	567	291	1723
Sore throat Ear ache Cough Bronchial problems Influenza	ARIs	523	783	1035	381	2722
Pneumonia		23	16	24	7	70
Fungal infections Sores, itching	MYCOSIS	33	32	25	10	100
Acarosis/mange Scabies, itching Boils, spots sangochupos	SKIN INFEC-TIONS	228	262	293	149	932
Anaemia Infected wound Paleness/pallor Bugs	ENTERO-PARASITES	310	395	216	201	1122
Malaria Probable malaria Fever	MALARIA	22 32 0	61 80 0	36 15 135	7 0 4	126 127 139
Eye pain	CONJUNC-TIVITIS	72	91	105	45	313
Vaginal pain Gonorrhea Chancres	STDs	12	12	10	3	37
Stomach ache	CO-LIC	43	45	33	28	149
Urinary pain	OTHERS			14	14	28
Snake bite		10	13	20	3	46
Ray sting						
Picadura de palo		20	12	7	7	46
Sickness		7	1	7	6	21
Machete wound		20	23	13	11	67
Wounds		15	31	17	7	70
Toothache		4	11	17	11	43
Fever		49	146	170	85	450
Headache		35	45	120	53	253
Bodily pains		25	42	29	16	112
Respiratory problems		4		4	3	11
Dengue						
Chicken pox						
liciadura						
Knock/blow						
Haemorrhage		1	2	4	1	8
Fracture				1		1
Family planning						
Burns		3	1	2	1	7
Inflammation		5				5
Childbirth		3	3			6
Intoxication			1	1		2
Rheumatism					1	1
Spider's bite			1		1	2
Leishmaniasis			1	1	1	3
Pregnancy				3		3
Wound dressing		1	1	10		12
Other prevention activs				12		12
Total		1836	2640	2946	1347	8769

CASES TREATED BY PROMOTERS IN 30 COMMUNITIES • OAGP
Period: 1997 - 2000

COMPLAINTS		1997	1998	1999	2000	Total
Diarrhoea Diarrhoea, "cholera" Diarrhoea with mucous	ADIs		418	343	139	900
Sore throat Ear ache Cough Bronchial problems Influenza	ARIs		283	361	103	747
Pneumonia			211	175	50	436
Fungal infections Sores, itching	MYCOSIS		0	16	13	29
Acarosis/mange Scabies, itching Boils, spots sangochupos	SKIN INFEC-TIONS		657	349	100	1106
Anaemia Infected wound Paleness/pallor Bugs	ENTERO-PARASITES		184	144	79	407
Malaria Probable malaria Fever	MALARIA		157	133 17 4	63 2 3	353 19 7
Eye pain	CONJUNC-TIVITIS		185	189	71	445
Vaginal pain Gonorrhea Chancres	STDs		20	1	7	28
Stomach ache	CO-LIC		8	9	2	19
Urinary pain	OTHERS	119	30	14	163	
Snake bite			20	21	7	48
Ray sting						
Picadura de palo						
Sickness			21	3	2	26
Machete wound			10	48	22	80
Wounds			0	16	29	45
Toothache			32	54	11	97
Fever			0	8	1	9
Headache			139	260	108	507
Bodily pains			0	1	0	1
Respiratory problems			7	6	2	15
Dengue						
Chicken pox						
liciadura			6	3	4	13
Knock/blow			12			12
Haemorrhage			7	2	1	10
Fracture						
Family planning			2	1		3
Burns				7	5	12
Inflammation			3	1	45	49
Childbirth						
Intoxication						
Rheumatism						
Spider's bite					2	2
Leishmaniasis				5	7	12
Pregnancy				20	6	26
Wound dressing						
Other prevention activs						
Total			**2506**	**2229**	**891**	**5626**

CASES TREATED BY PROMOTERS IN 33 COMMUNITIES
ORDECONADIT • Period: 1997 - 2000

COMPLAINTS		1997	1998	1999	2000	Total
Diarrhoea Diarrhoea, "cholera" Diarrhoea with mucous	ADIs	449	449	511	247	1656
Sore throat Ear ache Cough Bronchial problems Influenza	ARIs	597	520	633	378	2128
Pneumonia		61	50	91	41	243
Fungal infections Sores, itching	MYCOSIS	21	12	22	28	83
Acarosis/mange Scabies, itching Boils, spots sangochupos	SKIN INFEC-TIONS	398	342	336	201	1277
Anaemia Infected wound Paleness/pallor Bugs	ENTERO-PARASITES	786	324	314	170	1594
Malaria Probable malaria Fever	MALARIA	5	0	0	0	5
Eye pain	CONJUNC-TIVITIS	177	96	78	42	393
Vaginal pain Gonorrhea Chancres	STDs	41	30	30	15	116
Stomach ache	CO-LIC	27	24	34	30	115
Urinary pain	OTHERS	7	7	8	8	30
Snake bite		8	7	4	7	26
Ray sting		5	5	5	1	16
Picadura de palo		13	3	11	4	31
Sickness		5	4	4	0	13
Machete wound		6	3	11	6	26
Wounds		11	15	8	52	
Toothache		24	19	21	18	82
Fever		22	30	25	119	
Headache		52	24	23	17	116
Bodily pains		42	15	41	25	123
Respiratory problems		30	18	22	26	96
Dengue						
Chicken pox		2	0	9	6	17
liciadura						
Knock/blow						
Haemorrhage						
Fracture		1	0	1	0	2
Family planning						
Burns				3	1	3
Inflammation						
Childbirth						
Intoxication						
Rheumatism						
Spider's bite		1				1
Leishmaniasis<						
Pregnancy						
Wound dressing						
Other prevention activs						
Total		2818	1985	2257	1303	8363

- Tuberculosis

At the start of the first phase of the project with OIRA, when we were told that there were a large number of cases of TB in the communities, we decided to work in coordination with the Atalaya health centre, applying the standards and logistics of the national TB control programme. Later, in the second and third phases of the project, this important work was extended to OAGP and ORDECONADIT, with the following results.

Pulmonary TB BK (+) in the three organisations
Period 1995-2000

	Cases diagnosed and treated			Cases being treated at project end	Total
	1st Phase	2nd Phase	3rd Phase	3rd Phase	
OIRA	26	41	9	5	81
OAGP		2	3	1	6
ORDECONADIT		22	12	5	39
		115		11	126

In the first phase, actual field work lasted five months. In the second and third phases, it lasted 18 months each time.

In the project area, we have participated significantly in the control of TB, not only diagnosing cases of TB with positive bacilloscopy (BK (+)) in 119 communities but also establishing a model of treatment for indigenous peoples.

In OIRA, there has been a considerable decline in the number of cases of TB with positive bacilloscopy, from 67 cases to only 14 in the third phase (November/98 – June/2000), largely ongoing cases that had previously been irregularly treated. In ORDECONADIT, the decline in cases has been smaller. In OAGP, there has been no significant work due to problems with the Oventeni health post laboratory (MINSA) in terms of diagnosis and control.

From the start, work was carried out according to a model that was compatible with the local reality, the components of which include:
- MINSA establishments (health centres and posts) organising the work with the community promoters within their jurisdiction.
- Trained promoters in each community able to:
  - Identify respiratory symptom
  - Take samples of sputum
  - Prepare microscope slides

- Take or send the slide to the corresponding health centre laboratory
- Collect the result
- Ensure the case (BK+) is seen by the health centre doctor
- Administer supervised treatment
- Take control samples of sputum
- Check weight
- Monitor contact
- Record progress on the treatment control sheet and in the treatment book
- Act, with their organisation, to avoid abandonment of treatment

- Identifying respiratory symptoms in an indigenous community is very easy. Everyone knows who has a cough, particularly who coughs at night. So a well-trained promoter can examine 100% of those with a cough. Some people with a chronic cough are reluctant to provide a sputum sample. The promoter must insist, with the support of the head of the community and other members. Similarly, the promoter must act if there is a risk of treatment being abandoned.
- If the result is positive (+), the promoter endeavours to take the patient to the health centre for a medical examination and to commence the required treatment. Sometimes, the health centre doctor may come to the community. Generally, when a promoter has the health centre's confidence in terms of his ability, he will perform the first stage of treatment in the community, with precise indications from the health centre professional as to how to administer medication to the patient. He will return with control samples and take more medicines as appropriate until completion of the treatment.

During the project's field work, the promoters were given sufficient training to be able to follow these steps and procedures. In the beginning, there was some resistance on the part of the health centre staff to place their trust in the promoter and they would insist that the patient be transferred from their community to the town for the duration of their treatment. This resulted in people returning home and abandoning their treatment in all cases. They failed to take into consideration the fact that indigenous people need to move with all or part of their family and that their survival in the town is thus impossible. For this reason, the project worked successfully towards a situation whereby patients with TB were diagnosed and treated within their community. We had to train the indigenous promoters and promote trust in them. We had to reach out to the communities, recognising and respecting their particular ways of life. We had to recognise their organisations as their valid representatives, both at community and federal level. Only then would it be possible to achieve successful results in the treatment of tuberculosis and other illnesses that require prolonged treatment, such as leprosy, leishmaniasis, sexually transmitted illnesses, etc.

The public and private health bodies that work with the indigenous peoples of the Peruvian Amazon need to restructure their services and adopt new strategies and methodologies that are in line with the needs, cultural characteristics and potentialities of these peoples. They must not impose or mechanically apply western methodologies, which is what the MINSA posts and brigades that visit the communities have been doing to date.

Another prevalent opinion found during the field work was that the indigenous "do not learn" and that "they do not have the ability to improve their nutritional status" nor to face up to the issue of abandoning treatment. This is not the case.

In March 1997, a woman was receiving treatment for TB in the community of Centro Pucani, administered by the promoter, under the indications of the health technician from the nearest health post, in the community of Boca Pucani. During monitoring, it was noted that the dosage of medication being given was far lower than required for the severity of the illness. It turned out that the health technician had made a mistake in the calculations and the promoter was giving exactly what he had been told by the technician. We have noted that the indigenous promoters are extremely disciplined, they have a great interest and desire to learn and they do so rapidly when the teaching is practical, that is, via demonstration.

After the brief experience of the first phase of the project, the second phase began in January 1997. The first patients diagnosed with positive TB (BK(+)) in the community of Boca Apinihua were a man of 36 years of age, and another of 41. The first was a new case, extremely thin, weighing 27 kg, and he responded well to treatment. After six months he was discharged, cured and weighing 57 kg. The second was a relapse, also thin, weighing 46 kg and, after eight months of treatment, she was discharged weighing 57 kg. Another case of TB (BK(+)) that caught our attention due to the patient's serious calorific and protein deficiencies was a patient in the Tahuanti community, a woman of 25 years of age, a new case, weighing only 27 kg. After six months of treatment she was discharged, cured, and weighing 48 kg. The first and third cases had lost a great deal of weight because they had been following diets recommended by traditional indigenous medicine prior to our intervention. From the start, we explained that they could eat what they wanted, that this treatment did not require a special diet. We recommended that they improve their food intake with all the available food they could. Astonishingly, they gained weight rapidly with just the produce of their own fields, rivers, lakes and the forest. At no time did they need to receive supplementary food from the national TB control programme.

When the health centre forced a patient to stay in the town for the duration of their treatment, abandonment of treatment was 100%. With our work, treatment has been extended to the whole population and abandonment has been reduced to a few isolated cases. One of these was in 1997, a new case in the community of Galilea, with one month to go before completion of the treatment. Under the influence of a "traditional healer", the patient moved his house to a place outside the community and stopped the treatment. He was found by the promoters but did not want to continue. Through the intervention of the headman of the community, the sectoral team and the field coordination, he was persuaded to finish his treatment.

Another two cases in 1998 in the community of Chicosa were resolved in a similar way. This demonstrates the importance of working with the organisations, both at community and federal level, forging a relationship and agreements with them, that is, in the intercultural context. This is a determining factor in the success of the health work.

This same model was used for the work in leprosy, malaria and leishmaniasis treatment, with the corresponding specifications.

• Leprosy

A total of five cases of leprosy were diagnosed in the communities of Puerto Alegre, Mapalja and Canapishtea, belonging to the ORDECONADIT organisation. The diagnosis was confirmed in collaboration with the Bolognesi health centre, and treatment of four of the cases was undertaken by the promoters. One case was continuing treatment at project end. If the Bolognesi health centre continues to seek out and treat cases with the promoters, leprosy could be fully controlled in this area within a relatively short space of time.

• Malaria

Malaria in the three organisations
Period: 1995–2000

Cases diagnosed and treated

	1st Phase	2nd Phase	3rd Phase
OIRA		150	200
OAGP		109	435
ORDECONADIT		11	
		905 (*)	

(*) 630 cases were diagnosed and treated by the promoters, of which 151 were probable cases.

242

The Sepa, Inuya, Tambo and Unini river basins are areas of endemic vivax malaria. Other forms have not been diagnosed. In 1997 and 98, there was an epidemic in Atalaya that affected the OIRA and OAGP communities. The project's sectoral teams participated in its control, particularly the promoters.

- Leishmaniasis
Leishmaniasis in the three organisations
Period: 1995-2000

	Cases diagnosed	Cases treated	Cases awaiting treatment
OIRA	49	20(*)	29
OAGP	62	28	34
ORDECONADIT	37	15	85
	148	63	85

(*) *1 case of cutaneous leishmaniasis in the OIRA community of Puerto Esperanza was treated with a preparation of a medicinal plant basis.*

There are endemic areas within each of the three organisations, primarily in the Urubamba river zone in OIRA, and in the upper part of the Unini river in OAGP. Particular emphasis was placed on work of diagnosis and treatment during the second phase, given that a significant contribution of glucantine was available from the Regional Health Department of Ucayali. But this was the only time. Following this, obtaining the medication required bureaucratic procedures to be followed via the health centres, with sporadic positive treatment. For this reason, there are many patients with cutaneous mucous forms awaiting treatment. In the last quarter of the project's third phase, one case of leishmaniasis being treated with a medicinal plant-based preparation was clinically verified in the community of Puerto Esperanza, in OIRA. This has been the only case clinically proven by us.

Infectious and parasitic diseases are prevalent. Both the mortality rate and the disease profile given in the previous tables depict social strata in an extreme state of poverty and lacking in health services. The incidence of infectious and parasitic diseases of the respiratory apparatus, intestine, skin and mucous membranes is very high, particularly in the communities located along the banks of the larger rivers and near the towns and population centres. The process of concentration of the indigenous population into communities, and the greater contact with western culture, have broken down and changed epidemiological perceptions and ancestral ways of life, forcing them to adapt to new conditions and ways

Vaccination campaign. *Photo: Jim Thuesen, 1993*

of life in a disadvantageous relationship that entails a high risk of succumbing to illness and dying.

It is important to stress at this point that, through the methodology used in the field work – work with the indigenous organisation, with mixed teams, travelling from community to community, recording, disseminating, evaluating and planning the work in each trip, with a minimum of six visits per sector in each phase of the project, respecting their organisation and their culture – it has been possible gradually to uncover the health problems of each community, each village, and to reach a good understanding with the communities of the origins and causes of these problems in order to build structures and ways of preventing and controlling them. It has, accordingly, been possible to build a local and coordinated health system in each community, made up of the human and therapeutic resources of indigenous medicine, reactivated and strengthened by the trained promoter and the functioning of a medicine chest with a permanent stock pile of medicines. To this must be added the implementation of referral and counter-referral systems between the community and the closest MINSA health centre, and surgical treatment for those patients requiring it in MINSA's regional and national hospitals.
In this way, the local community system has been linked into MINSA at local and regional level, guaranteeing integrated care of the project area's population, with an emphasis on intercultural community health.

PREVENTION, APPROACH, DIAGNOSIS AND TREATMENT

As in many other societies, patient care in indigenous communities takes place, first and foremost, within the home environment, during the appearance of the first signs and symptoms. If the illness continues, the vapour healer, promoter or shaman will intervene, primarily representing traditional medicine, due to a generalised perception that the illness has a spiritual origin and obeys the curses of nature or people. If the process continues or if it is recognised as an illness coming from outside, the intervention of the promoter and/or health post is sought, and so they must be sufficiently trained to act effectively. In serious, sometimes terminal, cases, and when distance permits, efforts are made to transfer the patient to the health centre.

According to our observations, indigenous medicine is very effective in cases that are recognised by us as disorders of the mind or anxiety. Medicinal and ritual interventions have a great psycho-therapeutic effect on the indigenous patient.
It is said that if a shaman is good, he will soon know whether the illness is within his competence and, when it is not, he refers it to western medicine. Nonetheless, we do treat many cases, generally in a serious state, that have already been treated by the "traditional healer". The people claim that only good shamans have this capacity for referral.

Within both the family and the specialist sphere, indigenous medicine makes use of numerous preparations, behavioural rules, diets, and ritual acts of therapeutic and preventive value. There are many preparations known as *piripiri*, which have a preventive and protective value, not only against illness but also in relation to economic and social activities (hunting, fishing, personal relations, etc.).

The promoter has been trained in each community and a great deal of work has been done with the population on preventive-promotional activities for the diagnosis, treatment and prevention of infectious illnesses: diarrhoea, intestinal parasitosis, acarosis, pyodermatosis, bacterial conjunctivitis, acute respiratory infections (ARIs) and complications, sexually transmitted illnesses (STIs) etc. For the control of tuberculosis, malaria and leishmaniasis, work has been carried out in conjunction with the national programmes via an agreement with the Ministry of Health's Regional Health Department of Ucayali (MINSA).

At the start of the project, we found a high prevalence of the six mentioned infectious illnesses, and we had the impression that the people "had learned to live with these complaints". They attributed them to curses of different origins, and attempts to cure them with their own natural resources had been unsuccessful. This is why they have said and continue to say that they need medicines from the pharmacy, alongside their own medicine, for illnesses "brought from outside". Consequently, with the exception of intestinal parasitosis, we had to demonstrate to them how to use pharmacological products and patiently explain, in their own language, through the promoter and/or sector coordinator, the epidemiology and western measures of prevention of such illnesses. This is how we achieved significant reductions in their frequency.

It is very important to note that, in ORDECONADIT, the practice of treating intestinal parasitosis with *ojé* [*Ficus insipida*] and *paico* [*Chenopodium ambrosioides*] was supported and promoted, administered by one woman and one man, both indigenous experts in the preparation and handling of the said medicinal plants. At the same time as undertaking activities of deparasitisation, they trained a group of interested people in each community through which they were subsequently going to extend their work to other organisations.

In the indigenous communities, the diagnosis of a patient is only done in private in exceptional circumstances. Generally it takes place in public, that is, before an audience of many people who turn up spontaneously. So when you are treating the case, you can take advantage of this situation to explain its prevention. A great deal of emphasis was placed on the need for clean water, sanitation, personal and environmental hygiene, specifying and emphasising each one depending on the particular problem at hand, but always bearing in mind the real possibilities for practical implementation. The team left personal, family and community tasks for the people on each visit.

Specific cases of illness and treatment
Examples

- At the start of the project, we realised that death through acute diarrhoea with dehydration was the main cause of death in all age groups. At the start of the field work in the second phase, the nurses were instructed to insist on the practice of oral rehydration. The nurse of the Urubamba sector in Atalaya, OIRA, had to treat a three-year-old boy with acute diarrhoea and dehydration in the community of Huao for two days and two nights. The opinion of the family and the whole community was that "the more liquid you give the more diarrhoea there will be". The nurse and the team did everything possible not to submit to this pressure. The family believed the child was going to die. But it did not. The child survived and recovered. This was the first case, and afterwards many more were treated. On very rare occasions, parenteral rehydration was needed, a technique in which the promoters were also trained.
- On cases of tuberculosis see page 239.
- In terms of respiratory symptoms, we found that there were many cases of chronic coughs with repeated negative bacilloscopy (BK(-)). This raised the problem of diagnosis. We know of two cases, an indigenous adult from the community of Lagarto Millar and a mestizo girl from the town of Atalaya, who received treatment - not through ourselves - without confirmation of diagnosis, and who, on completion of treatment continued to have a chronic cough. In other words, their clinical condition had not changed. In the community of Centro Pucani, we treated a group of 15 people with chronic coughs who we classified as affected by paragonimiasis from a clinical-epidemiological point of view. The eggs of the parasite were not found in the sputum or faeces of the patients in the samples that were taken to the laboratory of the National Health Institute (MINSA) in Lima, but the worm was found in crustaceans taken from the stream adjacent to the community and which some members ate raw. The fact that we do not have a competent laboratory has limited our work in relation to these problems; in all cases, they form very interesting research and treatment issues. For a start, the members of Centro Pucani community no longer eat the crustaceans and molluscs raw from the stream, and a group of 15 patients have received treatment with praziquantel, with good results.

Health awareness and organisation
Examples of Community Cases

- In the first months of the second phase of the project, the field work model was made concrete in practice, specifically for tuberculosis. The third patient suffering from pulmonary tuberculosis BK(+)* (TBPBK(+))** in the community of Boca Apinihua was a young

---

* BK: Positive bacilloscopy
** TBP: Pulmonary tuberculosis

man of 26 years of age, diagnosed in April 1997. He was a native of the community of Boca Apinihua where he had resettled with his wife and their three young children.

He first fell ill in 1992, and was treated by the Atalaya health centre where he was diagnosed with TBPBK (+) in August 1992 and received continued treatment of only 24 doses of a total of 82. Feeling somewhat better, he then abandoned the treatment. He could stay no longer in Atalaya. He again fell ill and returned with more symptoms to the Atalaya health centre where treatment was recommenced. He received only 50 doses out of a total of 105 in January 1995. He then again abandoned the treatment, slightly recovered, for the same reasons as before. But the young man now knew that his treatment would take eight months and he wanted to be cured. Full of hope, seven months later (August 1995), he went to the Ramón Castilla health post, a community near to Boca Apinihua, and which at that time had just begun functioning again. There he began a third course of treatment with an agreement to return every day to receive supervised treatment. He decided to settle close to the community of Ramón Castilla, but it was not easy, he had to work, to feed and care for his family. He did not complete one month of treatment.

Mixed medicine chest.   *Photo: Jim Thuesen, 1994*

It was then that he found out about the work we had been carrying out in his community of Boca Apinihua since January 1997. The first two patients with whom we started the work of the second phase had notably improved (page 239). The two promoters in Boca Apinihua, one of which was also the head of the community, told him of it and convinced him to return and settle in his community and undergo the treatment that they themselves were administering to the two patients mentioned. He learned that they were already working again, having started their treatment in a serious state. With this help and persuaded by his organisation at community level that this was the best way, the young man once more recommenced his treatment for the fourth time, and this time he continued it until his full recovery in January 1998.

- With regard to cases of abandonment of tuberculosis treatment, the case in the community of Galilea and in the community of Chicosa (page 242) should be noted. These were cases recovered and treated with the support of the organisation, primarily at community level, and they demonstrate the credibility and trust achieved by the project's field staff.

RELATIONS AND COOPERATION WITH THE PUBLIC HEALTH SYSTEM

Collaboration with the Regional Health Department of Ucayali (MINSA) has taken place primarily in three broad areas. In the implementation of tuberculosis, malaria and leishmaniasis control programmes; in the treatment of patients in MINSA health posts, health centres and hospitals; and in recognising the work of the promoters. In terms of TB control, very good work has been carried out with the Atalaya health centre in the 55 OIRA communities. In ORDECONADIT, good work was carried out, with some temporary problems in terms of the laboratory and medicines. In OAGP, good work was carried out on malaria, average work on leishmaniasis and very weak work on TB, the latter through diagnostic errors on the part of the laboratory. With regard to the training and work of the promoters in the project's indigenous communities, the Regional Health Department of Ucayali has formalised its recognition by issuing a card to each promoter, duly accredited by the training office and signed by its director-general. Patient treatment was undertaken in health posts and centres in the project areas and, occasionally, in the regional hospital in Pucallpa, with some exemptions in terms of fee payment.

In order to formalise this cooperation, two agreements were negotiated and signed, one for the second phase from September 1996 to August 1998 and the other for the third phase from September 1998 to August 2000.

Surgical campaigns

The first indigenous woman to be operated on was a woman from the community of Boca Cocani, who had suffered, for more than 15 years, from a giant tumour of the right parotid gland. The operation took place in the Dos de Mayo Hospital in Lima between November and December 1997, the diagnosis of pleomorphic adenoma of the parotid gland being confirmed. Three years on, Esther Campos Ríos lives a normal life in her community of Boca Cocani.

The impact of this case on the indigenous communities was enormous. Other cases soon came forward requesting operations. It was not possible to take everyone to the hospital. The idea of providing surgical treatment in Atalaya arose. This commitment was recorded in an agreement with the Regional Health Department of Ucayali for the second phase, with contributions from both parties, the Programme and the Regional Health Department. A surgical team from the Pucallpa regional hospital came to the Atalaya health centre from 12th to 15th May 1998 and operated on a total of 23 people, seven from the town and 16 from the indigenous communities of OIRA, largely hernias and some tumours. Some had more than one operation, resulting in a total of 27 surgical interventions. Two similar surgical campaigns were outlined in the agreement for the third phase, this time for all three organisations. These took place in June 1999 and July 2000. Implementation of these three surgical campaigns, which made the recovery and rehabilitation of 92 people possible, was a new and important experience, particularly for the indigenous peoples.

**Surgical campaigns carried out in Atalaya for the Three Project Areas
Period: 1998–2000**

	OIRA			OAGP		ORDECONADIT		
	1st c	2nd c	3rd c	2nd c	3rd c	2nd c	3rd c	
Patients operated on	23 (**)	26	10	11	6	9	7	85
No. of operations	27 (***)	28	10	15	9	11	8	101

c = campaign   –   (**) 16 indigenous   –   (***) 20 indigenous

**Patients treated in MINSA hospitals
Period: 1995–2000**

	OIRA	OAGP	ORDECONADIT
Patients operated on in:			
Pucallpa Hospital	7	4	10
2 de Mayo Hospital – Lima	1	–	–
Hospital del Niño – Lima	–	–	1
Satipo Hospital	–	1	–

A total of 24 patients have also been treated for emergency complaints (uterine fibroid, renal tumour, strangulated hernia, acute abdomen problems, accident and serious injuries), which patients, given the complexity of their conditions, had to be transferred to hospital.

Salting fish for drying.   *Photo: Cæcilie Mikkelsen, 2000*

Medical Aspects II: Nursing

By Sofía Vivanco Hilaro, a nurse. She worked in the Ucayali Sector of OIRA during the third phase of the Programme.

Nursing in native communities

Field nursing usually refers to performing duties in hospitals, health centres and health posts in urban or marginal urban areas, and in human settlements within the coastal or Andean social environment. Activities are implemented according to health objectives, applying national vertical health programmes and using the health department's pre-established strategies. Methods differ little from one place to the next.

My experience of two years of working directly with the native communities has shown that their different accessibility, geographical location, transportation (by river), culture and general ecological environment mean that work strategies to achieve health objectives and to apply national health programmes need to conceive of new "ways of working", adapted to the culture of each ethnic group, and in which there is the active participation of the organisations' leaders and the leaders of the communities themselves, and whereby the health promoters form part of the work teams.

Permanence, trust, solidarity, and demonstration are all tools that enable relevant health activities to be effectively implemented:

Permanence refers to living alongside the community and participating in the daily routine of the health team, that is, participating actively in its tasks, in the community work, the communal crops, meetings, festivals and other community activities.

Trust comes gradually as permanence progresses. It is very important to "be able to integrate", and this comes not only through one's presence. Communication and respect for the culture of others also help greatly in terms of "being accepted" and then becoming a part of the people.

Solidarity means sharing food, community activities (fishing, communal work), the joy, sadness, problems and triumphs because, to the people, the nurse is very important. Simple and concrete demonstrations of how to "treat" the patients, such as demonstrating behavioural changes and improvements in terms of prevention, require the active participation of community members and, particularly, the health promoters of each community.

Our trip through the native communities, staying in each one at least two days, used to take an average of three months, and included following-up specific cases, transferring laboratory samples and administering treatments from the community medicine chest in the presence of the health promoters.

The work of the health promoters, the formation of the medicine chest, management of medicines, and data recording are all important tasks to be performed in the community because they ensure that the health activities adapted to the local culture are managed in line with the national health programmes. To achieve integration of the health promoter within the health team requires ongoing, permanent training. Persistence in this alleviates weaknesses and gives results.

A different dawn

It is often thought that daily life goes on as usual when you move somewhere different, even when you go to live in the Amazon forest, an unknown place, known only from stories, photos or because you have heard of someone who has visited, but to experience it firsthand is something completely different.

The first night I slept in the rain forest, in the native community of Tahuarapa, I almost couldn't sleep, I was so homesick. I missed many things, my family, friends, work, and the nightlife. I began to think of many things. I had left behind me a life of comfort and ease: here, things were very different, needs would not be quite so easily satisfied and I would have to adapt to the environment, to the natural resources and, above all, use my creativity to obtain the things I needed.

It was 5 p.m. and I had to sort out my bed, that is, hang up the mosquito net by its four corners. Well, I didn't know how to do that, it was a complete puzzle to me. Just where do you start, where do you attach it? What a weird thing! I gave up and called Javier the boat pilot to help. He laughed and said, "You'll soon learn and then you'll do it on your own. Don't worry, it's easy". He knew what he was doing, he did it in a flash! Next, I put down the plastic and then the mat ... and went to bed. So early, it was only 5.30 p.m, ... and the mosquitoes wouldn't leave me alone. Seven p.m. and I still couldn't sleep. The mat seemed very thin and my back was aching already, I couldn't find a comfortable position, tossing and turning. You could hear the noise of the Ucayali river clearly. The fruit falling from the trees sounded like someone throwing stones, the croaking of the toads and the noise of the birds, I couldn't make them out, and every so often something would scare me and I would shout, "Javier, what's that?" and he would answer, "It's nothing, go to sleep". What a night! I scarcely slept a wink.

Five-thirty in the morning, the sun was shining and up I got. Now... a wash and the toilet. But where? There was no tap, shower or private place for personal hygiene, everything was out in the open. So I went down to the Ucayali river, and I washed there. Rather unwillingly, I have to say, because the water's very dirty in winter. And what if I wanted a bath? It was so weird to sit in a canoe and throw water over myself directly from the river. Baths ended up being a very rushed and rather unpleasant affair.

Breakfast at 8 a.m. Javier and Alfonso, the sector coordinator, had prepared food: fish soup and boiled manioc. It was good but I missed a sweet breakfast with bread. No lunch that day, just dinner at 4 p.m. because what with the river rising there were no fish, and so to bed again. The memory I have of my first contact with the community members is very special. I was welcomed so warmly, everyone gathered round, looking at me and wanting to know my name, where I was from, what it was like. They also asked about "Nurse Juana" wondering whether "she'd be good, like Juana" but they didn't dare ask me. They talked in their own language and laughed, they laughed at my long trousers, long sleeved shirt and cap, because they wear very light clothes. They asked if I was hot. Of course I was, but what could I do? The mosquitoes didn't stop biting me and the *izango* jiggers would climb up your clothes in a flash to find somewhere to live on your body.

If they really want to welcome you, the people give you something, like fruit, manioc, smoked fish, salted fish, etc. Of course, they don't ask you first: Do you eat fish? Do you eat *sajino* [collared peccary]? Do you drink *masato* [drink from fermented manioc]? But, this way, you start making friends and you get used to the new way of eating. Of course, every so often you dream of cake, ice cream, roast chicken. Dream on and hope.

Trust and communication

Once we had made initial contact with a community, our next visit would be very different because everyone knew the nurse and coordinator were coming to visit the community to treat patients and train the promoters.

The community members would come up to you shyly, in small groups, and someone who spoke Spanish as well as their own language would come forward and say, "Nurse Sofia, have you brought any pills for infection?" I would say "yes, but who is ill? And he would point to someone, maybe a woman, hidden behind the others. I would ask her to step forward and, timidly and with embarrassment, in her own language for others to interpret, she would explain the problem. I found this way of talking to a patient - in front of other people - very strange. Likewise, examining a patient was sometimes rather difficult because they wouldn't let you see or feel certain parts of their body. As time went by, patients began to come to consultations alone but if it concerned a problem of the reproductive system, there was always great secrecy and much beating about the bush before you could actually find out what was wrong.

As time went by, they stopped calling me nurse and called me 'la Sofia', in other words, another person in their community. This rather unusual way of denoting someone, but one which showed great acceptance, would be given to any visitor that helped them.

Community meetings have formed an important part of our work, because this is where we can meet at least 90% of the community members and where we can find out about health problems, because here they tell each other their problems in order to facilitate the work. They give a rough idea of the illness so that it can be more easily identified.

Obviously, not speaking their language formed a barrier between myself and the people, but the participation of the health promoter, community leader and sector coordinator helped enormously in this work. I sometimes treated patients who came with their translator (another trusted community member) because they were too embarrassed to let anyone else hear their problem. There were no expressions of fear or of "what they will say if I am ill". The advantage of such collaboration in medical treatment is that the patients take pills as they are told and as they are shown with the help of the health promoter.

Training the health promoters

For each training session, a certain number of promoters were brought together. For them, this type of meeting represented "learning or getting to know a little more about what they had learnt". Without exception, they all had a sense of responsibility and commitment to their community. Being a promoter had given them a place in their community: they were no longer just another member but one that was providing a service, curing the sick. So the commitment to learn was great. There was always huge competitiveness, the promoter who knew more or who had more experience always stood out in each class, in each case treated.

The first training meeting was in the community of Unión San Francisco, which is two and a half hours downstream on the Ucayali river, where the Lagarto Millar stream joins it. Here, we brought together 17 promoters from the communities of Sapani, Santa Rosa de Laulate, Lagarto Millar, Aerija, San Francisco and Tahuanti.

Mauro was a 35-year-old promoter who spoke Spanish only with difficulty. He did so in a unique style but which hid a great deal of his charisma. With only second grade primary education, he was one of the promoters who never missed a training session provided by the health institutions such as the Indigenous Health Programme (PSI) or the Ministry of Health (MINSA). Of course, he had difficulty in writing clearly and rapidly and so, at this first session, he was always the last to finish and was writing until very late. But it was said that "he is already a recognised promoter, his face and name are known in the Ministry of Health in Lima because they said so at the hospital, and this is how it should be for the other promoters".

The issue of family planning, which touched upon vasectomies and sterilisation following a question from one of the promoters, caused reactions such as, "How is it possible to take away what God has given us? The Bible says thus you are born thus you must die. And it's not right that women are sterilised because we need to increase our population so that

the schools can function." Another opinion was that "while the hospital forces women not to have children by giving injections or cutting them open, the ADE (Atalaya Education Department) requires a minimum of 20 children to be registered for the opening of a school room and a teacher placement. They should reach some kind of agreement, we don't know who to believe". Such issues caused a great deal of negative reaction among the community members.

Examples: specific cases of illness and treatment
Witchcraft
A woman, 25 years of age and a member of the Pensilvania community, who was in a relationship with a community member from Tzipani, had a little girl of 5 years old. The woman said that a few months back, in January 2000, her husband had told her she was possessed by the devil. He suggested she needed treating and took her to the community of Tzipani, where he began to treat her with plants. He gave her *toé* (*Brugmansia sp.*), *ayahuasca* and other preparations, saying they would "remove the devil from her". In the hallucinations they caused in her, the woman said that "she saw the devil with the face of her husband pursuing her" and she lost control and began to run in any direction. She didn't say how many times she had taken the preparations but when she awoke in the countryside in Corintoni, she was very far from where she had started, and her daughter was no longer with her. From that moment she began looking for the child in the communities.

She arrived at the community of Cascada on 20th March 2000 asking for help to "remove the devil", because she still dreamt of the devil with the face of her husband pursuing her. Mr. Alfonso Gómez [a pseudonym] took her into his house and told her he would cure her. When asked about her daughter, she told us, "She must be dead, the people say the *tigrillo* [ocelot] has eaten her, if not why is she still missing?"

Working it out from her story, the child must have disappeared around two months earlier. What shocked us from the story was the woman's resignation in relation to her daughter, whom she gave up without having found any indication that she was dead.

According to Mr. Gómez, the woman was cured with *pinitsi for the devil* (an ashéninka herbal medicine) but she was told that if she didn't follow the diet the evil would come back.

The shaman leaving on vacation. Photo: Jim Thuesen, 1994

Strangulated hernia

On 10th March 2000, Mrs. Hortensia Flores (pseudonym), 52 years of age and from the Galilea community, arrived as an emergency case at the Atalaya Health Centre suffering from "witchcraft". This case was referred by the health promoter from her community.

Her husband told us, "A few months back my wife was complaining of pains in the stomach and, a couple of weeks ago, she started receiving treatment from the community 'doctor'. In the days that followed, she showed no signs of improvement and was in a great deal of pain, not eating. The treatment prescribed by the doctor was a diet, plant preparations and treatment with tobacco at night. The 'doctor' said that this 'ball' in the stomach was a curse, caused by witchcraft. On the ninth day she deteriorated and we asked the community to lend us the boat and engine to take her to hospital. We left the following day very early and when my wife arrived at the hospital she began to bring up a dark green strong smelling vomit."

The health team were in Atalaya at that time collecting sample results and, when the case was communicated to the OIRA office. We went to the Atalaya Health Centre but the woman had already died. The medical diagnosis was a strangulated umbilical hernia and kidney failure (hydroelectrolytic decompensation).

The term "curse" or "sorcery" is attributed to illnesses that are not recognised as such but, once they have had an opportunity of getting to know them, the people do call them by their real name, for example, a lipoma.

A hernia is one ailment that, when we first started working, very few community members knew of or requested help for but, once they understood the risks, they often came voluntarily to ask for surgery. This is why there was a considerable increase in the number of patients during the second surgical campaign.

Making use of plants for curing:

Uta or leishmaniasis

On 16th February 2000, the OIRA health team arrived in the community of Puerto Esperanza. As we began to treat the patients, a youngster came forward who was 15 years of age and had a cutaneous ulcer on his upper inside right leg measuring 6cm x 7cm. It was badly infected and we took a scrape sample of the skin.

That same day, we met with Mr. Ángel Ruiz – our herbalist – and he agreed to prepare a medication for leishmaniasis. So he went into the countryside to look for the *abuta* creeper [*Cissampelos pareira*] and, on his return, he began the preparation, with the participation of the promoters and community members. They produced the medicine and kept it in a bottle. Mr. Ángel gave dietary indications (not to eat chilli pepper) and prescribed treatment three times a day after cleaning the wound. The following day, the health promoter began to treat the ulcer as directed.

On 3rd March 2000, the sample was taken to the Health Centre and the scrape tested positive for cutaneous leishmaniasis. On 4th March, the notification and request for glucantine was made by the epidemiology department so that it could be dealt with by the Regional Health Department. We received no response to this request until early April.

Meanwhile, the results were surprising. On 3rd April 2000, whilst carrying out a monitoring trip with Dr. Luis Torres, we examined the patient and found that the ulcer had shrunk to 2 cm. x 3 cm. in diameter and, by May 2000, the sore had completely healed up.

Parasitosis

The use of *ojé* [*Ficus insipida*] as an antiparasitic has been commonplace among communities for some time, albeit prepared in different forms and with inexact dosages. Our experience of work in the Tahuanía communities, with the participation of the herbalist, Mr. Ángel Ruiz, who was trained by the AMETRA project– Pucallpa, has encouraged the careful use of this medication.

During the trip through the Atalaya communities from 15th February to 31st March 2000, Mr. Ángel Ruiz taught people how to extract, prepare and administer white *ojé* resin for the treatment of parasitosis, as well as the diet to be followed.

He administered the preparation to 49 patients, children and adults, particularly *"posheco"* (anaemic) patients, giving the dosage according to age.

Diet: no chilli peppers, no acids (lemon, orange), no strong *masato*, no sexual relations, for one week.

Contra-indications: not to be administered to expectant women or children under two.

Side effects: could cause sickness, nausea, weakness. Treat with warm sugared water.

The results after three days of administration were satisfactory. The comments of the people who had received the preparation were that they had passed small and large parasites, others had passed nothing. After one month, they looked physically well and had gained weight.

Pyodermatosis

In a promoters' training session in the community of Unini Cascada, there was an opportunity to prepare the *abuta* plant for the treatment of impetigo because, at that time, all the medicine had been used up and the number of cases was increasing.

With the participation of the promoters, vapour healers and community members, we managed to prepare eleven bottles that were shared among the promoters for use in their communities, to be kept in the community medicine chest.

The method of application of the preparation is as follows: First the mother washes the wounds well with soap and rinses them well, then dries them and, using a syringe, applies a drop of the prepared medicine to each wound, waiting for it to dry. This topical treatment is applied twice a day and improvements should be seen in three to four days. The results were very good, the promoters and community members said that it was easier than giving tablets to children.

Diarrhoea and sickness
While we were in a training meeting with the promoters and vapour healers, the son of one of them began to suffer from sickness and diarrhoea. The midwife, Mrs. Ana Cruz Otzonqui, who knows about medicinal plants, offered to prepare an infusion of herbs using the plant known as *rosa sisa* or *flor de tunchi* [*Tagetes erecta*] [sometimes called "Marigold" in English] mixed with crushed cow horn, cinnamon and oregano. She boiled it in a litre of water for five minutes, and they began to give the child teaspoons of this boiled water. They say it is also good for shock caused by "bad air". The promoters observed the case and the preparation of the infusion.

The following day, the diarrhoea was significantly better and the child's state had improved, so it was suggested that they should continue to give the child the liquid. In this case, no western medicine was necessary.

Similarly, there was an opportunity to observe Mrs. Iris Vásquez Nicolaspeque, a vapour healer from the community of Unión San Francisco, preparing an infusion of mango bark to give to her daughter when she had diarrhoea. She crushed the mango bark and boiled it in a cup of water and gave this preparation by the teaspoonful. The girl improved significantly. The vapour healer said that if the diarrhoea is treated early then it works well, but if it is left for a few days it becomes difficult, and the child has to be taken to the promoter.

In the beginning, all diarrhoeas are treated as mild diarrhoea and, if other signs or symptoms are identified, help is requested. Mild diarrhoea is attributed to "bad air", a shock, or a fall, and it is treated by the mother with the help of medicinal plants that she prepares herself or with the help of the vapour healer. However, diarrhoea that contains mucous, blood or that is accompanied by fever is referred to the health promoter because, they say, "it needs a pill".

Ashéninka design

Bridging the Gap between Western and Indigenous Medicine

By Bente Korsgaard, MD, and Jim Thuesen Pedersen, MD.
Representatives of the Karen Elise Jensen Foundation
and members of the project review team.

Introduction

At first glance, any attempt to implement modern western medical thinking in ancient indigenous cultures in the Peruvian Amazon while, at the same time, preserving traditional medical practices would appear to be a risky business for a foundation hitherto concerned with the funding of mainly high-tech medical projects with a well-defined outcome. This was our first thought when, in 1992, we became acquainted with the health project, which was presented to the Karen Elise Jensen Foundation. We had no previous experience of health work in tropical forest environments; one of us was working as a physician in occupational health and the other in respiratory medicine. However, life and death, illness and health are the cornerstones of any medical system. The concept of health in the West is, in essence, based on an analytic division of nature. Contrary to this, traditional medicine is often diffuse and synthetic, but well-integrated into the way of thinking of the culture concerned (Fock 1986: 95-118). We will shortly discuss some of these differences, which became apparent during our visits to the project area in the Upper Ucayali.

Western medicine

In the classical, mechanical model of disease within western medicine, disease is considered to be the result of a chain of causes. The process of disease is initiated by the combined effect of genetic and environmental factors, which are known as the aetiology of the disease. In the human body, a chain reaction of physiological, biochemical and morphologic nature is seen, which is called the pathogenesis, leading to the "error" in the apparatus and, thus, the disease (Wulff and Götzsche 1997:80-84). An example of this is lung tuberculosis, where the cause is considered to be known, although this is only partially true. The tubercle bacillus is a necessary causal factor in the development of the disease but it must be realised that natural phenomena always have a variety of causes. All diseases are multi-factorial, and deciding upon the cause is the result of a choice which reflects our interests (Wulff et al. 1986: 61-72).

Even though western medicine is, to a high degree, based on pure biological causal factors, social and psychological factors have always played a prominent role. Medical science is both a scientific and a humanistic discipline, attempting a holistic view of disease. However, western medicine is still highly influenced by a deterministic idea of causality based on science. Surgical as well as medical treatment is, thus, fundamentally based on rational thinking although, to this day, much treatment is still based more on tradition than on evidence.

Indigenous medicine

The indigenous concept of disease in the Upper Amazon is difficult to understand for a physician trained in western medicine, without a more thorough knowledge of the culture concerned. The late British anthropologist, Andrew Gray, who for a short period participated in the PSI health project in Madre de Dios, has given interesting descriptions of the concepts of health and disease in the Arakmbut culture in the Peruvian Amazon:

In the Arakmbut culture, health is not only physical health but must be considered in a broader context, comprising protection of the environment and the possibility of being self-supporting by relying on one's own resources. Disease can be considered as an indirect cause of the belief in souls and spirits, so-called animism. Disease and death can be inflicted on a subject by various evil spirits living, for example, in the forest or in the river. A number of plants and animals, for example, fish, tapirs and birds are similarly believed to be disease-inflicting. Disease can be caused by evil spirits in nature, by overfishing in the river or by gaining too much bag in hunting. Among the Arakmbut, excessive sexual activity in young people is also believed to debilitate the body. Sickness and death may be not only the fault of the victim but can also be inflicted by witches who are feeling hatred and wish to hurt a person. The witches use dangerous spirits who can attack a human being. Normally, the witches come from other villages, although they may live in the same community as the victim. Sorcery is considered very serious and could, particularly in the past, result in strangulation and drowning of the sorceresses once identified (Gray 1996: 159-176).

At the beginning of an illness, it is often regarded as a private affair but if the sick person does not improve over the course of a few days, she/he will receive the full attention of relatives and, in the case of a longstanding illness, of the entire settlement or community. The Arakmbut also distinguish between visible and invisible causes of disease. Diseases with an apparent cause, such as cuts and bruises, cold, headache, gastrointestinal upset and cough hit the body. They are caused by small accidents, hard work or exposure to much sun or rain and often disappear without any significant treatment.

The invisible causes are imputed to various evil spirits and may be difficult to treat. The contact with white missionaries in the 1900s led to great morbidity and mortality in many indigenous communities caused by, for example, yellow fever, influenza and various kinds of infectious eye disease, causing blindness. These diseases have been called "God's diseases" because the missionaries were believed to have caused them. (Ibid.) The immigration of poor colonists from other parts of Peru, seeking land, washing gold or collecting rubber has also been an important cause of serious and life-threatening epidemics amongst the indigenous communities.

Self-treatment of small ailments is common in the indigenous Amazonian communities - as it is in others - but traditionally the local healer is the key person when it comes to the treatment of more serious diseases. In addition, older healers have much experience in the use of traditional medicine, which can ensure the survival and growth of the local community, and in many ways they represent an intellectual elite with a holistic outlook. As we have experienced in the Upper Ucayali, there is a desire and motivation among the local communities to reinforce their own indigenous medicine, which has been losing force, and an interest in reconstructing a valid indigenous health concept. In this context, it is important that western medicine is not used as a means of power in the local community by key persons with access to western drugs. The Peruvian director of the Indigenous Health Programme, Lic. Juan Reátegui, is an Aguaruna from the northern Peruvian montaña, and has himself felt a dilemma, as a university-educated nurse, in implementing western medicine within traditional indigenous cultures of the Amazon [see the interview with Juan Reátegui Silva page 98 in Spanish edition]. He has emphasised the importance of regaining the part of indigenous knowledge that has been lost, and of formulating alternatives in the concept of health among the indigenous peoples. He stresses the significance of indigenous self-development and self-determination.

We encountered different attitudes in the local communities towards the use of traditional medicine versus western medicine. Some people consider that one should aim for traditional medicine as it is cheap, whereas, for example, the local teachers - who often administer the supply of western drugs - may prefer western biomedicine, partly because of its higher prestige in the national society and connotations of progress and modern development. In most indigenous groups, the shaman applies dreams and visions in diagnosing diseases and, in certain communities, all men and women can dream and treat to some extent, but only those who are regularly able to make a diagnosis are recognised as shamans. In other indigenous groups, curing songs are applied whose words are primordial and difficult to learn (up to 50 letters per word) and have many different meanings and should rather be regarded as names which hold spiritual power than words in the usual sense.

Indigenous medicine is dealt with by the local healers (*curanderos*),

The gentlemen Torres, Skielboe and Thuesen in the OAGP. Photo: Bente Korsgaard, 1998

vapour-healers (*vaporadoras*) and midwives (*parteras*). Training is given locally, combining treatment systems, and in many communities there are well-kept herbal gardens laid out to supply the village with plant medicines. However, certain species are considered to lose their powers once cultivated. There is a growing demand for knowledge of medicinal herbs and their effects, a knowledge which is often highly gender specific. However, each indigenous society has its own system, making it impossible to outline general rules. The cultural specificity of each group must be acknowledged and the variation in gender specific knowledge is surprisingly great. One example of this are the traditionally trained midwives, who obviously play an important role in a society where many children are born. The midwife employs, among other things, body therapy, including determination of the position of the foetus. But even this function - so intimately connected to the female universe - can also be exercised by men. Although the exception, we met male midwives in most of the groups the project was working with.

The vapour healers among the Asháninka (*vaporadoras*), mostly women, use vapour by cooking certain plants while the sick person, dressed in a traditional cotton tunic ("cusma" in local Spanish), straddles the pot boiling on the fire with legs wide while the vapours act on the body, including the airways, by leading the curing plant spirits into the sick person's body. The remains of the plants at the bottom of the pot show that the evil has been removed from the sick person's body. After the procedure, the patient is bathed with cold water. Although vapour healing is mostly the women's speciality, we have also come across a few men practising vapour treatment, and traditional male shamanism, such as the special tobacco shamanism, also has a few women practitioners.

There is an extraordinary biodiversity in the Amazon, with an estimated 40,000-50,000 plant species, only half of which have probably been identified. About 1,200 wild plants can be used for, among other things, medical treatment. In recent years, there has been significant interest on the part of international medical companies in exploiting the ancient indigenous knowledge of medicinal plants in order to develop new drugs without compensation, threatening the traditional Amazonian medicine by, among other things, taking out patents. In consequence there is a great need to protect indigenous intellectual property. According to literature, the use of plant medicine can be traced to around 1300 B.C. The most famous traditional plant medicine in the Amazon is very likely *Ayahuasca* or *Yagé* (*Banisteriopsis caapi*), a species of liana which, after proper preparation in combination with components from other plants (e.g. *Psychotria sp.*), is ingested by certain shamans who then fall into a trance of feeling at one with the universe through visions and a changed perception of time, space and sound. Some indigenous groups, like the Ashéninka, emphasise tobacco use instead of ayahuasca or in combination with it in a different sort of treatment. Apart from this, ayahuasca and other psychoactive drugs are used with apparently good results in the psychotherapy of drug abusers in a rehabilitation centre in Tarapoto in northern Peru. Another traditional drug which is encountered in most indigenous communities of the Upper Ucayali is "Cat's Claw" ("*Uña de Gato*": *Uncaria Tomentosa*) which has now become well-known world-wide due to a booming world market for alternative medicine. Cat's Claw, which is claimed to strengthen the immune system, has been marketed aggressively by the pharmaceutical industry in the US, Europe and Japan, and can now be found as capsules in any well-stocked drug store in all major cities of the world (El Dorado 1997: 51-71).

Becoming a shaman

A shaman may have 6 months - 3 years initial training before he or she attains the required spiritual state of mind, but it is estimated locally that 20 years of experience are necessary to be a fully qualified shaman. Potential shamans are selected from among youngsters who are believed to have the ability to make contact with the spirits. The young potential shamans are trained by older shamans either in their own community or in other communities where there is a lack of shamans. The training of the shaman student is aimed at illnesses with a spiritual dimension which, in fact, means most of them. During four months of training, the student shaman adheres to a special diet, ingests neither salt nor sugar and is sexually abstinent. He/she employs different drugs such as hallucinogens (*Banisteriopsis sp.*) and stimulants such as coca and tobacco, which are used while the older shaman controls the session by singing and other ritual performances. After some months of initial training, the shaman student may be able to cure simple diseases but the training continues, even if the shaman and his apprentice live in different communities, because spiritual contact can be created if necessary, e.g. by the use of tobacco to which the shaman student always has access. In general, the apprentices are taught about the powers and medical properties of plants through trances, visions and dreams.

The shamans are considered to be designated by the spirits of the ancestors and may easily make enemies. Shamans in the Upper Ucayali may either treat under the influence of ayahuasca or exclusively with tobacco but, in spite of their traditional training, the shamans may also use western drugs for certain complaints; it is important that they also use our western biomedical systems because the shamans in many societies are key persons with great influence. The shamans have the possibility of doing good but also the ability of doing damage to a person through sorcery. A fine balance is required. If the patient does not recover in spite of the treatment of the shaman, then the shaman may run the risk of being accused of sorcery.

Bridging the gap

The cultural gap between western and indigenous Amazonian concepts of health may, of course, result in unfortunate consequences. During an inspection journey, we visited a debilitated and emaciated man who had previously had tuberculosis. The professional staff in the project suspected that there was a recurrence of his tuberculosis, and the patient was given proper tuberculosis treatment. This was stopped, apparently due to side effects of the drugs. Later on, it appeared that the patient's brother, who was chief of the village and, furthermore, the shaman, had interfered with the treatment and had prescribed a diet which was probably the cause of the patient's aggravated condition.

There is apparently an understanding among the shamans to restrict their treatment mainly to the psychological causes of diseases or existential problems, while the treatment of what are considered physical diseases is handed over to promoters or nurses. However, the indigenous classification of what is physical and what is not is ambiguous and varies from context to context. Moreover, mistreatment by shamans of patients with physical problems does occur now and then. On one occasion, one shaman has thus, to our knowledge, treated a sick child by administering petrol. The project staff intervened and the child was treated properly. These cases illustrate the problems that can occur if there is not a mutual understanding between western and traditional medicine; however, it should be emphasised that such understanding is common and encouraged within the indigenous health programme.

It is a leading idea in the programme that traditional medicine and western medicine should complement each other, partly because traditional medicine is an integral part of ancient indigenous culture, which would consequently be strengthened, and partly because of a lack of access to expensive western medicine in the foreseeable future. The indigenous cultures have been much influenced by the various Christian missions but, in recent years, the Indians have developed a new self-confidence based on their own cultural values and the recognition of new rights. This project can contribute to such awareness raising. The combined anthropological and medical approach of the health project may, hopefully, avoid the creation of the problems that many western development projects have inflicted on vulnerable ethnic minorities over the years. It is important to create a sustainable health programme based on the individual, the family and the local community (Tarimo 1991:58-74).

Health for the individual and the family can be promoted through a healthy way of living, for example, through cleanliness, no-smoking (smoking has not hitherto been a problem among the indigenous groups involved in the project), good nutrition, and clean water that is protected against contamination. Hygiene and good sanitation go hand-in-hand with proper nutrition. Prevention of specific diseases such as malaria, diagnosis and treatment of diseases in combination with the use of any existing health service are other aspects of the health work for individuals and families.

The local community itself plays a major role in the health project, which is highly dependent on a kind of primary health care, with the involvement of the key people in the community such as the shaman, health promoters and the local teacher. It would be of great significance if the health project would lead to a formal education of assistant nurses - male and female - who would be firmly rooted in the local society just like the local teacher.

A reliance on traditional values and resources, in combination with basic western medical practices at nearly "barefoot doctor" level could, to our way of thinking, be a considerate and sustainable way of promoting health in the indigenous Amazonian societies.

Concluding remarks

On our first visit to the project areas in the Peruvian Amazon, we had only a vague knowledge of indigenous medicine. The combined medical and anthropological approach to the project fascinated us, but we were uncertain as to whether this dualism was going to work in practice. We are trained in modern biomedicine based on science, although it has to be admitted that many medical problems may not be solved by science alone.

Even after thorough preparation prior to journeying to Peru, someone will attain only a superficial knowledge of the indigenous concept of disease, a concept that belongs to another world far from our medical universe. Indigenous medical treatment is based on different modalities, as previously described, which as we understand it are applied to a number of well-defined somatic diseases, although the treatment is also used for psychic and psychosomatic disorders. It is impossible to make comparisons between the two medical systems. It is nevertheless interesting to observe that indigenous medicine also makes use of treatments which, in principle, resemble western methods of treatment, as for example: different ointments and drugs that are extracted from trees and herbs; vapour treatment, which has been used in various forms in the European medical system for centuries; as well as various kinds of body therapy which, in other variations, have been known for a long time in western medicine. We find it difficult to assess the role of psychotherapy in indigenous medicine but it occurs without doubt in various versions related, for instance, to vapour treatment and tobacco therapy. As previously mentioned, ayahuasca can put the shaman in a spiritual state giving him psychotherapeutic powers. The use of plant medicine is age-old in western medical culture, where many decoctions have been used in folk medicine. Nowadays, plant medicine is widespread in, for example, Switzerland, Austria and Germany and, likewise, alternative treatment has gained popularity in Denmark over the last decades, for instance the use of exotic plant species and preparations such as ginseng.

We are convinced that the collaboration between anthropologists and health professionals has been of great importance for the success of the health project. In order to introduce a health project in indigenous communities that are day trips away from governmental health centres, it is necessary to establish a relationship of trust with the population, one that includes respecting their way of life. This is, to our mind, best facilitated by anthropological expertise, and by trying to preserve traditional medicine and simultaneously make use of modern effective basic drugs aimed at prevalent diseases, e.g. tuberculosis and leishmaniasis; whereas indigenous medicine could, in our opinion, be used in particular to cure psychosomatic complaints. It is important that the indigenous population is instructed in using basic drugs as self-medication from a local medicine depot, which could be run by an indigenous assistant nurse.

The majority of the population in the world employs self-medication because there is no access to a proper medical service. Without doubt, basic health information and education in hygiene and sanitation would be of essential value for the state of health in the indigenous communities.

We believe that the health project - which is relatively cheap compared to other high tech medical projects - has created a sustainable health system that is largely independent of the governmental Peruvian health sector, which has difficulties in reaching remote areas in the country. We also believe that the medico-anthropological approach, with involvement of the local population, could be a model for future health projects in developing countries.

References

Elsass, Peter and Kirsten Hastrup (eds.).
1986   *Sygdomsbilleder.* Copenhagen: Gyldendal.

Fock, Niels
1986   "Sygdom, sundhed, liv og død." [Illness, health, life and death.]
        In: Peter Elsass and Kirsten Hastrup (Eds.). *Sygdomsbilleder.*
        Copenhagen: Gyldendal.

Gray, Andrew
1996-97 *The Arakmbut of Amazonian Peru, vol. 1-3.* Oxford: Bergkahn
        Books.

Perú Mágico
1997   Eldorado - Perú. *Revista Internacionál del Perú. No.6,* Enero-
        Marzo. Lima: ProdePeru.

Tarimo, Eleuter
1991   *Towards a Healthy District.* Geneva: WHO.

Wulff, Henrik R. and Peter C. Götzsche.
1997   *Rationel klinik, 4. ed.* Copenhagen: Munksgaard.

Wulff, Henrik R, Andur Pedersen and Raben Rosenberg.
1986   *Philosophy of medicine.* Oxford: Blackwell

Old specialist, the community of Nuevo Paraiso.　　　　*Photo: Cæcilie Mikkelsen 2000*

Photo page 273: Shipibo woman spinning.
Photo: Cæcilie Mikkelsen, 2000

Photo page 274: Coordinator Moisés Ramos, midwife Rosa Valera and
Ezequiel Augustín, president of ORDECONADIT.
Photo: Søren Hvalkof, Ucayali 2000

Shipibo-Conibo specialists and midwives.   *Photo: Søren Hvalkof, Ucayali 2000*

Yine representatives, Lower Urubamba.   *Photo: Jim Thuesen, 1998*

Don Luis, boat pilot and shaman, Ucayali River.   Photo: Jim Thuesen, 1994

A Yine woman explaining, Ucayali.   Photo: Jim Thuesen, 1993

Ex-patient and daughters, Ucayali.　　　　　　　Photo: *Søren Hvalkof, 2000*

Ashéninka women, Ucayali, after recovery.　　　　　Photo: *Søren Hvalkof, 2000*

Health promotor Martin and his family, Shumahuani,
Gran Pajonal.

Photo: Søren Hvalkof, 1996

Assembly in OAGP, Gran Pajonal.

Photo: Søren Hvalkof, 2000

Grandmother with grandchildren, Gran Pajonal. *Photo: Søren Hvalkof, 1996*

Young Ashéninka, Gran Pajonal. *Photo: Søren Hvalkof, 1996*

Ayahuasca vision.   *Art work by Noé Silva Morales, 2000*

Pascual

Pascual Camaiteri Fernández is President of the Ashéninka Organisation of Gran Pajonal (OAGP) and responsible for the Indigenous Health Programme in the area.

Introducing health into Gran Pajonal

It was rather difficult to begin the Programme, to gather the people in one place to talk to them about the Programme. For them, it was the first time that people had talked to them about a programme. As the person in charge, I talked to the chiefs of all the communities about the Programme to rescue and recover our customs, our languages, our dances. This Programme was going to work in all the native communities and the people asked me why there had been no such programme before. I explained to them that we had signed an agreement with some institutions so as not to lose our customs and, above all, to strengthen our organisation, the OAGP.

The chiefs told us that this Programme was good and welcomed us and gave us encouragement to work. Now the Programme has come to fruition, it's up and running and is more organised. The medicines are now being planted; there are now sheripiaris and vapour healers. It has truly been a success and the communities now have their promoters. This is what the communities were told, that the Programme was seeking to leave something, leave a future, for when the programme no longer existed. Now, unfortunately, the Programme is coming to an end. The people now trust us and we are getting to know the nurses and the coordinators better. The coordinators even talk to the women about health, how to care for their children, how to feed them and improve their lives.

Now the communities are already sowing their gardens, they have their medicine chests, their community centres, and are well-organised. Some communities have not grasped it all very well but when they see how the other communities are working, they will want to do the same.

The Programme ends in July but we are going to continue working, with our sheripiaris and by supporting the promoters, through the purchase of medicines, restocking the medicine chests. We will go on working and coordinating for ever.

Esther

Esther Chiri Santiago is the PSI coordinator in Gran Pajonal. She lives in the community of Ponchoni. This is where OAGP has its base and offers space to the Programme. She has worked for years as a leader and expert on the issue of Indigenous Women with OAGP, being very active in support of her organisation.

Organising the women

I first worked with the Programme in 1996, when we visited the communities of Gran Pajonal, seeing how we could re-assess our indigenous medicine, such as the *ivenqui, pintsi, chocawontsi*, etc. We are also organising because, previously, we did not realise that we had value as women but now, in actual fact, we have the same rights as men within the organisations. In the native communities, we have decided that the women should learn our indigenous medicine, how to cure, how to use western medicine. We are also rescuing our human resources, our doctors, sheripiaris, vapour healers, even our promoters, too, because we had forgotten our customs, our indigenous medicines. But now we are working with our indigenous medicine, we have even sown these plants around our house, in our fields.

The communities have rescued their medicines, sowing them around their houses. We have visited the communities and motivated them to produce, for example, textiles, *saratos* [bags], *cushmas* [cotton tunics], baskets and so on. Thanks to the Indigenous Health Programme we are going in the right direction and the women are now participating in the Women's Organisation. We are now encouraging them to sow quite a lot of cotton. We have two types, one is red, the other white. We are also encouraging the dying of this cotton and we now have our own colours. The women are now making their cushmas at home and the community members are asking us when they will have enough to be able to sell. So it would be good if the Programme could support or encourage more handicrafts.

Thanks to the Programme, we now have our sheripiaris and our vapour healers, who have been able to teach and who are leaving students behind them. We would also like to thank the organisation, for it takes good care of the communities. This is why we have worked for four years, leaving our families, our homes, to go from community to community and, through these efforts, we have achieved our desired objective.

Thanks to the Indigenous Women's Organisation of Gran Pajonal [OMIAGP], there are now far fewer complaints on the part of the women of mistreatment by of their husbands. We also tell the women not to give their under-age daughters away to be married. Such things now rarely occur, nor are men with two wives as common as they were before. In the communities, we tell the women there are laws that support us.

President of OAGP, Pascual Camaiteri, with his grandson. Photo: Cæcilie Mikkelsen, 2002

Voices III: Leaders, Promoters and Patients

Martín

*Martín Incaniteri Ema is 34 years old. He is Ashéninka belonging to the commu-
nity of Shumahuani in Gran Pajonal, where he works as a health promoter. He
was initially trained by a Swiss missionary who has worked for many years in
Gran Pajonal supporting the communities and also supporting the Indigenous
Health Programme through the regional organisation, OAGP.*

Continual education

I began to train in Ponchoni with Miss Liselotte from the Swiss Mission,
because then I knew nothing. She taught me to work with medicines and
has given us training on several occasions. She has even shown us how to
carry the patients to the communities [ed.: after treatment outside]. When
the training ended, we came to the community to give talks to our community members.

The training has helped me to solve problems of sickness and diarrhoea, coughs and tuberculosis. I was taught all of this and we often go to
Ponchoni to receive more training. Now they are teaching us how to use
medicines, how to treat patients and they are sending us to our community for practical experience.

Miss Liselotte told me that, as I had started as a promoter, I was still
not going to receive a salary, that I had to work to support the community, and she gave me the medicines to enable me to begin. I began to treat
all those who came to the post, children and their mothers. I told them I
did not have much medicine, that I still needed further training in medicine and that later, I would bring them more support.

In Oventeni, we were given training in giving injections. At first I
was the only one, but more promoters came later. These included my son-
in-law Daniel and now we are working together. Now they are going to
give us the medicines to give injections.

Sometimes the community members don't want to help us for they
say that we know nothing, that we will go astray, and they don't realise
that we are going to continue being educated, for the good of their children and of the community. We also have our other work, for example, I
have my fields.

The promoters have to be called upon when something serious hap-
pens, for example a snake bite. For snake bites, we also have wild herbs.
This is *piripiri* that I have sown here and also *ivenqui*, which is used for a
jergón [*Bothrops pictus*] snake bite. The nurse tells us that we have to use
traditional plants, and that we have to have a plot on which to sow them

and explain to people how to use them. But there are still some that have not sown.

Here in the community, my dad is the sheripiari and he has helped the community. There are also vapour healers working well and they are supported with western medicines. When there is an injury that the promoters cannot cure with western medicine, then the vapour healer takes over. My stepmother Laura is a vapour healer and has learnt quite a lot, she even has two students, one is my nephew. It is not only women who can be vapour healers. The sheripiaris also have apprentices.

Sometimes the nurses come to the communities to talk to us and they ask the community members how we are working and, if there are no problems, we continue our work.

The nurse went to Chequitavo and we went with her to receive training before returning to our community to give talks, about how to avoid falling ill. They taught us that you must wash your hands before eating, to prevent illnesses. As we are two promoters, sometimes one of us goes to the training session and the other stays to treat patients. Last time, my son-in-law went to the one in Catoteni.

Miss Isolina told us that the Indigenous Health Programme is coming to an end and she came to say goodbye to us. We gave her a good send off, butchering a cow.

Martín's sister, Shumahuani, Gran Pajonal.   *Photo: Søren Hvalkof, 1987*

Viviano

Viviano Huaris Chunisho is 23 years old, and promoter from the Ashéninka com-munity of Quemporquishi in Gran Pajonal, trained by the OAGP.

Western and indigenous medicine

I put my name forward for a position as voluntary promoter because I wanted to help my community and, thanks to the nurse, María Isolina, from the Indigenous Health Programme, we are on the way to being good promoters. I have already been on several training courses in different communities. First in Quemporquishi, twice, then in Bajo Chencoreni and, lastly, in Shumahuani. Then I started practising and I learnt to cure ill-nesses such as infections and also venereal diseases.

Through our coffee fields, we are able to continue to purchase west-ern medicines. We sell coffee in order to restock the health post's medicine chest. We also work with the sheripiaris and vapour healers and we would like to thank the Programme for the guidance it has given us with indige-nous medicines, such as the medicine for snake bites, *manqui* [snake in Ashéninka], for example, which is called *catahua* [*Hura crepitans*] in Spanish. It is a sap that is produced when a particular tree is cut, and this milky sap is rubbed into the snake bite every day.

Esther (centre), with the precidency of the OAGP.   Photo: Søren Hvalkof, 2000

Edgar

Edgar Camaiteri Viriña, Ashéninka from Gran Pajonal, is 27 years old. He is the promoter in Quirahuanero, which is the neighbour community to Catoteni, and belonging to the OAGP.

Inspiration and use

My community put their trust in me by appointing me as a promoter. As we have two professionals here, they have been training us for the past four years in how to cure the illnesses that exist in the community.

I have attended five training sessions now so I have a little more knowledge than the others in treating patients who come to the health post. In addition, as promoters we came to an agreement with the community that each member would contribute 10 kg. of coffee for sale in order to buy medicines, so that we would not lack anything and we would be able to continue treating our patients. Therefore we thank the Indigenous Health Programme for having supported us and having given us an idea of what we can do, in order to be able to work with the sheripiaris and vapour healers, and to be able to work with both kinds of medicine, both that of plants and western. If we cannot cure, because an illness is due to some form of witchcraft, we take the patient to the sheripiari or to the vapour healer. We work with the whole community and with the chief, well, they appointed me as promoter. This is why I would like to say: thank you, the Programme has been very useful.

Photo: Søren Hvalkof, 1986   *Grinding maize, Gran Pajonal.*

Rómulo

Rómulo Leiva Rosi is Ashéninka, originally from the community of Catoteni, but now living in Anexo Quirawanero. He works for OAGP as a health promoter and coordinator in Sector I, covering 13 communities of Gran Pajonal.

Organisation and promotion

The organisation appointed me as promoter after I had participated in many events, seminars, workshops and assemblies. I talked to my family about it as it is a very responsible job. I have eight children; four are at the bilingual primary school in Catoteni and one at the Mañarini agro-industrial college. My family agreed to my joining the Indigenous Health Programme in order to gain some experience. I attended a training workshop for coordinators and I found out what the aims were and what my role as field coordinator would be, and also what you had to share with the communities, because indigenous health is holistic, you cannot look at health without looking at the whole environment.

The first area of work that has to be carried out is to look at the community's organisation, because to go to a community that is not organised is a waste of time. My first job was to visit the 27 communities with the work team, a coordinator and a nurse, and to hold meetings to find out where to start. I learnt that the first thing is to organise the community and then seek out and promote the human resources such as sheripiaris, vapour healers, and others with knowledge of indigenous medicines. We have to interview the oldest people in the community, for they are the ones with the most knowledge. They always ask us why we are seeking the sheripiaris now, because previously they had been forgotten. We tell them that we have an organisation supporting us and that this is a way of strengthening our organisation.

As Sector I coordinator, I have 13 communities under my supervision and in them there are 18 sheripiaris. Each sheripiari has his students, around 14.

The sheripiaris came to the organisation's most recent Congress and I told them that we have rescued 95% of our indigenous medicine. We have *piripiri*, which we call *ivenqui* and which has different uses. *Manquivenqui* is piripiri for snake bites. *Charivenqui* is very useful for serious wounds and *wañurivenqui* is carried as a charm if there is some kind of confrontation. *Pinitsi* is *pusanga* in Spanish, which is used to hypnotise and quieten people. You try to tranquillise them with this. There are many varieties of piripiris and herbs and I have in my notebook a report on how to use them. Sometimes there are herbs in one community that are not used by another. We are trying to re-evaluate this and share it with those who do not know it, so that they share what they are doing with others. This is an achievement of the Indigenous Health Programme. The aim is to re-evaluate our culture, our arts, the songs for example, handicrafts such as arrows, bows, drums. Also the *inkishiwantsi* and *inkishorentsi*, which are dances for festivals. The women enter spinning round, following the men. It is very pretty and we have also endeavoured to prevent this from being forgotten, we encourage that they continue to practise their dances. I am an Ashéninka but I grew up outside my culture. But this does not mean that I have forgotten my culture. I am always here with my people.

All the knowledge I have acquired I have to share with my family and my community.

The secondary school, OAGP, Gran Pajonal.   *Photo: Cæcilie Mikkelsen, 2002*

Efraín

Efraín Inuma Torino, from the Shipibo-Conibo people, was born in 1970. He is a teacher and mayor of the district municipality of Tahuanía. He was the first indigenous mayor of the district and has recently been re-elected for a second term.

Being Indigenous Mayor

I was Secretary of Minutes and Archives for the organisation ORDE-CONADIT and, from there, my indigenous brothers chose me as municipal candidate. The authorities looked down on some leaders, saying that they were incapable, would not show up, that the mestizos were the ones that were capable. But, thanks to some young students who visited the local town, we realised that it was time to elect an indigenous mayor. The people cast their vote in the elections of November 1995 and, since 1996, I have held this very responsible position. I would like to thank the native communities, my Asháninka and Shipibo brothers. In response, I have worked harder, I have implemented more works in the native communities. Of course, they all wanted to know why a particular community did not have a school, a radio or a satellite dish like the *mestizos*. When I first started, I gave some communities these kinds of things or communication equipment. Thanks to the united work of the councillors, most of them Asháninka and Shipibo, we came to agreements with the communities and became strong, this was why we were elected by the communities and why we are now working hard.

For the second election, we held a congress in the community of Betijay where, after much criticism, both constructive and destructive, I was once more chosen as candidate for mayor, together with Mr. Andrés Encinas López, who represented the Asháninka community. It was not easy to take over a municipality and continue working as one thought fit. We have had to withstand such strong blows, as Cesar Vallejo says in one of his poems, setbacks that we sometimes thought would suddenly destroy us, or remove us from the municipality and enable them to say that we natives are incapable. But with our limited experience we have had to defend and, together with brother Andrés, represent the native communities. Now the *mestizos* are moaning. In the future, others will have the opportunity to ensure that the indigenous continue in government and, thankfully, since 1995 ORDECONADIT and OIRA have had a joint strategy that has led us to this triumph.

I would like to thank the donor for the Health Programme, together with the organisations OIRA and ORDECONADIT, who supported the project, and all the people who were involved with the indigenous communities. I can tell them that many of my patients have been saved thanks to this Programme, and that the promoters from the different communities and the nurses have always shown great concern for the indigenous communities. I feel that the Programme should not come to an end, and I would suggest they support us for another couple of years, until the work is consolidated. The state has never given the necessary attention to patients coming from the communities. But many people have been treated through the indigenous health project.

Efraín and his vice-mayor.   *Photo: Søren Hvalkof, 2000*

Moisés

Moisés Ramos Maynas from the Conibo people was born in the community of Betijay. He is 25 years old. In 1998 he was elected as Secretary of Minutes and Archives of the organisation ORDECONADIT. He subsequently held the post of Health Programme coordinator for the Shipibo-Conibo sector.

Working with the communities

On 10th August 1998, Dr. Jim arrived together with brother Juan Reátegui, who is a qualified nurse, and Dr. Luis Torres. That day, the Shipibo-Conibo people elected brother Ezequiel as president of the organisation and appointed me to coordinate the Health Programme. In October, I left to visit the three communities. First I saw the work of the first phase of the project and its continuation. In the first trip, we held meetings with the community, we coordinated with the community chief and then we organised an assembly to explain why we were visiting them. In all the communities, we looked at what human resources they had, the *onanyas* [shamans], midwives and vapour healers. We call the midwives *vaque byabo* in Shipibo and the vapour healers, *quamis*. They were given recognition by us. During my first trip, they also recognised me as a leader and coordinator. We both got to know each other and we have worked with 25 *onanyas*, 4 students, 5 bonesetters, 18 birth attendants and 19 vapour healers.

The community was quite supportive and when we called the assembly, the entire village came. We told them how to build family gardens, where they could sow plants, those that exist around our houses and those found in the wild in the highlands and lowlands. Then we worked largely with the *onanyas*, because they know the plants well. We sowed the plants that they knew and also the *piripiris*. The authorities have also helped us a great deal and I would like to thank them, for example, for restocking the medicines.

At first, the community members were confused and they said that the funding agency had donated the medicines and many said that the promoter did not want to treat them. But we told them that the medicines were not a gift but an endowed stock of medicines. And they didn't understand what endowed meant. With the little they give us, we ourselves have to work, for example, in communal fields, or logging. Other communities have sold some of their produce and are replacing the medicines. Then they understood. The promoters are now trained and they have medicines. I remember that, previously, the communities had no medicines but now they can be seen in all the communities. Not in great quantities, but they do have them and the most important thing is that they have the basics and they also have their family gardens, with medicinal plants. Not long ago, we held a meeting with the shamans and we discussed with them what they thought about the project coming to an end. They said that no-one could take from them the knowledge they have, they were going to continue working just the same, as they did before, training pupils, teaching interested people - that is their work. The same goes for the midwives and vapour healers, for they don't need training, they have learnt from their ancestors.

We have all worked, the community members, the midwives, the vapour healers, the *onanyas* themselves, and also the *sheripiaris*.

Culture and organisations

I am grateful for having gained this experience. I am now 25 and have two years' experience as a leader. When I arrive in the communities I tell them that we have to learn to value our medicinal plants once more, those that were used by our ancestors. What is it that makes the indigenous people more interested in western things than traditional ones? With the guidance we are giving them, they are beginning to realise what the cultural side of things is all about. Before, they didn't listen to the music that they listen to now. Before, our grandparents danced with drums, but now in the big festivals everything is with music. They must realise that we have to value our culture, including our handicrafts such as ceramics and fabrics.

We had problems in some communities as employers have entered without consulting anyone, without making agreements. We had to find a solution to a problem in the community of San Fernando de Vainilla. There a man had married an Asháninka who lived there and he wanted to organise the whole village, dividing it, causing problems between the Shipibo and Asháninka. We coordinated with the president and the team and we held an assembly, so that they would not continue to go in the wrong direction, so that there was no revenge between brothers and we were thus able to resolve this problem.

Manuel

Manuel Sangama Flores is 25 years old and comes from the Ashéninka commu-
nity of Nuevo Paraíso. He is coordinator and promoter for the 21 Asháninka and
Ashéninka communities that are members of the Indigenous Regional
Organisation of Tahuanía district, ORDECONADIT.

Legitimising the sheripiaris

At first, I knew nothing of the aims of the project, we just worked to rescue the human resources, the *sheripiaris*, vapour healers and midwives.
Previously, the sheripiaris were not recognised. They lived hidden in the
countryside, they were persecuted, tortured, killed. The people called
them devils, witches. But when the Indigenous Health Programme came
along, we rescued the sheripiaris and strengthened the midwives and
vapour healers. We visited the communities asking for them, but they told
us that the sheripiaris lived far from the community, that they were afraid
they would be beaten, whipped or killed. So they were living in hiding.
But when their children fell ill, the people would go and bring the sheripiari to the community. And when the children were cured, the people
would pay by giving him a canoe, a cushma or other things.

When the people embarked on the second stage of the Programme,
all the sheripiaris were happy for they were now being recognised. We
told them that they were already recognised in the organisation, that they
were no longer persecuted, that they could work in peace, curing and
teaching others.

They only used to cure their children, grandchildren, their family.
But now they are curing within their community. There is a great deal of
illness in the community of Toniromashi, and there is a sheripiari called
Alberto, and Mario Díaz is a sheripiari and promoter. They are working
well, curing patients. Here in Puerto Alegre we also have our sheripiari,
who is working really well. He is happy that we have given him supplies
and he would like to thank the Programme and AIDESEP. The organisation supports them and now they feel relaxed and happy in the community in which they work. The sheripiaris say they are going to continue
working and teaching their children, grandchildren and even their wives.
In other words, they do not want to lose their knowledge, so that in the
future their children can continue to teach and cure the community.

I have now been working with ORDECONADIT for four years. We
have our expert, vapour healer and midwife. They teach us how to use ojé
and I am practising a little with medicinal plants. I know a lot about cur-

ing bites, from snakes, scorpions, spiders and other insects that you find in the forest. I am always practising and I have saved several patients. We have an *ivenki piripiri*, which is very effective for snake bites. We have gathered this knowledge from our sheripiaris, our vapour healers and our midwives.

I have written a list of all the medicinal plants, their dosage, treatment, diets. When a snake bites you, then you always have to keep to a particular diet, such as fish cooked in our style. I have many medicinal plants to make you a hunter and other things too.

Carlos

Carlos Vasquez Vasquez is a member of the Asháninka people, he is 34 years old and has, at different times, been president of OIRA and responsible coordinator for the PSI.

Leaders in the field

In this Programme, the promoters are very clear about what their role is, and so are we and the communities as well. We are working via an agreement with the nurses from the health centre and in coordination with the health promoters.

Everyone wants the project to continue. The promoters have said that they are going to continue with the work in their communities, as the villages have placed their trust in them. This is why they were appointed promoters.

I would like to thank NORDECO for having supported OIRA through AIDESEP in this project. OIRA must continue, it has to continue with the work that has been planned together with the Programme Director, Juan Reategui.

It is important that the Programme Director and I are in the communities, that the communities' problems are not dealt with in the offices. It is important that we are there, so that they can listen to us, so that they know the goals of the project. We also want the AIDESEP leaders here in the communities because, as I have said, problems can't be resolved in an office.

We want indigenous people to be trained as health promoters because the others who come are not used to it here. The trained indigenous promoters from among our people have to work with the communities. This is what the whole institution wants.

Javier

Javier Prado Pishica, 38 years of age, was one of the founders of his Asháninka community of Tzinquiato or Nuevo San Francisco, and was previously its chief. He has worked as a voluntary promoter on the different health programmes for 11 years. Now he is working as a promoter with OIRA in the Atalaya zone.

Experiences with different health programmes

I have been trained and I have learnt how to handle and administer medicine. And this is what I enjoy doing, treating patients and using traditional medicines as I do now. This is what our organisation, OIRA, has accomplished so that we do not lose our traditional medicine. I enjoyed this training and practical work a lot. I haven't studied much but I am still training, thanks to OIRA, which is giving us guidance.

Now we have a post or health centre here in the community and we also have a little medicine. With what funds we have we are also buying more medicine.

I have my wife and my children, who are also starting school. Now I am a volunteer but I have to go out and work to maintain my children.

We have three promoters here and we need more training. I don't know what we will do now the health project has been cut short.

I have 11 years' experience of this work. I have worked for the organisations [Save the] Children and ADAR since 1988 and they trained me, so this is why I want to support my community. I have experience but the second promoter is giving me guidance, teaching me and, as I say, we need more training.

Misael

Misael García López is 18 years old and promoter in the Ashéninka community of Boca Cocani in the upper Ucayali, trained by the Programme through OIRA.

A young promoter

I was trained as a promoter in 1995 and, here in the community, we work hard caring for the sick. We treat patients with all kinds of illnesses, and deliver babies. Sometimes, the nurse has to leave the community, and we are left here in charge.

We administer all kinds of medicines, for tuberculosis, malaria, pneumonia and for fever. We work the communal fields in order to replace the medicines and last year we organised a sports event to raise a little money.

There are three of us working as promoters in the community and, as the programme will soon be coming to an end, we would like more training, for the good of the community.

Orlando

Orlando Díaz Kinini is 29 years old and health promoter and chief of the Asháninka community of Tzinquiato, located in the Urubamba sector, belonging to the regional indigenous organisation, OIRA, Atalaya.

The beginning of the Programme

The Programme was started here because we had no medicines with which to cure our sick and we had to ask our organisation for help. We had been asking them for help for many years and the president himself had come on several occasions to observe the patients here, and he saw that we had nothing to treat them with. Some time later, the organisation began to give us help and so the Health Programme was developed.

We have always asked for our indigenous traditional medicine to be developed. Now we can develop the medicine of our forests once more, like our ancestors, and not leave it abandoned. We want to use it like our Asháninka fathers and we want to develop it once more. We know some of the medicinal plants, such as sedatives, but we don't know all of them. You have to go to the person who knows these kinds of plants, a *sheripiari*. We provide support, along with the sheripiaris and the vapour healers, by providing various medicinal plants.

Cholera

Cholera reached us here and we had around ten people ill but then the Programme arrived, with nurse Otilia, who came to the community. When we did not have rehydration solution she taught us how to use a plant from our region, with warm water, a teaspoon of salt and sugar. Coconut milk can also be used as a medicine and this helped us greatly. There was not one death.

The people of Tzinquiato are happy with the Health Programme. We are happy with what it has taught us and we would like to thank the people involved. But we also want the Programme to be continued, and not to stop just like that. There is so much more we could learn about the forest plants.

Mercedes

Mercedes is Ashéninka. We met her in Boca Sapani in Ucayali, where she told us her personal experience of the surgical campaign.

A hernia

Let me tell you how the pain started. I was carrying beans and I fell from a bridge. That was how the hernia started and, as it got worse, I started to get headaches as well. I didn't tell anyone about the hernia, I kept it hidden, but when it got really bad I told nurse Juana about it and then Dr. Torres came to see me. He told me that a surgical campaign was coming to Atalaya and that they could operate on me there. When the doctors came to Pucallpa, they moved me so that they could look at me and told me I had a hernia and operated on me. They asked me how I felt and I told them that I had headaches, that I felt sick and that I just wanted to lie down. But now I am fine. OIRA treated me, that is where my nephew Carlos is, and the nurse Juana, the doctors, they all helped me, they gave me pills. Whenever I was in pain I told nurse Juana, who treated me. They also gave me good food to eat.

Now I feel much better and I have no more pain. I can work and carry a little manioc but not too much, so that the problem doesn't return.

Antonio

Antonio Zapata Campos is from the Yine people; he is 42 years old and a member of the Santa Clara community in the lower Urubamba zone.

A renal cyst

I had a sickness known as a renal cyst [a kidney disease] and I suffered for five years, nearly six by the year 2000. I want to thank OIRA, who came here to the communities, and I thank nurse Beatriz. I told them personally that I had this illness, that it was affecting me greatly and that I could not breath, the pit of my stomach was closed. I thank OIRA for their help, for they were kind enough to support the communities, and Dr. Torres, who also came and saw my illness. He registered me for an operation in Pucallpa. The time came and on 18th April they took me to Atalaya where I spent two days. On the 24th we travelled to Pucallpa and on the 25th we went to the hospital with Dr. Torres to analyse my illness, and they told me it was a renal cyst. They analysed my whole body and told me to collect my results on 2nd May. When I returned they made me stay in the hospital for an eight-day diet. On 10th May I was taken to the operating theatre and they took a huge tumour out of me, weighing 1.7 kg. The doctor told me they had also had to remove my right kidney. Now I only have the left kidney and the doctor told me to take it easy and follow a strict diet for a year in order to recuperate. Then, slowly, I was to carry small weights until I got used to it. I recovered well from the operation, I was more concerned about my younger children whom I had left alone here but, in any case, I got back home OK, and I don't feel any pain. Now I am back to normal and I don't feel any pain. This is all I can say about my illness. Thank you very much.

The Future of the Indigenous Health Programme

By Juan Reátegui, Director, PSI-AIDESEP

The current situation

During its eight years of existence, the Indigenous Health Programme (PSI) has managed to rescue - from virtual oblivion - a group of men and women who have been maintaining the health traditions of their peoples. These wise people of the communities: sheripiaris, onanyas, vapour healers, traditional midwives, were stigmatised by western culture, particularly by the churches, who branded them as "witches", while rejecting and marginalising them. Through this project, and with the support of the communities and their organisations, the PSI has put these specialists back at the forefront of their communities, and has achieved a candid re-evaluation of their roles.

The PSI has also brought about a situation in which the indigenous populations, who have always visited their specialists in spite of religious and social pressures, can now approach these people without the slightest unease and are able to renew a general knowledge of their culture and its values. As a corollary of this, the knowledge of medicinal plants and teaching plants that their ancestors passed down so many generations is being preserved. The knowledge of *pinitzi, ivenki (piripiris)*, of hunting, fishing and gathering techniques in each community and each family has begun to be re-evaluated because the PSI promoters are not only indigenous leaders but also health professionals and specialists recognised by their organisations and their communities.

Meetings are beginning to be held between indigenous specialists, and between these specialists and their organisation and the health promoters with western knowledge, with the result of creating a climate of trust and harmonious co-existence, beyond all conflict. This has all been made possible by the PSI. The wise people, sheripiaris and others, have taken up their role as transmitters of culture once more, by teaching about their diets, agricultural and hunting techniques, as well as the preparation, use and handling of medicinal plants. The knowledge lost over many years of colonisation – both internal and external – is once more being developed in both young and old alike.

The PSI's professional nursing staff have trained the western Health Promoters, giving them not only information but also some basic resources to facilitate their work. These qualified promoters manage a Communal Medicine Chest, stocked by various sources, one of the most important being the community.

A commitment has been made by the communities, through their own decision-making mechanisms and systems, to restock the communal medicine chests by means of community cooperation. In some cases, *ad hoc* economic activities are being undertaken, in others they have agreed to cultivate a "community plot" for the chest. In yet others they have agreed to contribute part of their harvest, to contribute products or to organise events. The fundraising or sale will be used to restock the chests.

All these communal and individual forms of contribution demonstrate the importance the communities give to the System and show that they have made it their own. Moreover, this self-sustainability of the medicine chest ensures its long-term viability.

A sub-system for surgical care has been created for situations when community members may require it. This sub-system functions through coordination and cooperation between the Programme and the Ministry of Health.

Grassroots leaders and indigenous community representatives have been incorporated into the care system, and have committed their efforts to ensuring that the system that has been set up does not grind to a halt.

In short, the indigenous health system in the area of the rivers Tambo, Urubamba, Alto Ucayali and Gran Pajonal, the geographical area in which the PSI is located, is functioning under the management of local and community leaders and leaders of the regional federations of indigenous peoples.

The future project

The indigenous communities of the Amazon have the strength and conviction to maintain their health system. However, the AIDESEP leaders consider that, given the condition of the indigenous populations and the paucity of state services, this will be a very slow and costly process for the indigenous peoples.

That is why we are working to produce viable proposals in support of the community health promoters and indigenous medicine specialists who are working in the remote Amazonian communities and towns that have formed a part of this project.

In addition, the success of the Programme has led us to consider the best way of reproducing it elsewhere. In other words, we need to design a strategy to ensure that the Health System of the upper basins of the Ucayali and lower reaches of the Tambo, Urubamba and Gran Pajonal can be replicated in other areas with similar health problems. That is, where there has been an abandonment of indigenous medicine due to ideological and cultural pressures, and where there is still a lack of western medicine due to the people's poverty and the state's negligence.

If we are to accomplish these goals then there is an urgent need to mobilise human, economic and financial resources, such that the following tasks can be rapidly implemented:

A) Maintain a dynamic monitoring system for the Health System developed by the Project, which means designating and committing special funding to a monitoring and feedback project, in order that the work achieved is not lost and progress can be made in terms of self-management on the part of the communities themselves as well as their leaders; and:

B) Create, in the short term, a mechanism for logistical and technical professional support of the ongoing Health System, besides implementing new projects in the indigenous areas of greatest priority, as part of AIDESEP's global strategy of indigenous health policies.

One of these mechanisms is the planned Amazonian Intercultural Health Institute (INSIA), which will form the human resource training institute required by the health system and a centre for research, recording and dissemination of indigenous health technologies. These two priority tasks require technical and professional support, which will only be possible if we gain funding from international donors. The state will also need to commit itself to cooperation, and so an inter-institutional cooperation agreement has been established with MINSA's Institute for Human Resource Development (IDREH), which is providing management support in order to gain funding from MINSA's *PAR Salud* [Ministry of Health Programme of Support to a Reform of the Heath Sector].

In short, we propose to develop health alternatives for the indigenous peoples of the Amazon, implementing a model of treatment and care that is appropriate to the cultural diversity of the indigenous peoples, by training indigenous technicians in intercultural health and by training MINSA's health staff in an intercultural approach.

Visions and perspectives

Given that we are a representative institution of the indigenous peoples of Amazonia, we have the enormous task of leading them toward their historic destiny, which is none other than that of autonomy, self-determination and the human and sustainable development of future generations. We know, like our brothers among other peoples and our ancestors, that before setting off we need to know where we are going, that it is not possible to follow a route if we do not know our destination. For this, we want to unite the utopias of our peoples in one common utopia. Not in the sense of a rather absurd "Utopia" but in the sense given to it by our brothers from the Colombian Amazon, who say,

"Utopia is on the horizon; take two steps towards it and it moves back two steps; take ten steps towards it and it moves back ten steps. So, what is the use of utopia? It is this: to make you move forward."

Coordinator and boat pilot Luis Cushmariano with daughters. Photo: Søren Hvalkof, 2000

We want to walk, we want to progress, but we can only do this if we set our sights on a utopian horizon that reflects our most intimate aspirations as Amazonian peoples at the historic time our generation has been given to live in. Our utopia, which is presented in the form of a vision of the future, is this: that in the coming twenty years, the Amazonian peoples will have achieved full human development, with autonomy, exercising self-determination, and having forged a truly multicultural and multilingual Peruvian national state, in a world at peace and harmony with nature and with all men and women of the world.

Thus expressed, our vision of the future would be the ultimate objective of all Amazonian peoples and their organisations. The immediate and longer-term tasks could be divided into the categories outlined below.

Short-term plans

Our short-term plans are in fact set in the medium to long term. However, we could consider within an immediate timeframe those projects which, if they are not implemented this year or the next, would put at risk our medium-term plans.

On a general level, we are concerned at the absence of concrete policies for implementation of Article 8.j of the Convention on Biological Diversity. We have received the reports from the 5th Meeting of the Conference of Parties to the Convention, held in Nairobi in May 2000, in which indigenous peoples continue to show their concern at the lack of recognition of "our territories"; at the absence of control over bio-prospecting on the world's indigenous territories; and at the absence of clear standards for the recognition of the intellectual property of indigenous collective knowledge, including the repatriation of those resources being held *ex situ*.

All this still goes on, despite the fact that, in the meetings in Nairobi, the state authorities showed themselves to be highly concerned at the degradation of our planet, at the irreversible ecological disasters, and at the plundering of genetic resources developed and preserved by our peoples.

We are also concerned that a detailed inventory of our resources has not been undertaken, including the knowledge produced by our peoples over thousands of years. The western anthropologists and molecular biologists cannot produce this inventory because their vision is distorted by specialisation. We want to carry out our own inventory of resources, which would include indigenous technologies and which, unlike western technologies, are imbued with our world vision, our values and our faith. This inventory must be drawn up before the laws to be approved by the states signatory to the Convention dictate to us what is our knowledge and what is not, what is the knowledge available to businessmen and what must be negotiated with the indigenous peoples.

We are concerned that we must provide immediate support for the Indigenous Health System created by the PSI. We have formed the Amazonian Intercultural Health Institute (INSIA), which will be responsible for training the Intercultural Health Technicians in order to improve the indigenous health system already created and other systems to be created in the coming years in other areas of Amazonia. The task of the Amazonian Intercultural Health Institute will be not only to train the human resources required by our system in the area of health but also to research our natural resources and our collective knowledge of indigenous medicine and biodiversity.

Medium to long-term plans

Whilst it is clear that everything is urgent for the indigenous peoples, there are projects that can only bear fruit in the medium to long term. Such is the case of the education of our children, the building of cross-border dialogue with peoples in other states with which our territories overlap, equality of rights, quality of life for indigenous peoples, autonomy and self-determination.

Our children must be educated in the mother tongue of each child. In spite of scientific studies showing that the development of a child's basic capacities must be undertaken in that child's mother tongue, the schools in the Amazonian communities find it impossible to do this because the state is unable to provide true bilingual intercultural education, as described in the Ministry of Education's directives. The Ministry hires *mestizo* teachers who speak only Spanish. Text books are not produced in indigenous languages. There are no educational radio programmes in our languages. In other words, the dominant culture continues to implement an educational policy of acculturation, of imposition of western culture on new generations of Amazonian peoples, accompanied by new rhetoric.

We would like to have the strength and necessary resources to provide true bilingual intercultural schools, in which our children are educated on the basis of a skilful and consistent use of our language, the vocabulary of which contains all the values and knowledge of our ancestors, and the survival of which will guarantee our identity as peoples. We would like to have the necessary resources to be able to put an elder of our peoples in the community schools alongside the bilingual teacher, so that the oral heritage of our culture is not lost through the intrusion of western writing. We would like to have an Editorial Fund to publish all the books the schools need in their own languages, besides the recordings and videos that we could make with the wisest elders of our peoples.

Our schools attract the least qualified teachers. Some teachers consider a posting to a rural Amazonian school as a form of punishment. More classroom hours are lost here than in schools in the towns, even though these latter schools are the ones that lose most classroom hours in South America as a whole. The texts are appropriate to large cities and to western culture. In their "citizenship" classes, the children of indigenous peoples have to learn how to cross the road when the light is green! We are concerned about all these things and we would like to have the strength and resources to change them.

We Amazonian peoples are considered "exotics" in our own land. Thousands of people, also nationals of Peru, see us as exotic beings worthy of visiting on holiday. Others consider us as mere objects to be used in the logging industry, to the extent that we worked as slaves in many regions until less than ten years ago. Our daughters are taken to the city to do the hardest of work and the vilest of activities. Our leaders must fight a fierce battle to get the municipalities to control the "work" of girls in bars and brothels.

We are working, and will continue to do so, to ensure that our fellow Peruvians recognise us as equals in law, as being from a different culture but with equal rights. We will always be open to intercultural and empathetic dialogue with other peoples from the coast and mountains of Peru.

In the medium to long term, we aspire to being citizens, of the same class as other Peruvians, enriched by our cultural and linguistic differences. We want our identity as Amazonian peoples to be considered not as a disadvantage or burden for the state and Peruvian society but as a significant advantage and benefit that will, in the final analysis, help the people of Peru as a whole to escape the vicious circle of poverty and ignorance.

Mrs Rosa catching armoured catfish.   *Photo: Cæcilie Mikkelsen 2000*

Yine design

7. Prospects

Towards a Training Programme for Indigenous Health Technicians

By Juan Reátegui Silva, Director, PSI-AIDESEP

The indigenous health system a gold mine[1]

It is estimated that around 7,000 medical preparations used in the West come from plants brought to light by indigenous pharmacopoeia. Some 80% of the world's population depend for their health on knowledge and products derived from indigenous health systems. To this must be added the countless bacterial organisms and fungi found in indigenous soils and which are used for a variety of remedies, from anti-depressants to testosterone, from antibiotics to antimycotics, to name but a few. The pharmaceutical industry derives around US$32,000 million every year from this traditional germ plasma. Another two-thirds of the world's population survive on the basis of knowledge provided by indigenous peoples in relation to their ecosystems, animals, insects, microbes and crop cultivation methods. In the United States alone, foods used as medicines, the so-called nutraceutical sector, represents an additional US$27,000 million of trade.

However, it is not yet possible to construct our national health system on the basis of its own wealth of indigenous biotechnology. Peru does not recognise the many possible contributions the indigenous health systems of the Amazonian rainforests could make to its health programmes, previously recognised internationally as the main repositories of pharmacopoeic knowledge.

It is this reality that will now be examined, with the aim of isolating a set of processes and broad outlines that could be incorporated into a training programme for indigenous health technicians in the Peruvian Amazon. The objective is to effectively reverse the key health problems present in the region by making use of the potential offered by the indigenous health systems themselves.

To the rejection of indigenous biotechnology on the part of national health programmes must be added an indifference to the biodiversity that forms its necessary counterpart. This is, in turn, undervalued in state-approved health programmes.

Amazonian ecosystems are thus disintegrating, with a consequent and significant impact on health systems in at least three key areas, and yet this crucial process is not being taken into account in official health programmes:

Firstly, this breakdown is, in itself, linked to the development of increasingly significant illnesses, such as the Ebola virus, HIV or AIDS, dengue, Hanta virus, malaria (*vivax* and *falsiparum*), leishmaniasis, and increases in acute diarrhoea and ARIs (Acute Respiratory Infections), to name but a few. This is attributed to the delicate and complex interchanges or balances established within tropical ecosystems between parasites, hosts, predators and prey in the development of different types of infection. Forest destruction and man's interposition in the existing exchange cycles of such ecosystems lead to a proliferation of these illnesses.

Secondly, with the destruction of the ecosystem that forms the basis of indigenous biotechnology, we will lose the possibility of continuing to seek and find new medicines that could be of use in the struggle against leukaemia, cancer, osteoporosis, blood pressure or diabetes, etc. In the United States, for example, nine out of every ten medicines on general sale come from a natural source. Only one in ten is manufactured synthetically. However, less than thirty per cent of known plant species have been analysed in terms of their possible medicinal value. It is estimated that one-tenth of these species, including around 1,400 forest species, could comprise active ingredients for use in combating cancer.

Thirdly, the loss of carbon in the Amazonian ecosystem seriously affects water cycles, climate change and the ozone layer, all of which have a dramatic impact on human health, by causing drought, flooding, global warming and other global climate change, and increasing the possibility of contracting, among other things, various types of cancer.

The tropical forests as a whole conserve, on average, 500 to 600 tonnes of carbon per hectare. In contrast, a hectare of pastureland conserves no more than around 5 tonnes of carbon. And agricultural activity retains only around 25 tonnes of carbon per hectare. The difference in quantities of carbon retained by a complete forest or pasture or agricultural land is therefore immense and directly transforms the density and distribution of insects, bacteria, viruses, parasites, rodents and various invertebrates. These latter are characterised by their lesser adaptive capacity, due to their greater capacity for mutation in relation to vertebrates and mammals, including man.

Culture, science and economy in the Indigenous Health System

Concepts of Amazonian indigenous health stress the dynamic balance that a human being must establish with his natural and human environment in the context of the multiple interrelations that develop, along with a capacity to "understand" the language with which this environment in turn permanently "talks to him", through a constant and attentive study of the signals produced by the different biotic and abiotic species around him. Indigenous Amazonian cultures are profoundly dialectic, open and fluid, in themselves and in the health systems they have been able to develop.

The anthropologist, Reichel Dolmatoff, partially illustrates this point in the context of a discussion on the Tukano indigenous people of Colombia, noting:

"Nature does not constitute a physical entity separate from man which he can, thus, confront or oppose ... as a distinct entity. Occasionally, man may unbalance nature, due to his malfunctioning as a component within it but he can never divorce himself from it.

Man is considered an integral part of a game of supra-individual systems which – biological or cultural – transcend, go far beyond, the individual lives of people and within which survival and the means of supporting a certain quality of life is made possible only when the evolution of other forms of life is permitted, according to their particular or specific needs, as established in the myths and mythological traditions" (1971:4).

From a similar point of view, others have arrived at an interpretation of the genesis of health problems:

"Many illnesses (including those of greatest incidence, such as parasites and respiratory infections) originate in illnesses related to "lifestyles" ... such as changes in settlement patterns, unsatisfactory nutrition, inappropriate diet, lack of care in domestic hygiene, a breakdown in the rate of birth control, etc.

In many cases, the disorders come from an alteration in the basics, be it through an anomalous response of nature (quality, quantity and variety of foods, depredation of basic resources, contamination, oil spillages, floods) or through the malfunctioning of group relations (damage through witchcraft, loss of the ethical economy of reciprocity or redistribution, resource competition on the market, coercion and pressure on the part of non-indigenous groups, etc.) or through decline in the individual himself (diet, hygiene, physical and spiritual strength, paid work, etc.).

Besides there are many illnesses to which the deactivated sources of indigenous wisdom cannot offer a solution and which are causing real devastation (rabies, hepatitis B, tuberculosis and malaria).

In other cases, they formerly had antidotes for illnesses but they are no longer known or used or they have forgotten how to use them (ojé for parasites, quinine for malaria etc.) through a lack of ability to develop their culture through their own systems of knowledge transmission.

Internal mechanisms for spiritual rebuilding are not working properly as the activators of these mechanisms (shamans, traditional healers and specialists) are often persecuted, misunderstood, disabled, with no confidence in themselves and considered more as an anomaly than a privileged component of a health system" (García Hierro 1995: 24-25).

In summary, the relationship between indigenous peoples, biodiversity and global health is indisputable, as is the critical interaction between forests, human health and indigenous economic culture. All this is based, in turn, on a cultural management of the relationship between science, health and economy, which the national-level health systems are still incapable of understanding and, far less, incorporating viably into the way in which they handle the human health challenges in the Amazon region.

A regional health system based on a number of unresolved problems[2]

As a result of the nature of their integration into the wider political economy, the indigenous peoples of the Amazon region are currently demonstrating alarming health statistics.

Infant mortality varies between 99 and 153 in every one thousand live births. In 1992, in Alto Amazonas Province alone, an under-5 child mortality rate of 16.6% was recorded. It is estimated that 77% of child deaths under the age of one are caused by diarrhoea and acute respiratory infections. Both illnesses are extremely sensitive to the changes in the production system with which the indigenous peoples of the region are currently being confronted. In this same context, mother and child malnutrition is being detected, also closely linked to imbalances in the trophic chains within the rainforest, related to deforestation and changes in living and work patterns encouraged by the *mestizo* teachers, health workers and religious people.

Tuberculosis is considered to be present in around 55% of indigenous settlements, leishmaniasis in 39% and malaria in 68%. There is, in addition, an extremely high prevalence of hepatitis B and hepatitis delta (HVB and HVD). To all this must be added high fertility rates, in turn related to high levels of maternal mortality, repeated pregnancies and reduced intervals between these pregnancies.

The imbalances that have arisen in the relationship established by the Amazonian indigenous peoples with their natural and human environment are linked to a conglomerate of living conditions that are currently under pressure, such as insufficient land provision, cultural pressure, changes imposed on the economic strategies of the domestic unit, irregularities in access to protein sources, the nucleation of relatively high-density communities and the associated impact on availability of sources of clean water and multiple strategic resources, in addition to the chemical contamination already prevalent in many areas. And this list is not exhaustive. Fish coming from the rivers Napo, Tigre and Corrientes, for example, contain mercury, cadmium and other toxic substances, caused by oil exploitation. The indirect environmental health problems caused by these new living conditions in turn lead to an increase in various associated problems such as parasites, infections and skin diseases.

Faced with the above, the national health system responds with isolated and sporadic vaccinations; poorly equipped health posts; badly paid health technicians who, as such, rarely do their jobs properly; health promoters from the communities themselves who are also not paid; largely incomplete, inappropriate and irregular medical provisions; insufficient staff and budget allocations for the dimension of the problems encountered; a lack of reliable statistics and the presence of official bureaucratic procedures that end up slowing down the minimal levels of capacity that exist to respond to the challenges presented by the health sector in the region.

However hard they try, the health staff and, in particular, the health technicians that implement health programmes at regional level, particularly in indigenous settlements, are unable to access professional training that is capable of dealing with the challenges they face. It is an option that simply does not currently exist. Given this situation, we now propose some technical points that should be taken into account in the future development of such professional training.

Elements for the design of a locally effective indigenous health system

The points raised so far corroborate the fact that there is currently no health system capable of responding relevantly to the potentialities or specific health problems found among the Amazonian indigenous peoples. The main criticisms of the existing health system define, simultaneously, the essence of the challenges to be resolved in the region.

Turning the order of presentation on its head somewhat, the key points can be summarised as follows: (1) health programmes are formulated at national and regional level, with a total ignorance of indigenous health systems; (2) the definition of health objectives, targets and achievements is inconsistent with the indigenous health reality; (3) the current handling of indigenous health problems is fragmented; (4) there is strong discrimination of the possible conceptual contributions of the Amazonian indigenous peoples and their health systems; (5) a huge inability to effectively coordinate with the people, structures and local indigenous organisations in the area of health continues to persist; (6) an unconnected handling of the fundamental relationship between the forest and human health in the Amazonian region persists; and (7) there is a refusal to incorporate local human and material resources, in terms of the cultural and biological diversity present among the Amazonian indigenous peoples.

Given, nonetheless, that it is impossible to design an indigenous health system without the national and regional health staff being trained in it, it is here proposed to embark upon the long path towards achieving this by designing a system for training indigenous health technicians, a system that is appropriate to the challenges and potentialities present in the region.

This proposed work of human resource training will, in turn, enable the future incorporation of different work parameters within official Health Programmes, parameters that have meaning and relevance at regional level.

The new skills to be included within a training process for indigenous health technicians would need to cover at least four fundamental areas of work, in an alternative system of formal and informal schooling:

Firstly, the training process cannot be detached from the multiple indigenous realities in which the staff would carry out their work as technicians. This involves the need to combine a basic and essential knowledge of general health issues, coming from western science, with an appropriate knowledge of each specific reality in which we are considering working, given that this completely changes the nature of the challenges, potentialities and specific results to be considered in each case.

Secondly, the development of a greater understanding of the social epidemiology of indigenous health among the Amazonian peoples is essential and, more precisely, of the health problems to be expected under specific patterns of coordination between the human "condition", the "condition" of the ecosystem and the expected condition of "indigenous health". The result would be the integrated management of health problems as an important prevention tool and proposals for simultaneous treatment.

Thirdly, the central guarantee for the functioning of any proposal is that it must necessarily be coordinated with the central bodies for representation and organisation of the Amazonian indigenous peoples. It is only in this way that it will be possible to know: (1) if a health programme or technique is responding effectively to the current health problems; (2) what needs to be done to understand and respond appropriately to current health problems; (3) existing local capacities and human resources with which we need to coordinate, including traditional midwives, herbals specialists and shamans; (4) what traditional knowledge, medicines and techniques can be employed at local level; (5) how the medical problems encountered and the situations of social disruption caused by activities of settlement, extraction and continuing geographical isolation are coordinated and interpreted at local level; (6) what forms the decentralised primary health care systems need to take; and (7) what type of agreements need to be established with each Departmental Health Section in order to effectively coordinate the local organisational efforts in the area of health with the public and collective health care services.

It is clear that programmes established from a western "civilisatory" approach have been incapable of alleviating the health problems of the Amazonian indigenous peoples. To start to consider the culture of regional indigenous peoples is not part and parcel of an indigenist plan but a product of the need to build effective health programmes based on existing problems and potentialities.

SAPIA[3] – The health initiative of the indigenous peoples of the Americas

On 13th and 18th April 1993, in Winnipeg, Canada, the Sub-Committee on Planning and Programming of the Pan-American Health Organisation held a working meeting on indigenous peoples and health, attended by 68 people from 18 countries of the Americas. Delegates from indigenous organisations, peoples and nations were present, along with international organisations, non-governmental organisations and official government delegates.

The Winnipeg Meeting, proposed among others by the official Peruvian delegation, recognised the need to contextualise indigenous people's health within the surrounding geopolitical and social reality and in

Educating the new generation, Gran Pajonal.   *Photo: Søren Hvalkof, 1986*

the context of the various historic processes underway. It agreed to adopt the following fundamental principles: (1) an holistic approach to health; (2) the right to indigenous self-determination; (3) the right to systematic participation; (4) respect for and revitalisation of indigenous culture; and (5) reciprocity in all relationships that take place.

It was thus acknowledged that:
"(a) The health situation of indigenous peoples is determined by an historic process the result of which has been dependency, loss of identity and marginalisation; (b) the indigenous peoples of the Americas have a shorter life expectancy than similar groups in national society, higher mortality rates and a different and changing morbidity profile depending on their quality of life, social position and level of acculturation, as well as their different exposure to the risk of falling ill and dying. Indigenous health is, to a large extent, determined by conditions of habitat and the new challenges raised by impoverishment and the process of modernisation; and that (c) health, the processes of health-illness, and the indigenous people's own health systems are cultural systems" (PAHO/WHO - CE 111/20, 1993: 8).

Of the different challenges emerging from the SAPIA initiative, some are primarily of a general nature and relate to coordination between international institutions, governments and indigenous organisations.

But there are further two challenges that have a bearing on the crux of what a new professional technician specialised in indigenous health would have to achieve:

"The challenge presented by the lack of appropriate and sufficient knowledge and information on the health of indigenous peoples in the face of the imperative to act and achieve immediate impact demands the design of strategies that will enable both adequate knowledge and information to be created while working ("learning on the job") and the knowledge and information created through experience to be systematically saved ("learning from what has been done and from what is being done") ...

... it is essential to simultaneously tackle all dimensions of the initiative at all levels ..., placing particular emphasis on local level experiences and processes in which actions that demonstrate their concrete impact and viability are required. In this way, we are seeking to create responses that are as varied and different as the situations and indigenous people requiring them, such that these experiences can form a body of knowledge and arguments to feed into and replicate other processes and actions ...

It is considered that cooperation must be organised around two key themes: (i) the principle of indigenous participation in management and implementation ... from the very start; and (ii) in the horizontalisation of a coordinated programme of cooperation activities ..." (ibid 10, 15-16).

This implies the formation of new human capital within the context of appropriate educational strategies that highlight at least three crucial points. The first is the formulation of curricula appropriate to the global issue of Amazonian indigenous people's health. The second is the training of human capital on the basis of a combination of western knowledge and experience and that which is unique to each indigenous people. The third revolves around the vital need to consult, coordinate, monitor and feed-back each stage of implementation of the training of new technical health staff with the representative bodies of each indigenous people, as an essential "barometer" of the implementation of any health programme being undertaken among them.

AIDESEP's indigenous health programme

With a very rare logic of work in the Amazonian indigenous world, the Inter-Ethnic Association for the Development of the Peruvian Rainforest, AIDESEP, established the Indigenous Health Programme (PSI) in 1991. With direct and important work experience in Alto Amazonas (Loreto), Madre de Dios and Atalaya, a region bordering onto three departments, Junín, Cusco and Ucayali, the PSI now proposes sharing, disseminating and institutionalising the essence of its project and achievements by means of a new stage, through the Training of Indigenous Health Technicians, initially in Ucayali.

The PSI has worked in various fields, in a simultaneous and integrated manner, directly linked to the indigenous health system. Given that the current proposal for Training Indigenous Health Technicians relates to

Ucayali, we will focus correspondingly on the work undertaken on the basis of that region, that is, Atalaya.

The PSI has worked, and made vast innovations with regard to the general work being undertaken with rural and indigenous Amazonian peoples, in the training of 219 health promoters, directly within 119 communities, through the visits of technical teams to each of the three subzones of the general area of Atalaya.

Each team has comprised a coordinator delegated by the corresponding indigenous organisation, a female indigenous traditional midwife or vapour healer, and a female nurse. Through these teams, it has been possible to visit each community two to four times a year to promote a complementary alternative indigenous health programme capable of coordinating, with impressive results, the shamans, midwives, traditional healers, herbalists, other local doctors, specialists in western medical practice, and indigenous representatives from the three regional organisations: OAGP (Ashéninka Organisation of the Gran Pajonal), OIRA (Indigenous Organisation of the Atalaya Region) and ORDECONADIT (Organisation of Native Communities of the Tahuanía District).

Faced with a considerably high prevalence of tuberculosis (TB) among the Shipibo-Conibo and Asháninka peoples of the Atalaya region, the promoters managed to detect and examine 65 cases of TB, coordinating and cooperating with the nurses for their treatment, and for control and prevention within their own communities.

With this, the main cause of abandonment of TB treatment was effectively counteracted: the simple fact that neither a patient nor his/her family can survive the treatment time required *outside* their respective communities. Two important additional variables in the abandonment of treatment, which were counteracted by the promoters' direct handling within the communities, were the lack of trust in health staff and the tendency to abandon medication once an improvement was seen in the apparent symptoms.

With a combination of medicines, procedures and indigenous and western specialists, the PSI managed to effectively identify and treat a significant number of health problems in Atalaya, in clear contrast to the experience of other medical services in the area. In the case of malaria, an additional 211 cases were diagnosed and treated between 1996 and 1998. In the case of leishmaniasis, 102 cases were diagnosed and 39 treated. Sixty-three cases are awaiting treatment. In both cases, however, that of malaria and leishmaniasis, the necessary corresponding medicines are lacking. In the same period, 1996 to 1998, 3,248 cases of intestinal parasitosis and nutritional deficiencies were diagnosed and treated; 496 cases of acarosis (mange) and pyoderma (bacterial skin infection); 294 cases of acute diarrhoea and dehydration; 140 cases of bacterial conjunctivitis; 99 cases of gonorrhoea; in addition to pneumonia and snake bites, among other things, including some cases that required minor surgery.

Lessons learned for the new training of Indigenous Health Technicians

It can be concluded that the main lessons of the PSI, as implemented in Atalaya, have been built around three basic exercises: (1) a direct rapprochement between western health specialists and the indigenous communities themselves; (2) greater appreciation of the local pre-existing indigenous medical staff; and (3) the coordination of indigenous medicinal plants and medical practices with various options coming from western medicine, under the supervision of the PSI.

These three points, however, constitute the external "symptomatology" of a far deeper and latent process, on the basis of which the PSI has had to build its work:

The first one, of a crucial nature, revolves around the territory and the natural resources within it. The PSI is being implemented in a zone which, only five years previously, was under the control of employers who held the indigenous peoples of the area in virtual slavery.[4] In this context, the shamans and local cultural resources had to be "hidden", and thus deeply devalued within the prevailing productive system. Compounding this adversity were drug trafficking, the neighbouring prison of Sepa and the political violence of the Selva Central.

Up to 1988, physical aggression, private imprisonment and beatings, forced labour, disappearances, kidnappings, fraud, threats, rape, child labour, murders, illegal detentions, the destruction of crops, etc., were all taking place.[5] The Ministry of Work and the International Labour Organisation (ILO) had to intervene with serious complaints at national and international level to put an end to the abnormal living conditions that persisted in the area as the main way of obtaining resources and indigenous labour for logging and cattle ranching.

Clearly the PSI emerged on the basis of an intense process of destruction and a completely inhuman treatment of the indigenous populations of Atalaya, even though they were the legitimate heirs of the environment and its destiny. A recovery of the indigenous health system under these conditions assumes, as noted throughout this document, access not only to medical resources and specialists appropriate to the health problems of the indigenous populations but, in addition, the restoration of the man/man and man/land relationships, which had been seriously damaged.

In this context, AIDESEP is initiating a quiet (but nonetheless dramatic) process of recovering the indigenous territory of the area. In less than a decade, more than a million and a half hectares of land have been titled in Ucayali, providing a sound basis for the subsistence of its inhabitants, who had been living under conditions of slavery only a few years previously. Currently, in coordination with the regional indigenous organisations, AIDESEP is implementing a project on the local use and management of sustainable resources, aimed at income generation, which is a necessary and inevitable complement to modern daily life, even in this context.

Following the abolition of slavery in its physical form in the area, servitude came in another form, this time spiritual, under the supervision of various Christian churches. Predominant among these were the Baptists, but also denominations of Pentecostal, Israelite and Catholic origin, aimed at making indigenous people once more feel inadequate and useless.

To understand these variables was a basic condition for being able to move on to working in the area of health. Moreover, both "memories", that of the slave-using employers and of the religious moralisers, persisted not only in people's minds but also in many physical habits in the region. To recover the indigenous health system would require confronting daily life, daily tasks and, hence, both "spectres", although neither one directly.

To reconstruct the fabric of a human relationship and a functional mode of interaction between the outside world and one's own, without ever entering into a direct confrontation with either of the two "spectres" of the past, was a condition of the PSI's work. This condition was just as - or more - important than the first three variables already mentioned: those of physical rapprochement with the communities, appreciation of their own indigenous health staff, and the incorporation of traditional resources and plants.

In summary, it can be said that the appreciation, consolidation and conservation of indigenous territory is as least as important as medicine itself for the appreciation, strengthening and conservation of health among an indigenous people, insofar as the first condition is necessary for the effective functioning of the second. Moreover both are inextricably linked, not only in theory, as at the beginning of this chapter, a few pages back, but in daily practice, as in the case of Atalaya. Even more dramatic, this case is not an exception and, furthermore, has provided important lessons, unrivalled in terms of creating a wider process of generating indigenous health mechanisms, as in the case of the Training of Indigenous Health Technicians, which will be the next step forward.

In conclusion, any process of Indigenous Health has to consider the situation of the territorial environment, including the economic and productive processes at work within it, along with the social systems of indigenous organisation, education and religion that are present, as determining factors in the form that identity and self-esteem will assume, and without which there can be no possible generation or reproduction of an integrated health system.

Notes

1. This section has been written on the basis of the following bibliographical sources: Brack 1998; Bundes, et al. 1996; COICA 1999, 1997; Estrella 1995 a and b; Rural Advancement Foundation International 1994; USDA Forest Service, 1995.
2. This section has been written on the basis of the following bibliographical sources: AIDESEP 1997 and Barclay 1998.
3. Salud de los Pueblos Indigenas de las Americas – Health of the Indigenous Peoples of the Americas – trans. note.
4. See, particularly, Hvalkof 1998.
5. See García Hierro 1998.

References

Asociación Interétnica de Desarrollo de la Selva Peruana [AIDESEP] and Instituto Nacional de Salud [INS]
1997   Prevalencia de Marcadores Serológicos para Hepatitis Viral B y Delta en Pueblos Indígenas de la Amazonía Peruana. Lima: Cooperación Española/Cooperación Amazónica.

Barclay, Frederica
1998   Perú: Perfil Socioeconómico y Cultural de los Pueblos Indígenas de la Amazonía. Lima: World Bank: Washington. [Manuscript]

Brack, Antonio
1998   "Comunidades Indígenas Amazónicas: Centros de Conocimientos Tradicionales." In A. Brack (General Coordinator) *Amazonía Peruana Comunidades Indígenas, Conocimientos y Tierras Tituladas: Atlas y Base de Datos.* Lima: GEF/UNDP/UNOPS. Pp. 201-255.

Bundes, Joske, Bertus Haverkort and Wim Hiemstra
1996   *Biotechnology: Building on Farmers' Knowledge.* London: Macmillan.

Coordinadora de Organizaciones Indígenas de la Cuenca Amazónica
1997   *Entre lo Propio y lo Ajeno: Derechos de los Pueblos Indígenas y Propiedad Intelectual.* [Ramón Torres, ed.] Quito: COICA/IBIS/ Climate Alliance/Berlin Senate .

1999   *Biodiversidad, Derechos Colectivos y Régimen Sui Generis de Propiedad Intelectual.* Quito: COICA/OMAERE/OPIP.

Design Project for Technical Education and Professional Training
1997   *Títulos Profesionales Familias de Salud Estética Personal Servicios y Asistenciales.* Lima: Spanish Agency for International Cooperation / Ministry of Education.

Estrella, Eduardo
1995a   *Biodiversidad y Salud en las Poblaciones Indígenas de la Amazonía.* Lima: Amazonian Cooperation Treaty.

1995b   *Plantas Medicinales Amazónicas: Realidad y Perspectivas.* Lima: Amazonian Cooperation Treaty.

García Hierro, Pedro
1995   *San Lorenzo: Salud Indígena, Medio Ambiente, Interculturalidad.* Lima: AIDESEP/Terra Nuova.

1998   "Atalaya: Caught in a Time Warp." In Pedro García Hierro, et al.,
        Liberation through Land Rights in the Peruvian Amazon, (eds.
        Alejandro Parellada and Søren Hvalkof), pp. 13-80. Copenhagen:
        IWGIA.

Gerardo Reichel-Dolmatoff
1971   *Amazonian Cosmos: The Sexual and Religious Symbolism of the
        Tukano Indians.* Chicago: The University of Chicago Press.

Hvalkof, Søren
1998   "From Slavery to Democracy: The Indigenous Process of Upper
        Ucayali and Gran Pajonal." In Pedro García Hierro, et al.,
        Liberation through Land Rights in the Peruvian Amazon, (eds.
        Alejandro Parellada and Søren Hvalkof), pp. 81-162.
        Copenhagen: IWGIA.

Pan-American Health Organisation/World Health Organisation
1993   *Salud de los Pueblos Indígenas.* Washington, D.C.: CE 111/20.

PROMUDEH / World Bank
1998   Amazonian Consultation on the Indigenous Development Plan.
        Report of the Workshop held in Iquitos from 1st to 5th June 1998.
        [Draft].

Ruiz Gironda, Rosa
1998   Perfil Ocupacional del Técnico en Saneamiento Ambiental
        Basado en Competencias. Lima: National School of Public
        Health/ Ministry of Health.

Rural Advancement Foundation International
1994   Conservación de Conocimientos Autóctonos: Integración de Dos
        Sistemas de Innovación. New York: United Nations Development
        Programme/UNDP. [Manuscript]

USDA Forest Service, International Programs
1995   *Forests and Human Health.* Policy 13.

World Council of Indigenous Peoples
1993   La Cooperación Internacional y los Pueblos Indígenas: Breves
        Notas para la Segunda Consulta Inter-institucional sobre los
        Pueblos Indígenas y el Desarrollo en América Latina.
        Washington, D.C.: World Bank.

The editor drinking masato in the Ucayali.   *Photo: Rune Hvalkof, 2000*

Epilogue

Søren Hvalkof, compiler and editor.

Summarizing the experiences

If asked whether the Indigenous Health Programme in Atalaya and Gran Pajonal had been a success, the answer would have to be a resounding yes. The Programme succeeded in raising awareness among the indigenous population in over 120 communities on the issue of health and helped them organize themselves and set up sustainable systems to continue monitoring their own health situation and simultaneously take action to improve it along the way. It recognised and legalised indigenous health practices and certified individuals with special knowledge on this topic, such as shamans, vapour healers, herbal medicine specialists and mid-wives, as specialists on a par with conventional nurses, physicians and other heath practitioners within our western bio-medical tradition. This official recognition of the value of these indigenous specialists meant that years of repression and ridicule by the Church, missionaries, doctors, school teachers and non-indigenous officials could be shaken off, genera-ting a renewed pride in indigenous culture and tradition, and greatly rein-forcing the interest in self-organising and maintaining a health service sys-tem in the communities.

This recognition served to integrate both indigenous and western medical practices within a holistic approach to community health service and linked it to the Peruvian public health system. In specific terms, it meant that agreement was reached on identifying and treating specific endemic and epidemic diseases locally, of which tuberculosis (TB) was of particular interest. Decentralised treatment of TB has been an unqualified success in the Programme, contrary to most other experiences from mar-ginal rural areas in the developing world.

In general terms, this meant that the communities could benefit from the public system and infrastructure far more efficiently and that agree-ments could be made with larger regional hospitals and health centres to accept indigenous patients without social security registration, which is normally a requirement if medical costs are to be covered. Public social security health insurance in Peru is available only to people with regular work and income, and certainly not to indigenous subsistence producers, who are most often turned away from hospitals.

This linkage between indigenous health services and the public health system suddenly made the indigenous world visible in the public sphere, a visibility that caused a growing interest in the indigenous health issues and opened up new opportunities for the communities and organisations involved to ensure a better public health service for the future. It also generated an interest among health planners and executives with regard to the structure and methodologies used in the Indigenous Health Programme, an organisational interest that now seems to be crystallising in the establishment of a new health technician training system and school for publicly certified Indigenous Health Technicians.

We know from monitoring and evaluating the project's development that the PSI is greatly appreciated by the communities in the area, and that the people it is targeting have as a whole expressed their satisfaction and stated that it has improved their quality of life. The Programme has accumulated, analysed and filed figures and statistics from all communities and has developed case records for all people and patients involved. And yet we cannot statistically prove that the general health conditions of the indigenous population have improved in the region. We have no absolute and objective statistical instrument by which to measure this. No baseline studies were available when the Programme began operating in Atalaya, existing statistics were highly unreliable, fragmentary and never covered the indigenous communities in any systematic way, nor was there any ethnic differentiation in the statistical approach to data sampling. This is still the case in the public system. It would thus be easy for any devotee of positivist philosophy and methodology to claim that the Programme cannot be judged as we are unable to prove that any change has occurred in the general health situation.

And yet what we can prove is that the people it was intended to benefit do believe they are better off now than they were before the Indigenous Health Programme began operating. We can prove that seve ral individuals have been saved from certain death, which from a moral standpoint alone could justify the whole project, and that many more have been cured from diseases that would have made their lives intolerable. We can also prove that the indigenous population has taken responsibility for their own health situation in the communities and developed systems and methodologies that make this sustainable. Moreover, we can prove that the PSI has strengthened the indigenous people's ability to control their own development and future. On this basis, we feel justified in calling the project a success.

Doubt remains, however, as to whether regional and national indigenous organisations will be able to maintain the supervision and back-up required at community level after the end of this Programme. It is clear that no indigenous organisation in Peru is able to carry the burden of such a project by themselves, and that they will be dependent on external funding and support for some time. It seems crucial from this perspective that the public health system in Peru should gradually take over financial responsibility and establish cooperation agreements with indigenous organisations at all levels. Such cooperation must acknowledge the integrity of the indigenous organisation, indigenous concepts of health and their ways of operating. To support the indigenous organisations to achieve such cooperation and to continuously sustain a high level of activities at community level, experienced NGOs could help with the logistical and planning aspects, as the public system has very limited capacity for implementation.

PARAMETERS FOR SUCCESS

In general, rural health programmes and projects in the developing world are not known for their overwhelming success, particularly in areas with multiple ethnic and linguistic groups, strong power hierarchies of colonial origin and unequal power relations between indigenous and non-indigenous populations, difficult access and undeveloped logistical structures. We feel it important to highlight some of the conditions and premises that we see as having been fundamental for the positive outcome of the project in Peru. We will first look at some of the structural prerequisites and then emphasize some of the functional characteristics.

Structural prerequisites

One of the issues central to an understanding of the momentum the PSI has gained in Atalaya Province is the political and spatial organisation. As mentioned in the introduction to the book and in the historical analysis in chapter 2, the regional indigenous organisations grew out of a long organisational process and struggle for their rights to land and territories. AIDESEP, their national indigenous organisation, supported by Danish development aid, carried out a large-scale land titling programme in the years preceding the current health project. They succeeded in obtaining titles to hundreds of communities, which were legally registered, surveyed, demarcated and titled. It was the organisational and political effect of this process that made the subsequent health project feasible. It built up a structure and network that reached from the local family in the community, with its internal committees and authority structures, through the regional organisations to the national and even international organisations that link up with overall policy makers at the national and international level. Through this structure, they challenged hitherto unquestionable power asymmetries, and radically succeeded in altering them once they had obtained titles to their communal territories, thus gaining the political power of landownership.

These local structural conditions must occur alongside international structural patterns favouring the linkage to funds and political back-up. This was provided by the international indigenous movement and its strategic alliance with environmental groups, which have allied with them and put the question of indigenous peoples' rights and resource management issues on the international agenda, making the connection between international and local agency possible and workable. It could be said that these structural conditions are both an outcome of and a reaction to the growing globalisation, to use a post-modern catchword.

In summary, the central structural issues that have been the *sine qua non* for the successful realization of this rural health project are:

- Legislation recognizing indigenous rights to land or territory, self-administration and government, and rights to bilingual education, health practices and similar exclusive indigenous rights.
- The existence of an organic organisational structure at community, local and national level that *de facto* represents the people, and which has the ability to take viable decisions and execute these and related activities.
- That fundamental power asymmetries were addressed prior to the implementation of the health programme and indigenous rights given exclusive priority.
- That unequal land tenure structures were altered, indigenous land rights were recognised and implemented in the form of the demarcation and collective titling of indigenous community territories.
- That sufficient infrastructure, transportation and communication systems existed or could be established, operated and controlled by the communities and their organisations.
- The existence of an international structure relating to indigenous issues, making linkage and partnership between the funding agency and the implementing organisation possible and feasible.
- That structures existed making linkages to other social sectors and public (health) systems possible.

Functional aspects

As mentioned above, the existence of an organisational structure has been crucial to the feasibility of the Programme. The clearest expression of this is the Native Community (*Comunidad Nativa*), a formation of recent date, originating as a spin-off from the Agrarian Reform period of the 1960s and 1970s, when cooperatives and peasant communities were legally instituted in the Andean highlands[1].

In the Amazon, the formation and registration of Native Communities was a response to and adaptation of this agrarian legislation. A Native Community in the Peruvian Amazon today is not necessarily a hamlet or other nucleated settlement but normally identical to a local territory belonging to a specific local indigenous group. It may or may not have nucleated settlements within its borders but people normally live dispersed in small extended family units composed of a few families with a tendency, however, to form larger settlements or hamlets along major waterways. Whatever the settlement pattern, the territory is a functional social unit, knit loosely together by kinship ties and similar social relations. If such social units, called communities and defined by a circumscribed territory, had not existed, it would have been impossible to take decisions, delegate responsibilities and carry through the health service functions. In other words, the high degree of participation would not have been possible. The social function of the community as an "autonomous", a self-regulating, system is thus a prerequisite for the application of the health work undertaken by the Programme. In addition to this comes the good functioning of all the adjacent organisational structures, of which the regional organisation has been the most important in terms of coordination, logistics and legitimacy. The regional indigenous organisation is primarily a political organisation, representing the indigenous interests of the different communities in the region. A "region" in this context most often coincides with a civil administrative unit such as the province or district. In order to institute the health programme as a sustainable initiative, it must be the regional indigenous organisation that takes on responsibility and appropriates the programme. This can only be done in practice. To understand what this is all about, the regional indigenous organisation must not only be responsible for the administration of funds and staff but also for all logistical arrangements, infrastructure, relations with the public sphere and civil society authorities. To facilitate this function as the institutional and political link between the communities on the one side and the world of regional resources and politics on the other, it was decided that every regional organisation should appoint at least one of its political leaders to be responsible for their version of the PSI, and that each field team (of nurse, indigenous specialist etc.) should also include an appointed coordinator from the regional organisation to accompany and support them on the community visits. In this way, the information flow and linkage between the indigenous organisation and the local communities and their families would be guaranteed. This proved to be very efficient, creating a synergy that also strengthened the regional organisations politically. In this context it is very important that the indigenous political organisation is seen as an integral part of a successful health programme and that it is supported accordingly to improve its functionality.

However, the competence of the regional organisations also has its limits. One cannot expect these organisations to have the necessary insight, expertise and personal resources to design and define the philosophy and overall strategy of a large health programme. Nor can they be expected to have the necessary capacity to mainstream it to fit into the national system, nor to fundraise internationally and in general promote their interests on the national and international arena. This is where the national indigenous umbrella organisation comes into its own. It was AIDESEP that had the necessary network on a wider scale to do this and it was AIDESEP that defined the philosophy behind the Programme, an ideal model which, once put into action, was obviously modified to fit the reality of the real world of the Amazon forest. But the control and political guidance of AIDESEP as the overall organisation responsible for implementation was as important as the rest, and it also received some core funding to cover its operational costs. It is very important in this context to repudiate statements that are often heard from non-indigenous persons working in parallel organisational circles, be they affiliated with NGOs or government institutions, that the indigenous organisations have no real legitimacy and that their leadership is unconnected with their grassroots and out of touch with the communities. The organisational structure that this health programme works through to reach out to the communities proves that this was not the case, and that none of the organisational levels in the hierarchy were superfluous.

Another functional aspect of the implementation strategy was the approach to monitoring and supervision on the part of NORDECO and the funding agency, the Karen Elise Jensen Foundation. NORDECO was given responsibility for administration and for supporting AIDESEP in the design, execution and administration of the project. NORDECO was, so to speak, the Karen Elise Jensen Foundation's guarantee that the project was feasible and appropriately supervised, for the latter had no experience of either indigenous peoples or Latin America. NORDECO, with years of experience in evaluating and developing rural projects in developing countries, knew that it would be difficult to convey the intricacies of the indigenous world of the Amazon to the board of the funding Foundation, composed of rational thinking Westerners, particularly in relation to a health project that was supposed to integrate two incongruous cosmologies.

Accordingly it was decided that the Foundation should appoint one or two representatives to participate alongside NORDECO staff in every monitoring trip to the project areas where the Programme was being executed. This turned out to be an excellent idea, as both "recipient" communities and the "donors" established a personal relationship, a partnership, which overcame all the expected communication problems, unfolding into a very dynamic process of project development. It gradually merged into a common experience and could almost be called a phenomenological approach to project implementation, an approach we highly recommend. On the other hand, the Danish parties concerned did not wish to be present on a daily basis nor to employ a permanent representative in Peru. Apart from the costs of such an arrangement, it was considered undesirable to have an "outsider" intervening in local affairs; we preferred that the organisations themselves take responsibility. The idea was for the Danish donors to visit and intervene at certain times if necessary, but not to have a permanent presence. This is called a "recurrent intervention strategy", a "hit-and-run" tactic. And it worked very well, leaving the locals to solve their own problems once they had been helped to identify them. The Programme opted for frequent reviews, particularly in the early stages, when quarterly joint visits from the foundation and PSI-AIDESEP were common. Later, when the Programme had gained a functional form, such visits were limited to biannual reviews.

These frequent visits made it possible to maintain a very dynamic project development, with constant changes to the design and adjustments to the logical framework. In brief, the project did not strictly follow a predetermined log-frame or any other rigid blueprint for its realization and goals, rather it was based on a trial-and-error strategy, a very pragmatic approach which, however, does require recurrent intervention and frequent reviews. Goals, indicators, means and actions could thus constantly be adjusted to inputs from reality and fed back into the system, perpetually proceeding towards successful outcomes with high participation from the community members and their authorities.

The most important functional aspects of the above named factors can be summarised as follows:

- Well-defined, organised and functioning communities able to take decisions and participate on equal terms.
- Collective landownership (community land titles) counteracting existing power asymmetries.
- A functioning hierarchy and network of indigenous organisations, from community level to the highest national level.
- A functioning communication and transport system within this organisational framework.
- A trial-and-error project design, with a dynamic and pragmatic implementation strategy (vs. a rigid log-frame approach).
- A monitoring and supervision strategy characterised by recurrent intervention and frequent field reviews.
- A long-term perspective of implementation and few time constraints to execution.
- A partnership between donors and beneficiaries, characterised by the active participation of funding agencies' board members in field reviews.
- Diversified health approaches, characterised by respect for ethnic differences and interpretations.

Finally, it should be emphasised that, had it not been for the very skilled, dedicated and committed field staff in the teams, who overcame unimaginable hardships to reach the communities, visit the dispersed families and offer them training and help, this project would have come to nothing. The nurses, in particular, gave of themselves greatly in their extraordinary efforts to make the Indigenous Health Programme a reality. Many of these young women, coming from urban areas far away in the Andes or in Lima, had children and families whom they did not see for most of the year, as they were spending 11 months at a time in the field with little contact to their homes, a sacrifice that was compensated by nothing more than salary levels only symbolically higher than those of the public sector. We all appreciated their commitment and their humanity greatly, for this was the driving force and motivation behind the project, making the dream of an Indigenous Health Programme come true.

Postscript, November 2002

When the editor visited Atalaya and Gran Pajonal in November 2002, the general situation in the zone had taken a disturbing turn. Logging activities had accelerated and spread due to fear from the contracting companies of the implementation of new legislations regulating extractivist activities. The ribbing off of the last hardwood resorts was unfolding indiscriminately and heavy machinery was penetrating even the remotest corners of the rain forest, without any control or legitimacy. Simultaneously oil and gas exploration activities had been booming in the entire region. According to the regional authorities, there were strong indicators that the indigenous communities were suffering an alarming increase in venereal diseases, particularly syphilis, apparently due to the increasing presence of oil and lumber workers in the area. Although no systematic information on the prevalence of HIV and AIDS is available, it is beyond doubt that this disease too is spreading to the indigenous population under the present conditions.

Confronted with these massive problems the indigenous organisations are in a state of despair. The synergetic effect of the Indigenous Health Programme has vanished with the expiration of the projects in the three areas of operation. On the other hand the new project, expected to continue the process with the establishment of the public School of Indigenous Health Technicians, has been considerably delayed by bureaucratic obstacles in the public decision making structures, both nationally and internationally. There are great expectations and a desire in the indigenous communities that this Programme will continue, but each day that it is delayed disappointment and resignation are growing. It must be emphasised that the situation presents an extraordinary opportunity for the entire health sector and the NGOs, to reactivate the structures and functions already established through the Indigenous Health Programme – PSI. It would be erroneous and absurd not to take advantage of this exceptional opportunity.

Note

1. Cf. Roger Plant and Søren Hvalkof: *Land Titling and Indigenous Peoples in Latin America.* Technical Paper Series, Inter-American Development Bank. Sustainable Development Department, Indigenous Peoples and Community Development Unit. SDS/IND, Washington, D.C., 2001.

Going upstream against the current.   *Photo: Jim Thuesen, 1993*